The Desert Movement

The Desert Movement

Fresh perspectives on the spirituality of the desert

Alexander Ryrie

CANTERBURY PRESS

Norwich

© Alexander Ryrie 2011
Maps © Bill Johnson 2011

First published in 2011 by the Canterbury Press Norwich
Editorial office
13–17 Long Lane,
London, EC1A 9PN, UK

Canterbury Press is an imprint of Hymns Ancient and Modern Ltd
(a registered charity)
13A Hellesdon Park Road, Norwich,
Norfolk, NR6 5DR, UK

www.scm-canterburypress.co.uk

Quotations from *The Sayings of the Desert Fathers*, translated by
Benedicta Ward SLG are used by kind permission of Cistercian
Publications, Collegeville, Minnesota

British Library Cataloguing in Publication data

A catalogue record for this book is available
from the British Library

978 1 84825 094 9

Typeset by Regent Typesetting, London
Printed and bound in Great Britain by
CPI Antony Rowe, Chippenham, Wiltshire

Contents

For our grandchildren
Ella, Andrew, Kate, Fiona, Duncan
following their way through life

Preface

It was while I was visiting the convent of the Sisters of the Love of God in Oxford many years ago that I first came across the volume of *The Sayings of the Desert Fathers*, translated by Sister Benedicta Ward SLG, and my interest was aroused. This is a collection of some of the sayings of the monks, including Antony the Great, who withdrew to the deserts of Lower Egypt in the period from the third to the fifth centuries CE. On acquiring my own copy I became fascinated by the stories and sayings of these strange, sometimes apparently crazy men. I knew they 'had something'.

During the following years I read and pondered all I could get hold of about the desert monks, and gradually and imperceptibly I found myself being influenced by their outlook on life. Then as time went on more and more texts about men and women of the deserts of Upper Egypt, Judea, Gaza and elsewhere became available in English, some of them only very recently, and I began to realize that Antony and the 'Desert Fathers' of Lower Egypt were not the only desert monks. I read with fascination of people such as Shenoute, the powerful and controversial Coptic monastic leader, of Onnophrius, a solitary hermit hidden in the remote desert in the far south of Egypt, of Chariton living in silence in a 'hanging cave' halfway up a cliff in a Judean wadi, of Syncletica glimpsed only once after she had lived 28 years alone in a cave near the Jordan, and a great many others. And I realized that in addition to those whose stories we have, there were many, many more, unseen and unknown, scattered in cells or monastic communities throughout the desert areas.

The records demonstrate that during these early Christian centuries there was a widespread movement to the desert, taking place not only in Lower Egypt but in various parts of the Middle East; and that all the monks of this desert movement had something in common – an approach to Christian faith and living which was unusual, radical and totally demanding, an approach which we may call 'the way of the desert'.

It became clear to me that the modern interest in the 'Desert Fathers' has usually been centred on too small a part of the desert movement. To understand it fully, it will be useful to do something that, as far as I know, has not been done before – to cast our eyes more widely, and take a comprehensive look at all the areas of the movement; to consider the form it took in the various places where it arose, and to examine both what they had in common and how they differed with regard to their monastic organization and their spiritual life. In this way we can hope to reach a deeper and more comprehensive understanding of the way of the desert.

This book is an attempt to do that. It is a description of the desert movement and the way of the desert, including the stories of the leading figures, based on the sources and historical records that are available to us from all the desert areas. It is not an attempt to propose a 'desert spirituality' for the twenty-first century; but I hope that the accounts in the book may not only be of interest in themselves, but may also provide a basis and an encouragement for people today who may want to develop and pursue a spirituality of the desert for our own time.

Sandy Ryrie

Introduction

The Desert Movement

The period from the third to the seventh centuries of the Christian Era witnessed one of the most extraordinary movements in Christian history. Thousands of people, both men and women, in Egypt, Palestine and other parts of the Middle East, took themselves off to the desert to live as monks and hermits. They were remarkable people, living lives of great asceticism, sometimes individually on their own and sometimes in monastic communities, deliberately enduring great hardship, and spending their time in silence, prayer and meditation, in obedience to their understanding of the Christian Gospel. This 'desert movement', as it may be called, took place not only in Egypt but in various parts of the Near East and the eastern Mediterranean, wherever there was at hand an area of wilderness and solitude.

It has been customary to think of the desert movement as starting with Antony, known as Antony the Great, who, about the year 285, moved into the desert of Egypt to live an ascetic life in solitude. Antony's move was not, however, entirely new: it was one further chapter in a history which extended back over many centuries in different places. Behind Antony and the desert monks of Egypt there lay a rich background and a long tradition of asceticism and monastic life of various kinds, not only in Egypt but in Palestine and elsewhere. To understand the desert movement we need to know something about this background.

The background of the desert movement

As far as Egypt is concerned, the most immediate background lay close at hand. Fragments of ancient papyrus documents recently discovered in Egypt have provided interesting and sometimes vivid glimpses into the ordinary life of those days.[1] Several of these refer to *apotaktikoi*, or 'renouncers'. These were Christian people, both men and women, who were living a life of celibacy and ascetic practice within the towns and villages of northern Egypt. The word is derived from the Greek word *apotasso* found in the Gospel of Luke, where Jesus says, 'Whoever of you does not renounce all he has cannot be my disciple' (Luke 14.33). The word *apotaktikos* 'indicated a person within the church who, on the basis of his or her Christian belief, renounced the traditional social patterns of Roman Egypt'.[2] Although they were called 'renouncers', they did not remove themselves to the desert nor did they entirely cut themselves off from normal society. Just how the *apotaktikoi* lived is not entirely clear: it seems that there were differing patterns of monastic and ascetic life. Some no doubt gave up their possessions, but they did not all do so: there is even evidence that some of them bought and sold property. But it is clear that ascetics of various kinds were to be found in Egypt in Antony's time, and that their presence formed part of the background to the desert movement in that area.

The desert movement was not, however, confined to Egypt, and much of its background is to be found elsewhere. There is good reason to believe that there were Christian people practising asceticism, and perhaps even living in monasteries, from a very early date, possibly even from New Testament times. Indeed, evidence from the Gospels themselves points in this direction. In St Matthew's Gospel in particular there are several reported sayings of Jesus which suggest that some people in the

---

1 See especially Goehring, *Ascetics, Society, and the Desert.*
2 Goehring, 'Through a Glass Darkly', p. 68.

early church believed that there were two kinds of Christians: those who aimed to be 'perfect' on the one hand, and ordinary Christians on the other. Jesus' words to the rich man, 'If you wish to be perfect, go, sell your possessions, and give to the poor ... then, come follow me'; his call to his followers to 'humble themselves'; his commendation of those who had 'left houses or brothers or sisters or father or mother or children or fields, for my sake'; his calling some to follow him when he 'had nowhere to lay his head'; his telling his disciples that they must 'lose their life' for his sake; and his statement that there were some 'who have made themselves eunuchs for the sake of the kingdom of heaven'[3] – all these sayings were taken by some to be a call to the ascetic life, and were regarded as providing something of a foundational commission for monasticism. Their presence in the Gospel tradition seems to demonstrate that there were those who practised an ascetic life from the first days of the church. Similarly, St Paul's discussion in 1 Corinthians 7 shows that he believed that there was a place in church life for those who chose to remain celibate. Some years later, the writer of the *Epistle of Barnabas*, writing perhaps in Alexandria, seems to have known of the existence of monks of some kind, since he expressed disapproval of those who chose to 'live in solitude' (*monazein*).[4] Similarly, the *Gospel of Thomas*, an apocryphal Christian writing of the first century, attributes to Jesus three sayings which refer to 'solitaries' (*monachoi*).[5] The distinguished third-century writer Origen, commenting on Matthew 19.21, assumed that the bishops were on the lookout for opportunities to found new monasteries.

More significant is what the church historian Eusebius says about Philo's description of the Jewish community known as the Therapeutae (discussed below). Philo, a distinguished Jewish writer of the first century CE, gives a detailed description of the

---

3 Matthew 19.21; 18.4; 19.29; 8.20; 16.25; 19.12.
4 *Epistle of Barnabas*, 4.11.
5 *Gospel of Thomas*, 16, 49, 75.

life of this ascetic community in Alexandria. Eusebius, writing in the early years of the fourth century, believed that Philo must in fact have been describing a Jewish *Christian* monastic community. Philo's book, he says, 'obviously contains the rules of the Church which are still observed in our time', and claims that this is 'a very accurate description of the life of our ascetics, apostolic men who were, it appears, of Hebrew origin, and thus still preserved most of the ancient customs in a strongly Jewish manner'.[6] Although most scholars do not agree that the Therapeutae were Christians, Eusebius' statements show clearly that there were Christian monastic communities existing both during and before his time. Indeed, earlier in his book Eusebius refers to two types of Christian, some of whom are apparently ascetics who are 'transposed in soul to heaven, leaving their mortified bodies on earth'.[7] Moreover there were some who believed that the Christian monastic life had been in existence since the days of the apostles. Cassian, referring to the fourth chapter of Acts, claims that 'the discipline of the cenobites (monks) took its rise at the time of the apostolic preaching'.[8] Just what form Christian monasticism may have taken during those early years is not clear, but it seems evident that it did exist, and that it formed a part of the background of the desert movement. In the words of O'Neill, 'Christianity always had it monasteries, as did the Judaism from which it sprang.'[9]

That this early Christian background of the desert movement is indeed closely linked to the Jewish background can be seen especially from two particularly interesting developments of an ascetic and monastic nature in Judaism. The first was the emergence of the Essenes. These were an exclusive group who withdrew from normal society and lived a life of strict obedience to the Jewish Law. The movement had two branches: a

---

6 Eusebius, *Ecclesiastical History*, II: 17:1.
7 Quoted in O'Neill, 'The Origins of Monasticism', p. 275.
8 John Cassian, *Conferences*, 18:6; see also *Institutes*, 2:5.
9 O'Neill, 'Origins of Monasticism', p. 286.

'party' and a 'sect'.[10] Those who formed the 'party' lived in towns and villages, married and engaged in normal occupations, but observed strict purity rules, limited their contact with other people, came together for a common meal at certain times, and contributed to a common fund. The 'sect' was a group who established a monastic community at Qumran in a remote part of the Judean desert near the Dead Sea. It was here that the well-known Dead Sea Scrolls were produced. These ancient documents, found in the mid-twentieth century in caves near the site and only recently published in full, give details of the life of the community. It was begun about the year 140 BCE, and survived until their buildings were destroyed by the Romans in 68 CE. Their life was governed by extremely strict rules. Membership was regulated by a demanding entry procedure. Members were required to surrender their private property, and to live in poverty. They engaged in manual work, both agricultural work to provide for themselves and the scribal work of copying texts, including biblical texts. They ate together twice a day, at the fifth hour and after sundown. They rejected the existing priesthood in Jerusalem and the worship of the Temple, followed a strict interpretation of the Law, and expected the coming of the Messiah. They were a group that 'incorporated many ascetic practices into its communal way of life. These practices included (at least for a major segment of the movement) a materially simple life free of possessions, temperance in food and drink, avoidance of oil, simplicity of dress, reserve in speech, desert separation (for those at Qumran) strict rules of ritual purity and of Sabbath observance – all part of a collective and individual discipline that made them in Philo's eyes "athletes of virtue"'.[11] The Essenes were a very distinctively and exclusively Jewish community with a passionate devotion to Jewish Law. Nevertheless, in its corporate life, its ascetic simplicity of life and its commitment to manual work,

---

10 Terms used in Sanders, *Judaism*, p. 342.
11 Fraade, 'Ascetical Aspects of Ancient Judaism', p. 266.

the Essene community was in some respects similar to some later Christian monastic communities. And their withdrawal into the desert is an important foreshadowing of the Christian desert movement.

The other Jewish development was the group known as the Therapeutae, mentioned above. This was an ascetic and monastic community which is described in detail by the Jewish writer Philo, writing in the first Christian century, in his treatise *On the Contemplative Life*.[12] Members of the sect were apparently found in various towns and villages in Egypt and elsewhere, but there were some who lived a kind of monastic life together in Alexandria. These were both men and women who, after giving away their belongings and leaving their families, moved to a place of solitude outside the city walls where there were gardens and 'solitary wild places'. They did so, Philo says, because they had been 'seized by a heavenly desire' and were 'possessed by God'. They kept the memory of God always unforgotten, prayed twice a day at dawn and dusk, and read sacred literature. They lived in houses which were neither very close together nor very far apart. They spent six days of the week alone, but came together on the seventh, the Sabbath, for a common assembly, at which an elder gave a homily, and they ate together a meal of bread and salt. Being committed to 'temperance' they ate nothing until after sundown, and some of them did not eat for three or six days. Every seventh week there was a special assembly when, after they had eaten, the President gave a long exposition of scripture. After that they sang a hymn and then kept a vigil, during which they formed two choruses, one of men and one of women, and performed a dance as they sang together until dawn. With the rising of the sun they offered prayers before returning to their own sanctuaries.

Here we have a picture of a Jewish community whose life was sufficiently similar to that of later Christian monasteries that, as

12 Philo, *On the Contemplative Life*, pp. 134ff.

we have seen, some believed that it must have been a Christian community. Their emphasis on poverty and the renouncing of personal possessions, on solitude, on the asceticism of limiting their eating, and their practice of coming together every week for a meal, for instruction and for prayer: all these were aspects of the life of later Christian monasteries. There is sufficient similarity to allow one eminent scholar to claim that early Egyptian monasticism 'had Jewish roots'.[13]

The *apotaktikoi* in Egypt, the early Christian solitaries and monasteries, and the Jewish Essenes and Therapeutae, together formed part of the background of the desert movement: the rich soil out of which it grew. These ascetic and monastic developments provided a fertile soil, but they were not the seed of the desert movement. The seed which was the source of the movement's life lay buried deep in the soil of the past, in the long history of the desert tradition of the Bible.

The desert tradition

Throughout the Bible, the desert has a special importance. The people of Israel believed that they owed their origin as a people to the desert and events that happened in it. If we are to understand the desert movement we need to take note of the significance of the desert in the Bible.

In both Old and New Testaments there are a great many references to the 'wilderness'. Both the Hebrew word *midbar* and the Greek word *eremos* refer to empty places of various kinds, not necessarily deserts of pure sand but places where scrub or thorn bushes may grow but where there are no cultivated fields or human dwellings: lonely, desolate places with little or no food or water. To the east and south of the land of Palestine there lay wildernesses of this kind. The people of Israel were always conscious that they lived not very far from the desert.

---

13 Pearson, 'Earliest Christianity in Egypt', p. 110.

They believed that their ancestors had been closely connected with this wilderness, and that this was where their faith originated. Whatever their historical basis, the stories of the Old Testament show how much importance the people of Israel attached to the desert and their desert origins. According to the stories in the book of Genesis, the earliest ancestors of the Israelite people, those we call the 'patriarchs' – Abraham, Isaac and Jacob – lived as pastoral nomads keeping flocks and herds on the edge of the cultivated land of Palestine, always in touch with the wilderness.

It is when we come to Moses that we have the most significant encounters with the desert. According to the tradition it was through him that the worship of Yahweh as their God was initiated and established, and this took place in the desert. Having fled from fear of punishment in Egypt, Moses found himself beside Mount Horeb or Sinai, deep in the wilderness of Sinai.[14] Here in the desert he encountered Yahweh, the God of the Israelites, in a 'burning bush', who instructed him to deliver the people out of slavery in Egypt. When they had escaped from Egypt they were to come to that mountain and worship him there in the desert. When eventually Moses freed them from their subjection, he led them across the Red Sea into the desert, to Mount Sinai. Here they encountered the presence of God in a fearful crashing storm, and were given the Law, which formed the basis of their life as a community. Throughout forty years they remained in the desert, being miraculously provided with food and water, and being led by God in their wanderings.

It was the experience of these desert years that formed the basis of the later religious life of the Israelite people. Its significance is echoed in other parts of the Old Testament, in the Psalms and in the books of all the major prophets.[15] The desert had indelibly stamped its character on the way people of faith

---

14 Exodus 3.
15 Isaiah 63.13; Jeremiah 2.6; Ezekiel 20; Hosea 9.10; 13.5; Amos 2.10.

in Israel viewed their God and their relationship with God.

The next great desert figure in the Bible was Elijah. He was one of the early prophets of Israel, later regarded as a type and symbol of the prophets. He was something of a wild man, dressed in a garment of haircloth with a leather girdle, an unpredictable man of the Spirit. He was a solitary figure generally regarded as a man of the desert. He once spent a long period living by himself in a lonely place, fed morning and evening by ravens sent by God. One story in particular links him with the wilderness: that of his journey to Mount Horeb (or Sinai), the mountain of Moses.[16] Here he too, alone in the desert, as Moses had been at the burning bush, found himself confronted by Yahweh, the God who made himself present not this time in crashing noise or fearful storm but in the mysterious 'sound of sheer silence'. Elijah appears in the Bible as a solitary, eremitical, ascetic, figure. Tradition has it that he lived alone in a cave at Mount Carmel, where, it is said, he was followed by Jewish hermits, and where, much later, the Christian monastic order of Carmelites was founded in the twelfth century CE. Elijah was one who provided a role model, example and inspiration for the Christian desert movement.

The next important desert figure was John the Baptist. In the Gospels John is portrayed as a desert ascetic, after the manner of Elijah. He was 'clothed with camel's hair and had a leather girdle around his waist' – a description that almost exactly matches that of Elijah (Mark 1.6; 2 Kings 1.8). Luke's Gospel says that when the child had grown 'he was in the wilderness until the day he appeared publicly to Israel' (Luke 1.80). And it was in the desert that he began to preach. He was 'The voice of one crying in the wilderness: Prepare the way of the Lord.' Jesus himself referred to John's ascetic lifestyle when he said that 'John came neither eating nor drinking' (Matt. 11.18). The parallel between John and Elijah is emphasized by the fact that he was widely considered, both by the people generally

---

16 1 Kings 19.

and by Jesus himself (Matt. 17.12), to be the new Elijah. It is not without significance that John the Baptist, the Forerunner who introduced the Messiah to the world and one of the most important figures in the New Testament, was in fact an ascetic of the desert.

Jesus himself, however, was no desert ascetic, but the Gospels make it clear that, following in the footsteps of his Forerunner, he had strong links with the wilderness. It is significant that the first thing he did immediately after his baptism by John was to retreat to the wilderness by himself for 40 days and nights, where he fasted and resisted the devil. Later there are frequent references to him going off by himself to the *eremos*, a 'lonely place', sometimes spending the whole night there in prayer. For Jesus as for others the desert was a place for meeting with God, as well as for struggling with the devil. And something of the same must also have been true for Paul, who records that after he had been given a vision of Christ on the road to Damascus, before doing anything else he 'went away at once into Arabia' (Gal. 1.17) to spend some time in the desert.

The theme of the desert thus runs right through the Bible. As we shall see, the monks of the desert movement who took themselves off to the deserts of Judea and Egypt and elsewhere were aware that they were continuing the biblical tradition. Everywhere in the literature of the movement there are references to Elijah and John the Baptist, the archetypal men of the desert in the Bible whom they looked back to in a special way as their prototypes and exemplars, whose tradition and way of life they were consciously continuing.

The miracles performed by monks of the desert were often described in ways which recall miracles in the Bible. The miracles were 'signs that God is working as strongly now as he did among the prophets and apostles'. They place the monks 'directly in the line of the biblical revelation of the power of God'.[17] One intriguing detail gives a practical illustration of the

---

17 Ward, Introduction to *The Lives of the Desert Fathers*, pp. 39f.

monks' awareness of their continuation of the biblical desert tradition. The clothing of the desert monks typically included a sheepskin or goatskin cloak, which they called their *melotê*. This was the word used in the Greek Old Testament for Elijah's special garment, in English usually called his 'mantle', which in a miraculous sign his successor Elisha inherited. The desert monks, in adopting a *melotê* as their symbolic garment, would be conscious that they were following in the footsteps and tradition of Elijah. It was from the biblical desert tradition and the example provided by Moses, Elijah, John the Baptist and Jesus himself that the desert movement drew its principal inspiration. As we shall see, all the monks of the desert were aware of, hearkened back to, and deliberately continued this biblical heritage.

The desert movement

The desert monks were therefore different from the *apotaktikoi* and others who lived an ascetic life in towns and villages, in that they took themselves off to the desert. Unlike others, they were people who, in James Goehring's words, 'withdrew spatially from the community'.[18] What distinguished them was their *anachoresis*, their withdrawal. For most of them this meant living physically in the desert, but there were some who separated themselves from the community while living on the margin between the desert and the town.

In the third and fourth centuries something was stirring among Christian people, causing this desert movement to spring to life simultaneously and spontaneously in a number of places. This was something new: a new spirit moving in the hearts of men and women, a desire to seek out the desert, a longing for the solitude of the *eremos*, the empty lonely place where one could be alone with God. It was not the result of one

---

18 Goehring, 'Through a Glass Darkly', p. 68.

person's initiative, nor did it emerge in one place from which it spread; it simply emerged in various places from the seed of the biblical desert tradition. The form it took was influenced, no doubt, by contemporary ascetic developments in Christianity and Judaism, but the movement itself was something different, a new plant growing from an ancient seed under the impulse of the Spirit of God.

There were three principal areas where the desert movement initially developed. One was Lower or northern Egypt, the place with which it has been most commonly associated. It was here that Antony the Great made his celebrated move to the solitude of the desert, to be followed by many others. The *Life of Antony* written by Athanasius, the collections of the sayings and stories of these monks and the accounts of their life written by visitors to the area have all served to make this the most well known of the places where the movement developed.

Rather less well known is the monasticism of Upper or southern Egypt. The monasteries of Pachomius have indeed been widely studied, but until quite recently less has been known of the monasteries of Shenoute, and less still of the anchorites isolated deep in the remote desert beyond Aswan, near the present-day border with Sudan. This area was linked in some ways with developments in the north, but it had its own characteristics and personalities.

The developments in the third area, the deserts of Judea, are also relatively unknown. Nevertheless, this area, with its long and close associations with the biblical desert tradition, and its proximity to the Christian Holy Places, was the spiritual heartland of the desert movement, the place where the seeds of the desert movement had been sown. It sprang up here independently of developments in Egypt, and also had its own special features and remarkable personalities.

Some other areas were also influenced by the movement. Mount Sinai, a place of very great importance in the biblical tradition, attracted monks and hermits from an early age. It was the place where John Climacus later wrote his celebrated *Ladder of Divine Ascent*, gathering up and expounding the way of the desert for monks of generations to come. And Gaza in southern Palestine, although not actually in the desert, became an important monastic centre, begun by monks from Upper Egypt and maintained by others who continued the desert tradition. Ascetic monasticism was also strongly developed in Syria and in the Cappadocia of Basil of Caesarea, but in both places it had a somewhat different character and did not essentially involve the desert.[19]

In recent years there has been a considerable interest in the monks of the desert, and much has been written about them in both scholarly and more popular works. Most writers, however, have concentrated very largely, if not exclusively, on the 'Desert Fathers' of Upper Egypt, to the extent that one might be forgiven for thinking that there were no others. Although the last two or three decades have seen the publication in English translation of a large number of texts from other places, especially from the lesser known areas of Upper Egypt, Judea and Gaza, there has been little attempt to look at all these texts together, and to see the developments in these various areas as parts of one desert movement.[20] This book is an attempt to do just that – to look at the movement as a whole and how it developed in the different areas, noting the similarities and the differences in the pattern of their monastic life, telling what we know of the leading figures, and describing what we can gather about the spiritual life of the monks and their purpose in embracing this extraordinary way of life.

The book is in two parts. Part One has three chapters which deal with the three main areas where the desert movement originated, starting with Lower Egypt because most is known about it, and concluding with Judea, the place of the bibli-

---

19 See the Additional Note, pp. 226ff.

20 Possible exceptions are the important books by Chitty, *The Desert a City*, and Harmless, *Desert Christians*, but even these do not discuss all the areas described here.

cal wilderness. A fourth chapter then deals with the place of women in the desert movement. The fifth chapter is an attempt to gather up the features of the movement as a whole, and to offer a general description of what may be called the 'way of the desert', both its external and its inner or spiritual aspects. Part Two deals with various ways in which this way of the desert was interpreted and developed by others, by the thinkers and systematizers Evagrius and Cassian, by the monks of Gaza, and by John Climacus of Sinai.

The aim of this book is to describe what we know of the desert movement from the writings of the time. It does not attempt to provide a 'spirituality of the desert' for our own day as has been done in several other publications.[21] A concluding chapter, however, presents some thoughts about some of the difficulties that the desert movement presents to modern readers, and goes on to point to what may be regarded as the main distinctive features of the movement when it is viewed from a modern perspective.

---

21 See for example the works by Rowan Williams, John Chryssavgis, David Keller, and Douglas Burton-Christie in the Bibliography.

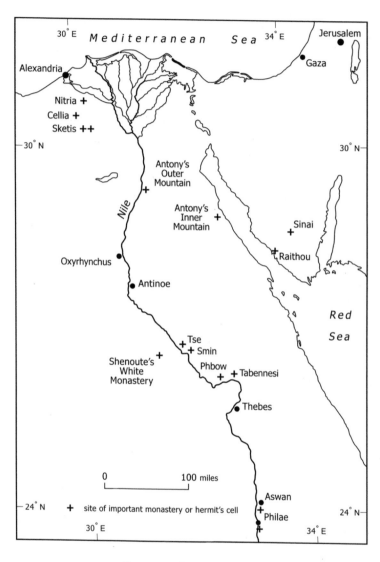

Lower and Upper Egypt

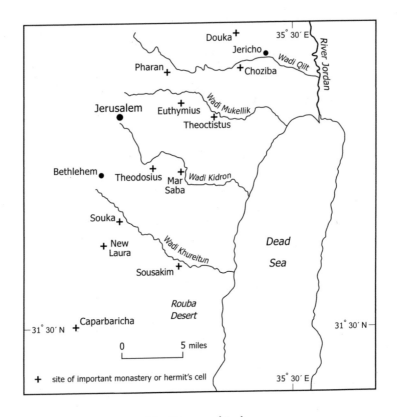

The Desert of Judea

PART ONE

The Original Areas

I

Lower Egypt

The place with which the desert movement is especially associated in most people's minds is Lower, or northern, Egypt. Here the long River Nile, having wound its way through hundreds of miles of desert, spreads out into a broad delta. Where it nears the Mediterranean Sea there are lakes and marshes, and also towns and cities. In those early years the principal city was Alexandria, a place of Greek language and culture. Other towns and villages were to be found inland, all along the Nile Valley. The desert, however, was never far away, and this is where some of the earliest desert monks were to be found.

Antony the Great

The desert movement in Lower Egypt is indelibly associated with the name of Antony, usually regarded as the great pioneer and initiator of the eremitic or hermit life. He was not in fact the first desert hermit, as we shall see. But it was Antony who became well known throughout the Christian world, mainly as a result of the *Life of Antony*, written by the famous Bishop Athanasius of Alexandria soon after Antony's death in 356 CE. Athanasius gives a vivid account of the monk's life, portraying him as a heroic figure, who spent his life in solitude, rigorous asceticism and prayer, and in single-handed combat with the demons. The book also provides an account of Antony's teaching and instructions given to fellow monks, and although we cannot be sure how much of this stems from Antony himself and how much from Athanasius, it gives us an early statement of the principles and purpose of the desert life of Lower Egypt.

The story of Antony's life is well known, but a brief rehearsal of it is essential if we are to understand the life of the monks of Lower Egypt. He was born about 251, and brought up in a Christian home. When he was aged about 20, a few months after his parents had died, he experienced what amounted to a call to the monastic life. In church one Sunday he heard in the reading of the words of the Gospel: 'If you would be perfect, go, sell what you possess and give to the poor, and come, follow me.' Feeling that these words were addressed directly to himself, he sold the land and possessions he had inherited from his parents and gave the money to the poor of the town. He first attached himself to a hermit living near his own village, and also visited and learned from others like him. Over a period of perhaps 15 years he continued to develop a life of asceticism, solitude and prayer. Towards the end of this time he shut himself in a tomb. Here the demons attacked him mercilessly, at one point leaving him apparently dead but not defeated. It was an experience which taught him how to overcome demonic attacks by prayer.

After this long apprenticeship in monastic discipline, he felt that he would better express his devotion to God by moving into the solitude of the desert; and having ascertained that his hermit mentor felt unable to accompany him, he set off by himself into the empty wilderness, taking a supply of bread with him. The bread consisted of dried loaves which could be kept indefinitely and soaked in water before they were eaten. He found a deserted fortress in which he barricaded himself in solitude. This place, some hundreds of miles up the Nile Valley from the Delta area, was what came to be known as Antony's 'Outer Mountain' – the word 'mountain' being a way of referring to the desert. He remained in this lonely cell for nearly twenty years, as Athanasius says, 'pursuing the ascetic life by himself, not venturing out and only occasionally being seen by anyone'.[1] He spent his time in prayer and in the struggle with demons, and fed on loaves left for him outside his cell by supporters twice a year. After 20 years some friends broke down his door and Antony emerged, totally unchanged in appearance. He continued in this desert place for many years, training up disciples and gathering a community of monks. In his account of this period of Antony's life Athanasius includes a long address said to have been given by Antony to these fellow monks, to explain the monastic life and encourage them in it. Many people from far and wide came to see him, seeking his guidance and his healing powers. In the year 311 he paid a visit to Alexandria to encourage and support Christians suffering from persecution. But soon he began to long for greater solitude, and leaving this Outer Mountain he retreated to a more remote part of the desert, further east towards the Red Sea. Guided by an inner voice and with the help of some Bedouin, he came to a place with which he fell in love, a hill with a small oasis and a few palm trees. This was to become his 'Inner Mountain', and became his base for the rest of his days, spent in silence, prayer and asceticism, supplying his bodily needs by making himself a small garden, and from time to time receiving visitors who made the journey to consult him. He made occasional visits to the Outer Mountain, and one more visit to Alexandria, this time to combat heresy. Two disciples who shared his desert retreat were with him when he died, aged 105, and according to his instructions they buried him in the desert, and told no one where he was buried.

Athanasius' biography became something of a best-seller, and through it the fame of this lover of solitude spread far and wide. It is our major source of information about Antony, but there are other sources as well. He is credited with having written seven letters, which have now been translated into English. Some have doubted the authenticity of these letters, largely on

---

[1] *Life of Antony*, 14.

the grounds that a Coptic monk who may have been illiterate could scarcely have written in this way. But being illiterate would not have prevented an intelligent and deeply spiritual man from dictating letters of this kind, and others believe that the letters give us a deep insight into his thoughts and attitudes. In addition, the collection of *Sayings of the Desert Fathers* includes a number which are attributed to Antony. From all these sources we learn something, not only of his way of life and ascetic practice but of his spirituality and his view of the purpose of the monastic life. In other words, these sources illustrate in a preliminary way some of the essential ingredients of the way of the desert which we shall discuss more fully in Chapter 5.

Among these ingredients was *solitude*. Having attached himself initially to a monk near his village who had practised the solitary life from his youth, Antony learned to love solitude. His moves into the desert, first to his Outer Mountain and then to his Inner Mountain, were made in search of greater solitude. He needed to escape from the presence and attention of other people, and to be by himself, alone with God. He sought not fame but obscurity, to conceal himself from other people. This does not mean that he had no concern for other people. His openness to sincere enquirers, his visits to the city to support the church, and his offering of himself in prayer were all done out of a concern for others, because he believed, as he put it, that 'our life is from our neighbour'.[2] Desert monasticism, as we shall see, took different forms, of which the eremitical life was only one; but it always included a measure of solitude.

Another basic ingredient of the monastic life was *asceticism*. Athanasius reports that from the start of his monastic life, before ever he retreated to the desert, Antony adopted a rigorous ascetic discipline, particularly with regard to sleep and food. He 'often passed the entire night without sleep', he 'ate once daily, after sunset, but there were times when he received

---

2 *Letters of Antony*, 6.

food every second and frequently even every fourth day'.[3] This control of one's eating and sleeping, to various degrees and in different ways, became the normal practice of all the monks of the desert movement.

It is clear, however, that for Antony these external practices were not as important as the inner discipline. Here we encounter one of the most essential concepts of the desert way.

In one of his reported sayings, he reminds his listeners of the words of Jesus: 'Take heed to yourselves.' And one story about him tells how he heard a voice saying, 'Antony, keep your attention on yourself'.[4] This instruction, to *attend to yourself*, forms the basis of the inner discipline. It involves knowing oneself, something that Antony mentions several times in his letters. 'He who knows himself', he says, 'knows God.'[5] He believed that our true nature is good, being 'made in the image of his [Christ's] image',[6] and that 'evil is alien to our nature'.[7] And so our task is to 'remain as we were made',[8] to know our true self and to remain that self. Attending to oneself is not, as some might think, a matter of selfishly thinking only of oneself, but an injunction to examine one's inner self, to seek the roots of sin within it, to take responsibility for it, and to continue to 'guard the heart' so as to prevent it from being taken over by corrupting thoughts or passions. It is this inner attention which leads to humility and repentance, and the refusal to blame or judge other people.

One of the most striking things about the *Life of Antony* is the description of his battles with the *demons*. Paying attention to oneself demanded constant vigilance and a struggle against them. When he was shut up in the tomb and in the desert fortress he was attacked by demons not just within his own

---

3 *Life of Antony*, 7.
4 *Sayings of the Desert Fathers* (hereafter referred to as *Sayings*), Antony, 2.
5 *Letters of Antony*, 3.
6 Ibid., 6.
7 Ibid., 7.
8 Ibid., 20.

mind but physically. Taking forms of all sorts, they struck and buffeted him, on one occasion leaving him apparently dead. Their object was to get him to yield to a 'spirit of fornication', and ultimately to abandon his monastic vocation. However we may interpret these descriptions of demonic attacks, it is clear that the struggle against the demons was basically an inner struggle, a warfare against the 'passions' within. In one of his letters Antony says that the demons 'are not visible bodily; but . . . we serve as bodies for them, for our soul receives their wickedness'.[9] The demons were at work, however, not just within the individual but throughout the world. His most-quoted saying shows how conscious he was of the widespread power of evil: 'I saw the snares of the devil spreading out over the world.'[10] The struggle against them is a life-long one, and the monk must 'expect temptations to his last breath'.[11]

This battle against the demons was not, however, fought with one's own strength. The demons were overcome by the power of prayer and the grace of Christ. So the principal task of the monk was to engage in *unceasing prayer*.[12] Constant prayer involved a continual offering of one's total self to God. In his letters Antony repeatedly urged his readers 'to offer yourselves a sacrifice to God in all holiness'.[13] 'Make your body an altar,' he counsels, 'and set thereon all your thoughts, and leave there every evil counsel before the Lord.'[14]

By praying in this way and calling on God's help in the struggle against demonic passions, one can be led closer to '*purity of heart*'. Attaining purity of heart was, as we shall see, one way of describing the purpose and aim of the desert monks. Antony himself is described by Athanasius as being 'ready to appear before God – that is, pure in heart and prepared to obey his

9 Ibid., 6.
10 *Sayings*, Antony, 7.
11 Ibid., 4.
12 *Life of Antony*, 3, 5, 55.
13 *Letters of Antony*, 5, 6, 7.
14 Ibid., 6.

will, and no other'.[15] Purity of heart was the way to be able to draw near to God, to be 'ready to appear before God', and it was this intimate relationship with God that was Antony's ultimate object. He advised an enquirer, 'Always have God before your eyes.'[16] It was because he himself did this that he was known as 'God-loved'.[17]

Part of a larger movement

Antony is regarded as the pioneer of this way of life, and he was looked up to and looked back to as a great exemplar of it. But, as we have seen, he was not alone, but was part of a larger movement. Athanasius in his *Life* says that Antony believed that ascetics should learn from 'the great Elijah',[18] thus providing a link with the biblical desert tradition. We have seen also that Antony owed his monastic training to other monks who lived the eremitical life before him near to his own village. And as we shall see, later on he had connections with monks from independent monastic developments in Palestine and in Upper Egypt.

Perhaps the fact that the desert movement did not simply start with Antony is most engagingly illustrated by the story of his meeting with Paul of Thebes, a story which bears retelling. It comes from Jerome's *Life of Paul of Thebes*, written probably in Antioch about 337, while Antony was still alive.[19] When Antony was 90 years old, the story says, and living in his Inner Mountain, 'during the night while he was asleep it was revealed to him that there was someone else further into the desert interior who was far better than him and whom he ought to go and visit'. This was Paul of Thebes, now aged 113

---

15 *Life of Antony*, 7.
16 *Sayings*, Antony, 3.
17 *Life of Antony*, 4.
18 Ibid., 7.
19 See White, Introduction to Jerome's *Life of Paul of Thebes*, p. 73.

years. Antony duly made his way on foot through the desert and, miraculously guided by a strange creature, he eventually found Paul's desert cell. After warm greetings the two prayed and gave thanks together, and then shared a loaf which had been miraculously supplied by a raven. Rather than having one of them break the bread, they broke it together by holding the loaf between them. Paul, being aware that he was about to die, asked Antony to go back to his own cell and bring a cloak given him by Athanasius to cover his dead body. On his return he found that Paul had already died. Wrapping his body in the cloak he buried him in a grave dug for him by two lions.

How much historical fact lies behind this tale is not clear, but the fact that the story was widely circulated testifies to the widespread popularity and influence of Antony.[20] The story also bears witness to the existence of a desert movement prior to Antony's own vocation to the eremitical life.

Lower Egypt: our sources of information

During the period following Antony's retreat to the desert, a large number of men and a few women entered the monastic life in Lower Egypt. It is impossible to tell whether they were all drawn there by the example of Antony, or whether some felt the call to the desert quite independently. We know about these desert monks from a number of sources. The one which attracts most attention is known as the *Apophthegmata Patrum* or *Sayings of the Desert Fathers*. This is a collection of

---

20 Images of Antony's meeting with Paul are found, for example, on at least four carved stones in faraway Scotland dating from the seventh and eighth centuries. One of them, the eighth century Nigg stone, shows a raven bringing the bread to them in the desert, recalling the story of Elijah in 1 Kings 17, as is mentioned in Jerome's account. It is worth noting that in it Antony, on returning after his meeting with Paul, says, 'I have seen Elijah.' This same stone shows two animals at the monks' feet, presumably the lions that dug Paul's grave.

sayings of the desert monks and stories about them, recalled by those who knew them, passed on originally by word of mouth, and later gathered together and written down. Some of them are arranged alphabetically according to the name of the person concerned, and referred to as the 'Alphabetic Collection'; and some, the 'Anonymous Series', are arranged systematically according to their subject matter. Sister Benedicta Ward's translations of a large number of these sayings and stories has made them especially accessible to readers of English. They have their own special character; short and pithy, sometimes enigmatic and puzzling, their meaning is not always immediately apparent. This is partly because the sayings were addressed mostly to particular individual hearers in circumstances which are not always known to us, and were not meant to be applied generally. Nonetheless, pondering them can reveal a depth of penetrating thought and insight which has relevance even today. It is these stories and sayings which have opened the world of the desert monks to modern readers, and aroused a great deal of interest.

Our other main source of information is the writings of a number of people who visited the monasteries of the desert to meet some of the leading figures and gather information about their life. The first of these was Palladius, who had embraced the monastic life in Palestine about 386. Shortly after that, being keen to learn about the Egyptian hermits, he travelled to Egypt, staying first of all in or near Alexandria for three years, and then spending longer periods in the monastic centres of Nitria and Cellia. He gathered a wealth of stories, of the monks, of their way of life, and of miracles they performed, and wrote them in a book, which became known as the *Lausiac History* because of its dedication to the emperor's chamberlain, Lausius. Some stories were based on Palladius' own experience, on places he himself had visited and people he had met, and some on things he was told by others. Although there is doubt about the historical reliability of some of the narratives, the *Lausiac History* provides us with a most useful source of information about the desert monks.

Shortly after Palladius, another group of visitors came to Egypt from Palestine. Seven Palestine monks, whose names are unknown to us, made a journey through Egypt in 394. They too gathered stories and sayings of the monks and hermits, and published their account in a volume known as *The History of the Monks of Egypt*.[21] This was later translated into Latin from the original Greek by Rufinus, a monk in Jerusalem who had himself visited Egypt, and who made some alterations to the original account.

Two other visitors to Egypt provide us with material of a different kind. Evagrius Ponticus, born about 345, and John Cassian, born about 360, were both able and intellectual men who, after spending time among the monks of Lower Egypt, gave deep thought to this way of life, and in the light of their experience wrote about its practice and principles. Both of these will be discussed in Chapter 6.

There are other, later works which include stories of the monks of Lower Egypt, including *The Spiritual Meadow*, written by John Moschos about 600, and various versions of the *Life of Daniel of Sketis*, a work about a sixth-century priest and monastic superior. In addition, there is a collection of fourteen letters written by Ammonas, a desert monk who succeeded Antony, and eleven of whose sayings are included in the *Sayings of the Desert Fathers*.

The monastic centres

The stories of the monks of Lower Egypt are based on three principal monastic centres. First there was Nitria, a promontory of desert extending northwards to within about 40 miles of Alexandria: a desert place, but one where water was

---

21 Published in English as *The Lives of the Desert Fathers*.

accessible. Amoun, who became one of the leading figures of Egyptian monasticism, is said to have been the first to move there about the year 330. He was a married man who had lived a life of asceticism for many years with his wife, but eventually decided, with her support, to move to a life of solitude. So Amoun built himself a cell in Nitria. He was soon joined by others, and a loose community of monks grew up, living in cells often grouped together around a respected elder monk or abba. The numbers grew enormously: Palladius claimed that at the time of his visit in about the year 388 there were close to 5,000 monks living there, following different patterns of life.[22]

As numbers began to increase in Nitria, Amoun longed for greater solitude. In the year 338, when in the course of a visit to Alexandria Antony came to Nitria, the two men walked out from there to a lonely spot some 12 miles to the south. Here Amoun made himself a new cell, in a place which came to be known as 'The Cells', or 'Cellia'. Others monks followed him there, including some who had 'already begun their training' in Nitria but now wanted 'to live a more remote life, stripped of external things'. The Cells thus became a second monastic centre, but one which was very different from Nitria. This was what Rufinus called the 'utter desert', where there was 'a huge silence and a great quiet',[23] and the monks lived alone in their cells at a good distance from one another, coming together only on Saturdays and Sundays in church.

The third centre was Sketis. This was a much more remote place, about 40 miles from Cellia, a low-lying valley, much of it below sea level, known today as the Wadi Natrum, a place where throughout the centuries nitre has been gathered. Reaching Sketis involved a long, arduous journey across a trackless desert where it was quite possible to lose one's way. It was here, to this unlikely place, that Macarius the Egyptian, another of the

---

22 Palladius, *Lausiac History*, 7:2.
23 *The Lives of the Desert Fathers*, Additions of Rufinus, XXII.8.

early ascetics, came in 330 and built a cell, making this his base for the next 60 years. Once again others followed, and before long Sketis became 'the most flourishing centre of anchoritic life', where the most renowned Fathers lived.[24] When Cassian came there sometime after 385 he found four churches.[25] The desert was, however, a lawless and dangerous place, and Sketis twice suffered devastation at the hands of 'barbarians', in 407 and 434, causing many monks to leave and go elsewhere, some to a place called Terenuthis[26] not far away, and a number to Palestine.

These, then, were the main monastic centres in Lower Egypt. Various forms of monastic life were found in them, with varying degrees of isolation from others. These were not, however, the only places in Lower Egypt where monks were to be found. We have seen already that there were monks living as hermits near Antony's village when he was young. Some of the stories of the desert also tell of occasions when a monk on his travels unexpectedly came across an unknown hermit living all by himself in some remote place. Palladius' *Lausiac History* contains stories of hermits living in a great variety of places. In addition, we know that there were coenobia, or organized monasteries, in the Nile Delta area, some of which were visited by Cassian and his companion Germanus.[27] When Palladius visited Egypt he spent four years in Antinoe, some 200 miles further up the Nile Valley from Sketis, where, according to his account, there were 1,200 monks living in monasteries, as well as anchorites living in rocky caves.[28] We know also of John of Lycopolis, a monk living some 60 miles further still up the river.[29] And while most of the accounts of desert monks are about men, there were also

---

24 Regnault, *The Day-to-Day Life of the Desert Fathers*, p. 6.
25 Cassian, *Conferences*, 10.2.3.
26 *Sayings*, Anoub, 1.
27 Cassian, *Conferences*, 18.1f.
28 Palladius, *Lausiac History*, 58.
29 *Lives of the Desert Fathers*, I.

large numbers of nuns living in women's monasteries and some anchoresses living alone in cells.[30] Most of these appear to have been near the towns or villages, but some were found deeper in the desert.

From all this it is clear that, by the nature of their calling and their way of life, many monks remained hidden from the public eye. They chose to live in remote places, where few people visited them and no one collected their sayings or stories about them. The sayings and stories we have tell us something about the well-known monks and hermits, and give us a window into the monastic life of the desert, but they do not tell us the whole story.

The leading figures

Although it is said that in the fourth century there were thousands of monks in Lower Egypt, we know of only a relatively small number of them. Benedicta Ward's translation of the Alphabetic Collection includes sayings and stories of 130 monks. These were some of the prominent and well-known ones, mostly monks regarded as elders or *abbas* to whom their disciples and others looked for example, advice and direction. Their sayings were often a response to someone who had asked to be given 'a word'. Here we take a look at some of these leading figures and a few of their most significant sayings and stories.[31]

Arsenius was one of the best known of the desert monks. He was unusual in that unlike many of the monks he was not a native Egyptian, but a well-educated Roman nobleman who had held a high post in the Emperor's palace in Constantinople. He was a commanding figure, perhaps not always liked by his fellow monks, but famous for his asceticism and his love

---

30 See Chapter 4.

31 The quotations in this section are all taken from the relevant sections of the *Sayings of the Desert Fathers*.

of silence and seclusion. The first stories recorded about him tell how he had prayed to be shown the way of salvation, and a voice had said to him, 'Arsenius, flee from men and you will be saved.' His love of seclusion is shown in a number of stories. In one, the Archbishop Theophilus and a magistrate came to see him and asked for 'a word'.

> After a short silence the old man answered him, 'Will you put into practice what I say to you?' They promised him this. He replied, 'If you hear Arsenius is anywhere, do not go there.'

He was once asked by one of his fellow monks why he seemed to avoid them. He replied,

> 'God knows that I love you, but I cannot live with God and with men. The thousands and ten thousands of the heavenly host have but one will, while men have many. So I cannot leave God to be with men.'

It was said of him that:

> When from time to time he came to church he would sit behind a pillar, so that no one should see his face and so that he himself would not notice others.

When he was at the point of death he made this comment on his long life:

> 'I have often repented of having spoken, but never of having been silent.'

Agathon came to the desert while quite a young man, but because of the quality of his speech he was soon recognized as an abba. He lived for a long time in Sketis with his disciple

Abraham, and had known some of the early pioneers of that place. He is said to have moved about quite a lot, building a cell in one place and then moving on. One saying reports that:

> It was said of him that he often went away taking nothing but his knife for making wicker baskets.

A saying of his demonstrates the importance of prayer in the struggle against the demons:

> 'Every time a man wants to pray, his enemies, the demons, want to prevent him, for they know it is only by turning him from prayer that they can hinder his journey. Whatever good work a man undertakes, if he perseveres in it, he will attain rest. But prayer is warfare to the last breath.'

This prayer involves recognizing one's weakness.

> A brother asked Abba Agathon about fornication. He answered, 'Go, cast your weakness before God and you shall find rest.'

John the Dwarf came from a village in Upper Egypt, where even as a child he had a desire to be a monk. After years of training by an abba, he himself became a popular abba in Sketis. He was known especially for his humility, as can be seen from a number of his sayings.

> One of the Fathers said of him, 'Who is this John, who by his humility has all Sketis hanging from his little finger?'

> He also said, 'Humility and the fear of God are above all the virtues.'

> Someone who came to see him praised his work, and he remained silent, for he was weaving a rope. Once again the

visitor began to speak and once again he kept silence. The third time he said to the visitor, 'Since you came here, you have driven God from me.'

Macarius the Great was one of two monks of that name. The other one was known as Macarius the Alexandrian and was a Greek-speaking monk from the city. This one, known as 'the Egyptian', was a Copt who before he became a monk had been a camel-driver trading in nitre. He was probably familiar with the Wadi Natrum, the place famous for nitre, and he is reputed to have been the first to make a cell there, and thus to have initiated the monastic centre of Sketis. Before moving into the desert he lived for a while as an ascetic in a village, and later, even after building a cell in Sketis, he seems to have travelled around to different places. There are stories of him dwelling for a while in 'the great desert', and of visits paid to Antony. A number of his recorded sayings suggest that he was particularly aware of his own sins, of the importance of not judging others' sins, and of being willing to accept blame even if it is not justified. To those who asked for a 'word' of advice he sometimes gave a brief reply:

'Do no evil to anyone, and do not judge anyone. Observe this and you will be saved.'

'Sit in your cell and weep for your sins.'

When asked about how to pray, he said:

'There is no need at all to make long discourses; it is enough to stretch out one's hands and say, "Lord, as you will, and as you know, have mercy." And if the conflict grows fiercer say, "Lord, help!" He knows very well what we need and he shows us his mercy.'

It was said of him:

> Just as God protects the world, so Abba Macarius would cover the faults which he saw, as though he did not see them, and those which he heard, as though he did not hear them.

Moses was a black-skinned Ethiopian. Before becoming a Christian and a monk he had been a robber with a history of violence. He was very conscious of himself as a sinner, in need of humility and repentance. It seems that even when some other monks abused and rejected him because of his colour, he had the humility and inner strength to accept this without complaint. When he was ordained a priest and clothed with a white ephod,

> The archbishop said to him, 'See, Abba Moses, now you are entirely white.' The old man said to him, 'It is true of the outside, lord and father, but what about Him who sees the inside?'

He refused to blame or find fault with others, saying,

> 'When someone is occupied with his own faults, he does not see those of his neighbour.'

Perhaps his most famous saying, one which was often repeated by others, is a true expression of the way of the desert.

> 'Go, sit in your cell, and your cell with teach you everything.'

Bessarion seems to have been something of a wanderer, moving from place to place. It was said of him that he had spent his life 'without trouble or disquiet'.

He seemed entirely free from all the passions of the body
... firm in the strength of his faith; he lived in patience ...
always suffering cold and nakedness, scorched by the sun.
He always lived in the open air, afflicting himself on the edge
of the desert like a vagabond.

One story tells how in his journeying he once came across an
unknown hermit living in a cave, who did not answer when
spoken to. Returning later, Bessarion found that the hermit had
died. On taking the body for burial he found it was a woman,
dressed like a man.

Filled with astonishment, the old man said, 'See how the
women triumph over Satan, while we men still behave badly
in the towns.'

Another brief story illustrates something of the way of the
desert.

A brother who had sinned was turned out of the church by
the priest. Abba Bessarion got up and went with him, saying,
'I too am a sinner.'

Syncletica was one of three women ascetics quoted in the *Sayings of the Desert Fathers*.[32] There are many sayings of hers
recorded in this collection, but no stories about her. We know
something of her, however, from a *Life* written not long after
her death about the year 460. She belonged to wealthy family
in Alexandria, and was well educated. After the death of her
parents she sold her possessions, and moved out of the city,
along with her blind sister, to live in the tombs on the outskirts
of the town. We shall encounter her again in Chapter 4.

32 These three are discussed at greater length in Chapter 4, which deals with
women's part in the desert movement.

Her sayings suggest that she emphasized the importance of achieving a balanced way of life. What distinguishes 'divine asceticism' from that which is 'determined by the enemy' is 'its quality of balance'. Ascetic practices should not be taken to excess.

'We who have chosen this way of life must obtain perfect temperance.'
'As long as we are in the monastery, obedience is preferable to asceticism.'

True asceticism also involves willingly accepting adversities that come unsought.

'This is the great asceticism: to control oneself in illness and to sing hymns of thanksgiving to God.'

And the really important things are prayer and humility.

'Prayer joined to fasting drives evil thoughts away.'
'It is impossible to be saved without humility.'

Poemen. There are a great many sayings and stories of Poemen in the collection, and as this was a very common name it may be that they originated with different people. Nevertheless, certain themes can be discerned among them. One is that of silence and secrecy.

'If you are silent, you will have peace wherever you live.'
'A person may seem to be silent, but if his heart is condemning others he is babbling ceaselessly. But there may be another who talks from morning till night and yet is truly silent.'
'The victory over all the afflictions that befall you is to keep silence.'

It was said of him that:

It was always the old man's way, to do everything in secret so that no one noticed it.

Another theme is the importance of being aware of one's own faults and of overlooking those of others.

He was asked, 'When we see brothers who are dozing at the *synaxis* shall we rouse them so that they will be watchful?' He replied, 'For my part, when I see a brother who is dozing, I put his head on my knees and let him rest.'

Similarly,

'If I have to go out and I see someone committing a sin, I pass on my way without reproving him.'

He recommended that if one sees someone committing a murder, one should say,

'He has only committed this one sin, but I commit sins every day.'

Theodore of Pherme, one of several monks called Theodore, was another educated man, who had been trained in Sketis, probably by Macarius the Great. After the first devastation of Sketis he moved to Pherme, a mountain to the north of the Wadi Natrum. He was aware of the need for the monk to be committed to what he called 'the work of the soul'. One of his sayings makes it clear that the desert life was not simply a matter of trying to find inner peace. When a young man came to him because he was troubled by his lack of progress, he said,

'Why have you become a monk? Was it not to suffer trials? Tell me how long you have worn the habit?' He replied, 'For eight years.' Then the old man said to him, 'I have worn the habit seventy years and on no day have I found peace. Do you expect to obtain peace in eight years?'

An important part of his discipline was ensuring that he didn't despise anyone.

> 'There is no other virtue than that of not being scornful.'
> 'The man who has learnt the sweetness of the cell flees from his neighbour but not as though he despised him.'

The desert way of life

It was suggested earlier that the desert movement had its roots and origin in the biblical desert tradition. When we turn to the records of the monks of Lower Egypt we can see that they were aware of this, and that they regarded Elijah and John the Baptist, the two most outstanding men of the desert in the Bible, as the great exemplars of their way of life. Cassian, recalling his years spent in the Egyptian desert, refers explicitly to 'those who in the Old Testament were responsible for the beginnings of this profession – namely Elijah and Elisha', and claims that the monastic garb derives from them, mentioning particularly the monks' goatskin, or *melotê*.[33] Similarly, the fifth-century church historian Sozomen, writing of the monks of Egypt, said, 'Elijah the prophet and John the Baptist were the authors, as some say, of this sublime philosophy (i.e. way of life).'[34] We have already seen that Antony regarded Elijah as the great prototype from whom desert ascetics should learn, and that he saw Paul of Thebes as another Elijah. Ammonas in his letters to fellow monks urges them to imitate the holy fathers who 'withdrew into the desert alone, men such as Elijah the Tishbite and John the Baptist'.[35] People said of a monk named Elias that 'the spirit of the prophet Elijah rested on him'.[36] And

---

33 Cassian, *Institutes*, 1.1.4, and 1.7. On the *melotê* see p. 11.
34 Sozomen, *Ecclesiastical History*, I, 12.
35 *The Letters of Ammonas*, XII and VIII.
36 *The Lives of the Desert Fathers*, VII.1.

Elijah is mentioned elsewhere in the desert records.[37] Clearly the way of life of the Christian monks of Egypt was not felt to be something entirely new, but a resumption of a much older tradition.

What, then, was this way of life like? The practical aspects of monastic life in Lower Egypt followed the pattern of Antony, described above. The first thing to note is that men or women who felt a call to it had to start by making a clean and decisive break with their old life. To begin with they had to give up or give away all their possessions. We have already seen how Antony sold his land and gave all he had to the poor. Many of the monks of Egypt will have been ordinary, poor village people who had little to give away, but there were some who had considerable wealth. For example, a very wealthy merchant of Alexandria with a business worth 20,000 gold coins, after encountering a monk named Paphnutius on a boat on the Nile, eventually gave away all that he had and went to live in a cave.[38] The important thing, however, was not what or how much one gave away, but the decision to make a clean break with one's old life, and leave 'the world'. This clean break involved an *anachoresis*, a word meaning, literally, a withdrawal to another place, but used to refer to a radical and complete renunciation of one's previous life, an abandonment of one's home, possessions, comforts, relationships and way of life, and a move into the empty desert. The desert represented, in symbol and in practice, a complete and utter dependence on God alone. It was, as we have seen, a severe and sometimes dangerous place, but one which had its own attractiveness. It is said that Antony, on reaching his Inner Mountain, 'fell in love with the place',[39] and the same was said of Paul of Thebes.[40]

---

37 *The World of the Desert Fathers*, p. 32; *Life of Daniel of Scetis*, p. 70.

38 *The Lives of the Desert Fathers*, XIV.18ff. See also XXIII.2, and Introduction, p. 34.

39 *Life of Antony*, 50.

40 Jerome, *Life of Paul of Thebes*, 6.

This *anachoresis* involved breaking the ties with one's family. In principle, monks of the desert had no family, and belonged only to God, and there are many, sometimes to us rather distressing, stories of monks' families who wanted to keep in contact, or who needed their help and support, and who were rejected. Poemen's aged mother came to see him with tears, and was greatly distressed when she was refused, until she was reassured that she would see him in the age to come.[41] Pior's sister was desperate to visit her brother, and under pressure from the bishop he went and stood outside her house to let her see him, but refused to look at her.[42] On the other hand, a monk who wanted to help his poor sister was told by his abba, 'Blood is thicker than water.'[43] Generally, however, it was believed to be particularly important for male monks to keep separate from women. There were indeed quite large numbers of women monks, most of whom lived near the towns or villages, although a few were in the desert, as we shall see. The deeper or 'great' desert in particular was felt to be a place for men. This is an issue we shall return to in Chapter 4.

On moving to the desert, the first thing a monk had to do was to find or build a cell. Cells in the desert were usually built of stone, and could be very small with just one little room, or larger with two. Some monks found caves which they turned into cells. They had very few furnishings in their cells: only a mat for sitting and sleeping on, possibly a small papyrus bale for a pillow or seat, and vessels for food and water.[44] Cells could be situated close to one another, often near to that of an abba, or they could be more isolated. Experienced ascetics could move far away into the great desert on their own, as Antony did. The monks of Nitria together formed a kind of monastic community, and the same was true to a lesser extent of the monks of Cellia and Sketis. They came together on

---

41 *Sayings*, Poemen, 76.
42 Palladius, *Lausiac History*, 39.1f.
43 *The Wisdom of the Desert Fathers*, 101, p. 32.
44 See Regnault, *Day-to-Day Life*, pp. 89ff.

Saturdays and Sundays for worship, the *synaxis* and Eucharist, and sometimes for a meal together, before returning to their individual cells. This was a form of monastic life which can be termed 'semi-eremitic'.[45] There were, of course, other forms as well. As we have seen, the writings of Palladius and Cassian make it clear that in Lower Egypt there were also some coenobia or organized corporate monasteries; but we are told very little directly about them.

The monks went into the desert partly in order to find solitude. In their cells the monks lived alone, but just how much solitude they had varied from one place to another. In Nitria the monks lived in individual cells not far from each other, whereas those who retreated to live the eremitical life in the great desert could sometimes spend months or years without encountering anyone else. All the desert monks, however, spent a great deal of their time in solitude, in order to be able to face their inner selves, and be alone with God. We have already seen how Arsenius did his best to avoid contact with others. Abba Isidore did the same: it was said of him that 'when a brother went to see him, he would escape to the furthest corner of his cell'.[46]

Solitude was, however, interrupted by the meetings between an abba and a disciple. New and younger monks attached themselves to an older, more experienced monk, in a relationship which had various elements. The disciple was expected to reveal all his closest thoughts and feelings to his abba, so that the abba could understand his inner processes and give advice about the struggle against evil thoughts. The disciple was also to be totally obedient to the abba, doing immediately and unquestioningly whatever the abba said, in order to learn humility. There are many examples of abbas prescribing unnecessary and pointless tasks simply to test the disciple's obedience. The most remarkable example is that of an abba

---

45 See especially Regnault, *Day-to-Day Life*, pp. 162ff.
46 *Sayings*, Isidore, 7.

who planted a piece of dry wood in the ground and ordered his disciple to water it daily until it flowered. When the disciple had done this without question for three years, it was counted as obedience.[47] 'Obedience', said Amma Syncletica, 'is preferable to asceticism. The one teaches pride, the other humility.'[48] Sometimes the relationship between abba and disciple lasted for many years, and the disciple could find himself caring for the abba in old age.

Once a disciple had progressed in obedience and humility he could be responsible for his own discipline and determine his own way of life. It was characteristic of the hermits of Lower Egypt that they each lived by their own rule, and that their ascetic practices varied from one to another. Some were more strict than others. Similarly, these monks were free to move about, to change the location of their cell, or to go to visit other monks to learn from them about their way of life. This freedom was a feature of the eremitic life.

Nevertheless it was a fundamental principle of this way of life that the monk should normally simply stay in his cell. The advice most frequently given to a new monk was that of Abba Moses quoted above: 'Go, sit in your cell, and your cell will teach you everything.'[49] A monk should not go out and about to relieve boredom or satisfy curiosity. To stay in the cell, no matter how tedious it was, was the way to be able to discern the inner motion of one's heart and resist evil thoughts. Abba Arsenius advised a struggling young man, 'Go, eat, drink, sleep, do no work, only do not leave your cell';[50] that is to say, even if a monk could not manage to maintain the rest of his ascetic discipline, he should still not leave his cell.

Staying in one's cell meant living in silence. Keeping silent, overcoming the urge to speak, was a fundamental part of the

---

47 A story found in *Sayings*, John the Dwarf, 1; and in Cassian, *Institutes*, 4.24.

48 *Sayings*, Syncletica, 16.

49 *Sayings*, Moses, 6.

50 *Sayings*, Arsenius, 11.

monastic discipline. Abba Poemen said, 'The victory over all the afflictions that befall you is to keep silence.' 'If you are silent, you will have peace wherever you live.'[51] Abba Ammonas wrote to his fellow monks, 'Those who depart from quiet are unable to conquer their passions.'[52] Even when a monk was with others it was important, as far as possible, to remain silent. Nisterus advised a fellow monk, 'Be silent, and when a conversation takes place, it is better to listen than to speak.'[53]

Along with the discipline of silence went the discipline of eating and sleeping. From the earliest biblical times food was always an issue in the desert. For the monks of Egypt strict control of eating was an important part of their way of life. Just how this was done varied considerably. We read of some monks who were said to have eaten so little and so seldom that it is hard to believe they could have survived. One is said to have taken food only once a week; one fasted completely for four weeks and another for five; one is said to have eaten only heavenly food miraculously provided for him, and another to have eaten only the bread of the Eucharist. Of a number it is said that they ate only raw vegetables or only dry bread. Some made a practice of fasting totally during Lent.[54] Most, however, did not go to these extremes, it being a common practice to eat a little every day, but not until after the ninth hour, or sundown. And while there are many stories of extreme fasting in the *Lausiac History* and the *History of the Monks of Egypt*, the words of the abbas recorded in the *Sayings* tend to encourage moderation. Poemen said that it was 'preferable to eat every day, but just a small amount'.[55] Sisoes told some enquirers, 'I eat when the need arises.'[56] Agathon commended a disciple who fasted till evening and then ate two hard biscuits,

51 *Sayings*, Poemen, 37 and 84.
52 *The Letters of Ammonas*, XII.
53 *Sayings*, Nisterus, 3.
54 *Lives of the Desert Fathers*, VI.4; VII.1; X.23; XI.5; XII.2, 3; XIII.3.
55 *Sayings*, Poemen, 31.
56 *Sayings*, Sisoes, 21.

saying, 'Your way of life is good, not overburdened by too much asceticism.'[57] And Amma Syncletica held that excessive fasting which lacked proportion was in fact 'determined by the enemy'.[58] None were in any doubt, however, that fasting was an essential part of the monasticism of the desert, and that the individual monk could decide how much and when he or she would eat.

The same is true of controlling and limiting one's sleep. It was common practice for monks to spend at least part of the night keeping vigil. The *History of the Monks of Egypt* reports that, 'Some of them never slept at night, but either sitting or standing persevered in prayer until morning.'[59] It was said of Arsenius that 'he used to pass the whole night without sleeping, and in the early morning when nature compelled him . . . he would snatch a little sleep and soon wake up again'. He used to say, 'one hour's sleep is enough for a monk if he is a good fighter'.[60] Bessarion is reported to have said, 'For fourteen days and nights I have stood upright in the midst of thorn bushes, without sleeping', and, 'For fourteen years I have never lain down, but have always slept sitting or standing.'[61] Others made a practice of sleeping for part of the night, and keeping watch for the other part of it.

How, then, did the monks spend their time? What did they do during these long hours of wakefulness, alone and in silence? Much of their time was spent in manual labour. This usually took the form of plaiting or weaving reeds or palm leaves, which they found near marshes. Palm leaves were soaked to make them soft, and then plaited or woven to form cords or baskets, which could then be sold either to an itinerant trades-man or in the town. This allowed them to buy their necessary supply of loaves, which were dried and kept for long periods.

---

57 *Sayings*, Agathon, 20.
58 *Sayings*, Syncletica, 15.
59 *Lives of the Desert Fathers*, XX.17.
60 *Sayings*, Arsenius, 14, 15.
61 *Sayings*, Bessarion, 6, 8.

This work of weaving was ideal for the eremitical life: it was done by one person alone, and occupied the hands, while the mind could concentrate on prayer or reciting psalms.

And it was prayer and reciting of psalms which was the main task of the monk. Once again, practices varied. Antony discovered that it was useful to adopt a pattern of sitting down and plaiting cord for a while, and then standing up to pray for a while. Prayers could be said in this way, but prayer could in fact continue all the time. Cassian tells us that the monks used what he calls a 'formula', repeating over and over again the opening words of Psalm 70: 'O God make speed to save us; O Lord make haste to help us.'[62] In this way a monk's attention could be focused on God all the time. In addition they would 'meditate' on the Psalms, a practice which involved the continuous repetition of the words in a low, murmuring voice. In doing this the monks were continuing a biblical tradition, as the Psalms themselves refer to this practice, using the word 'meditation' in the same sense.[63] Praying and reciting psalms in these various ways lay at the heart and centre of the monks' life.

The life of the monks was, therefore, an extremely hard one, involving withdrawal and renunciation; solitude, silence, asceticism of food and sleep, manual labour and ceaseless prayer. These features, illustrated here from the monastic life of Lower Egypt, were found in one way or another in all areas of the desert movement. They were part of a way of life which was characteristic of the movement as a whole. They represent, however, only the outward and practical aspect of this way of life. They were undertaken in order to assist them to achieve their principal objective, which was an inner and spiritual one – a topic we will return to after we have looked at the other areas of the desert movement.

---

62 Cassian, *Conferences*, 10.10.

63 Both the Greek of the LXX and the desert monks use the word *meletan* to describe this practice. See Ryrie, *Silent Waiting.*

2

Upper Egypt

If we move some 200 miles up the Nile from Antony's Outer Mountain we come to another important monastic centre. Here the river winds its way through a fairly narrow valley, with strips of cultivated land of about three to seven kilometres in width on either side of it, beyond which lies the desert. In the early centuries there were villages at intervals along the riverside. This was a populated but remote area, accessible mainly by boat, and far from the northern delta and the city of Alexandria. It was an area to which the influence of Greek language and culture did not extend; the local language was Sahidic, a form of the Coptic language different from the Bohairic of Lower Egypt.

Like Lower Egypt, Upper Egypt was in early years the home for various forms of monastic life. As we shall see, there were anchorites' cells in a variety of places; but it was its coenobia or monasteries which formed the distinctive monastic pattern of the area. If Lower Egypt is noted especially for the semi-eremitical life of its monastic centres, Upper Egypt is noted for its coenobia. There were several large monasteries here, many of them belonging to a group or family of monasteries founded and initially supervised by the great monastic leader Pachomius, and known collectively as the Pachomian Koinonia, or Pachomian Fellowship. But there were others as well, including the very large and not so well known monasteries of Shenoute.

As these monasteries were not situated in the deep desert, and as the monks were engaged in practical activities of agriculture, trades and commerce, some would not regard them as part of the desert movement.[1] But the desert was never far away, rising in a steep escarpment just beyond the cultivated land, and referred to by a Coptic word which meant both mountain and desert. This was a harsh and unwelcoming place, a place of demons, at the edge of which the dead were buried; but a place also in which there were hermits' cells, and to which monks from the coenobia retreated for silence and prayer. That is to say, the word 'desert' refers not only to a physical place, but, in the words of Tim Vivian, 'takes on two additional levels of meaning: the spiritual and the mystical. Not only was the desert a religious *place*, it signified a spiritual *way of being*.'[2] It is clear from the available texts that for the monks of the monasteries in the Nile Valley the desert was a constant presence, and directly or indirectly impacted on the life of the monasteries.

We shall take a look at each of these leaders, Pachomius and Shenoute, and the institutions they established, to get the flavour of this pattern of monastic life, before turning to what we know of the eremitic life in the area.

Pachomius and his successors

Pachomius is often put alongside Antony as a pioneer of early monasticism, Antony being seen as the great exemplar of the eremitic life, and Pachomius as the first great leader and organizer of coenobitic monasticism, although he was not in fact the first to establish a coenobitic monastery in Upper Egypt. The Pachomian movement generated a large body of literature, and a considerable number of documents about it have come down to us, most of them only recently translated into English. These include the *Life of Pachomius*, a document which was

---

1 See Goehring, 'Withdrawing from the Desert', in *Ascetics, Society and the Desert*, pp. 89–109.

2 Paphnutius, *Histories of the Monks of Upper Egypt*, Introduction by Vivian, p. 23.

probably written in Sahidic soon after Pachomius' death, and then translated into Bohairic, Greek and other languages. These different versions basically tell the same story, but with variations. Other documents include details of the rules of the Pachomian monasteries, the *Letter of Ammon*, and letters written by Pachomius and others. Together they provide a detailed picture of the monasteries, their founder and later leaders, and their rules and way of life.

The life of Pachomius

The *Life of Pachomius* tells the story of his life and work, and of his successors Theodore and Horsiesios. It begins by invoking the memory of Elijah and John the Baptist, the biblical desert heroes, and of the monks of recent times who had 'revived the conduct of the prophet Elijah',[3] indicating that Pachomius was to be seen as continuing the biblical desert tradition. Although, like other biographies of the time, it includes stories of extraordinary miracles, some of which modern readers may regard with scepticism, it provides a credible and detailed account of Pachomius' character and achievements. He was a Sahidic-speaking Egyptian, born about the year 292 into a pagan family. At an early age he was forcibly enlisted into the Roman army, along with a number of other young men. While they were locked up prior to being taken away for service elsewhere, they were visited by a group of Christians who gave them food and water. On learning that these people who showed such unsolicited generosity and care were Christians, he prayed to Christ, promising to give his life in service to humankind. On release from the army he went to a nearly deserted village, where he was baptized, and thereafter spent three years in solitude and in works of kindness to local people. Then, feeling the call to be a monk, he did what Antony had done at the start of his

---

3 *Pachomian Koinonia*, PK hereafter, Vol. 1, Bohairic *Life*, 1.

monastic life: he attached himself to one of the many monks in that area, an anchorite named Apa Palamon, who lived 'a little way from the village', and who was one of a number of anchorites who had 'settled on that mountain' (or desert).[4]

Palamon trained Pachomius in ascetic practices and prayer, including limiting food and sleep. It is said that when they found it difficult to stay awake during the night, 'they would go out to the mountain outside their cell, and carry sand in baskets from one place to another, giving their bodies labour so as to stay awake to pray to God'.[5] Pachomius himself is said to have 'made it a habit to leave his cell and to go often to tombs [in the desert] to pass the whole night there praying',[6] and to have practised 'mortifications in those deserts, in the acacia forest that surrounded them and in the far desert'.[7] That is to say, Pachomius was trained and formed as a monk in the ways of the desert. Seven years later, when he had gone 'across that desert' to a deserted village called Tabennesi, he had a vision of Christ instructing him to stay there and establish a monastery. He and his brother John built the monastery and together began a life of great ascesis. They adopted monastic garments, severely limited their food and their sleep, and engaged in the struggle against demons. Pachomius found himself attacked physically by demons, in the way that Antony had been in the desert.[8] According to the Greek *Life*, Pachomius regarded this ascetic life as a way of 'carrying the Cross of Christ', a phrase that echoes through his story. The particular nature of Pachomius' monastic vocation is shown by another vision he experienced about this time. An angel told him that it was the Lord's will for him 'to minister to the race of men and to unite them to himself'. Although he was trained in the desert, his was to be a life not of eremitic solitude, but of adapting the

---

4 Ibid., 10, 16.
5 Ibid., 10.
6 Ibid., 12.
7 PK, Vol. 1, Bohairic *Life*, 15; Greek *Life*, 11.
8 PK, Vol. 1, Bohairic *Life*, 21.

ways of desert spirituality in which he had been trained so that it could be lived out in a different setting, in service to others. The establishment of a coenobitic community did not, however, arise from 'a sudden disenchantment with the solitary vocation'. There was an 'unbroken thread of practice that ran from his earliest ascetic enthusiasm to the teaching of his final years'.[9]

Soon after that his first followers began to arrive. Three men came asking to become monks. Many others followed, some but not all of whom he accepted. Together they set to work and built a church for the people of the village, to which they themselves went for the Eucharist at weekends. Then, when the numbers in the monastery reached 100, they built a chapel in the monastery itself, in which they said their daily offices. Pachomius also began the formal organization of the community: a 'housemaster' was appointed and others were allocated particular responsibilities, and arrangements were made for the monks to wear a habit and do manual work, and for 'instructions' to be held every week to train the new monks in the monastic life.

Something was clearly stirring in the hearts of many people at the time, as the number of monks apparently increased at such an extraordinary rate that before long Pachomius was founding new monasteries. The first of these, at Phbow, a village a few miles downstream from Tabennesi, was eventually to become the largest and the main base of the Pachomian Koinonia. Soon afterwards, another was built at a place called Tse, and then another close by at Smin. Even Pachomius' sister Mary, whom he had declined to see in person, accepted his suggestion and embraced the monastic life. A building erected for her in the village by the monks became the first of three Pachomian women's monasteries. The Koinonia was even further enlarged by the inclusion of two other communities which already existed in the area, and whose 'fathers' approached

9 Rousseau, *Pachomius*, p. 126.

Pachomius asking him to organize them according to his rule.[10] Thereafter still more monasteries were established, bringing the total in the Koinonia to nine for men and three for women. Although all of these were in the Nile valley, none was very far from the desert or 'mountain', where the dead were buried and where one could retreat to for prayer and solitude.[11] A pilgrim site recently discovered in the desert not far from the Phbow monastery was probably visited by Pachomian monks.[12]

Among the first to join Pachomius was a young man named Theodore. He belonged to a prominent Christian family in the area, and is described as a devout person from his very early years. He had already led the eremetic life for some years, along with some pious old monks, before he sought out Pachomius and entered his monastery. He was soon recognized as 'second to none in ascesis and prayer vigils', and Pachomius realized 'that God would entrust him with souls after himself'.[13] Thereafter the story of Theodore becomes almost as important as that of Pachomius himself. From an early date Pachomius began to entrust him with a variety of responsibilities, and eventually put him in charge of the original monastery at Tabennesi. Things changed, however, when the monks, fearing for the future, urged Theodore to consent to be their leader in the event of Pachomius' death. Although, because of his self-effacing humility and his loyalty to his leader, he was very reluctant, Theodore eventually did give his consent. When Pachomius learned of this he immediately dismissed him from all his positions of responsibility, telling him, 'Withdraw by yourself somewhere, and pray to the Lord that he may forgive you.'[14]

Pachomius eventually died in May 346, apparently of the plague which had swept through the monasteries, and his body

10 PK, Vol. 1, Bohairic *Life*, 51, 54.
11 PK, Vol. 1, Greek *Life*, 146.
12 See Goehring, 'New Frontiers in Pachomian Studies', pp. 182f.
13 PK, Vol. 1, Greek *Life*, 36.
14 Ibid., 106.

was 'carried away to the mountain . . . and buried'.[15] Before his death he appointed another monk, Petronius, as his successor, but he too succumbed to the plague three months later, passing on the torch to Horsiesios. He, however, seems to have found growing tensions within the Koinonia too much to bear, and after four years appointed Theodore to take over from him. Theodore remained the 'father' of the community for the next eighteen years until his death in 368, leaving behind him a reputation for humility and holiness second only to that of 'our father Pachomius'. The *Letter of Ammon*, written about the year 400 by a monk who had lived in the monastery at Phbow under Theodore, tells of his powers of prophecy and healing, as well as his gentle but firm dealings with the monks in his care.

This was a time of success. The Koinonia grew still more to include eleven monasteries, and relationships with Archbishop Athanasius of Alexandria were strengthened. Success, however, brought an increase in possessions, which greatly distressed Theodore, with the result that 'he often used to put on hair garments and go up the mountain by himself. He would spend the whole night praying tearfully to the Lord and he would come down to the monastery in the morning.'[16] Before he died in 368 he persuaded Horsiesios, who had been much praised by Athanasius, to take over the leadership again. Horsiesios remained in this position until his death about 20 years later.

Pachomius as a person

So what sort of a person was Pachomius? His fame and significance rest mainly on two things. The first was his skill and ability in organizing and supervising monasteries and thus providing a pattern for coenobitic monasticism. Just how many of the rules given in documents available to us have come from

---

15 PK, Vol. 1, Greek *Life*, 106; Bohairic *Life*, 123.
16 PK, Vol. 1, Bohairic *Life*, 198.

Pachomius himself is not clear, but it seems certain that he was the first to compose a systematic monastic rule. 'He established for [his monks] an irreproachable life-style and traditions profitable for their souls in rules which he took from the holy scriptures.'[17] He laid down regulations and instructions for every detail of the life of his monks: regulations about the nature of the buildings; arrangements for a hierarchy of leadership and responsibilities; a scheme for entering the monastic life; rules to do with monastic garb, with eating, sleeping, manual labour, and worship; and arrangements for regular instruction in the faith and the monastic life. He prescribed punishments for those who transgressed the rules, including expulsion from the monastery for the most serious offenders. These rules and this pattern of organization not only governed all the monasteries in the Koinonia, but eventually influenced other communities as well, and set a precedent for later monastic rules in both east and west.

The other thing about Pachomius that impressed and inspired many people was simply his character and his faith. He was a charismatic figure, and was known also as a person of great humility. Although he exercised total control over all the monasteries in the Koinonia, he did not stand on rank. He was said to have 'submitted to the housemaster, being more humble than all others',[18] and to have regarded himself as 'the servant of all'.[19] When a new building was being erected, 'Pachomius was building the monastery with the brothers, carrying the clay on his back like all the other brothers'.[20] Although he supervised the monks very strictly, his aim was not to dominate, but to save the souls of the brothers. 'He was full of mercy for the old men or the sick or for the younger ones, and he cared for their souls in everything.'[21] He was known as a person of

17 Ibid., 23.
18 PK, Vol. 1, Greek *Life*, 110.
19 PK, Vol. 1, Bohairic *Life*, 61.
20 Ibid., 54.
21 PK, Vol. 1, Greek *Life*, 28.

remarkable discernment or clairvoyance, a gift he made use of in his pastoral care of the monks. Having learned, by his long experience of solitude in the desert, how to guard his own heart against the 'wiles of the devil', he was able to detect the workings of the demons in other people. He knew their thoughts before they revealed them to him, in a way that enabled him both to understand and to encourage, and also to expose and rebuke. His clairvoyance was so unusual that it aroused suspicion, with the result that he was summoned before a synod of bishops and monks to explain his gift. He was a man of deep prayer and of extraordinary visions. In keeping with the call he received from the angel at the start, his concern for others extended beyond the Koinonia. When he prayed, we are told, he 'would pray for the whole world'.[22] He is quoted as saying, 'May all, Jews, pagans, Christians, and even the barbarians be saved for the Lord, through our Lord and God Jesus Christ . . . and be found in the kingdom of heaven.'[23]

It was these personal gifts which seem to have made a very strong impression on those who knew him, so that his story was told again and again in different translations and variations, and which, together with his outstanding organizational ability, led to his being regarded as one of the great monastic pioneers, comparable to Antony the Great.

The way of life in the Pachomian monasteries

The way of life of the monks in Pachomian monasteries was determined and governed by a strict and detailed set of rules. Details of these are known to us from a number of documents which have come down to us, written originally in Coptic but available to us in their fullest form in a Latin translation by Jerome.[24] These rules come from a later period, but they have

---

22 PK, Vol. 1, Bohairic *Life*, 101.

23 PK, Vol. 2, *Paralipomena*, 41.

24 These include, as part of the *Pachomian Rules*, the *Precepts*, the *Precepts and Institutes*, the *Precepts and Judgements*, the *Precepts and Laws*; other

been developed and adapted from the precepts laid down by Pachomius himself, and there is no reason to doubt that they reflect the intentions of the founder.

The first feature of Pachomian monasticism was that it was based on buildings surrounded and enclosed by a wall. This wall symbolized *anachoresis* or separation: those who lived inside it had removed themselves from ordinary life and renounced the world. Entry into the complex was through a gate controlled by a porter. Strangers were not allowed free entry, and monks could not go out without permission. Within the wall there were the cells of the monks, a refectory, kitchen and bakery, a *synaxis* or meeting room, workshops, a laundry, an infirmary and a church or chapel. As the movement grew, these buildings housed a very large number of monks, perhaps eventually totalling 5,000 to 7,000 in all the monasteries together.[25]

When someone came asking to become he monk, he was asked if he was ready to renounce the world, to give up all his possessions, his home and his family. He was kept outside the door for a few days and taught the Lord's Prayer and some psalms. If he seemed 'ready for everything' he was taught the basics of the monastic discipline, and then given his monastic garb and assigned his place in one of the monastic houses.[26] Eventually he had to learn the New Testament and the Psalter by heart, and if he was illiterate he had to learn to read.[27] All the Pachomian monks had to be literate.

The life of the monastery was supervised by a hierarchy of people appointed by the 'father' of the whole Koinonia. Each monastery was governed by a 'steward' and his 'second', and was divided into a number of houses, each with its 'house-

---

information is given in Jerome's *Preface*, the *Paralipomena*, the *Letter of Ammon*, the *Regulations of Horsiesios*, and two short pieces known as the *Draguet Fragments*, all found in Vol. 2 of the *Pachomian Koinonia*.

25 Figures given in Cassian, *Institutes*, 4.1, and Palladius, *Lausiac History*, 32.8, respectively; Jerome's figure of 50,000 (*Preface* 7) must be an exaggeration.

26 PK, Vol. 2, *Precepts*, 49.

27 Ibid., 139.

master' and his 'second'. The supervision and regulation of the day-to-day life of the monks, down to the very last detail, in accordance with the monastic rule, was in the hands of the housemasters who had the power to punish offenders. Under them others were appointed to special responsibilities. Each monk had his own rank and place in an established order, which determined where he sat or stood at meals, at worship and at gatherings of the monks. Within the house, each monk had his own cell, although it seems that as time went on and numbers grew it became necessary to have more than one in a cell.[28]

The day started with a *synaxis*, or gathering for prayer, of all the monks in the monastery, in their allocated ranks. After that, much of the monks' time was spent in manual work, to which they were assigned by the housemaster. Some worked in fields, and some were engaged in cooking and baking or crafts of various kinds – Jerome refers to weavers, tailors, carriage makers, fullers and shoemakers.[29] At the end of the day they gathered in their houses for the 'Six Prayers', before retiring to their cells for the night. As was done elsewhere in Egypt at that time, the Eucharist was celebrated in each monastery on Saturdays and on Sundays, and attended by all the monks. In addition, every week there were three 'Instructions' or teaching sessions, one on Saturdays and two on Sundays, for all the monks of each monastery, given by the steward or by the father of the whole community; and two Instructions, one on Wednesdays and one on Fridays, given by the housemasters in each house. These were to provide training for the monks both in the monastic discipline and in the spiritual life.

The rules about eating and sleeping were not harsh or severe, but were aimed at achieving 'that pursuit of discomfort for its own sake which seems to have characterized some more solitary

---

28 Palladius, *Lausiac History*, 32.2; PK, Vol. 2, *Precepts*, 87f.
29 Jerome, *Preface* 6, in PK, Vol. 2.

ascetics'.[30] Except on fast days, meals consisting of bread and vegetables were served twice a day, with some kind of 'sweet' distributed afterwards.[31] Individual monks could restrict their diet further[32] or undertake fasts if they wished, but no one was 'to fast beyond his strength'.[33] Additional kinds of food were given to any who were sick. Monks spent the night in their cells, and had to sleep on a reclining seat without lying down completely,[34] so as to keep themselves alert; but it seems that there were no strict rules about hours of sleep. Pachomius himself made a practice of spending the night alternating times of sleep and times of prayer,[35] and it may be that this was the recommended practice for others.[36] Individuals were apparently free to decide for themselves about the extent of their ascetic practice. In other ways also the regime was flexible. Monks were allowed to visit their parents or families if need arose, especially if they were sick, and could even visit women relatives.[37]

Although the ascetic practice was in some ways not very severe, there were very strict rules governing behaviour generally. There was a general rule of silence: monks were not to talk as they worked except about holy things;[38] there was to be silence during the *synaxis* and at meetings, and in the bakery where there seemed to be a particular temptation to talk.[39] Since the monks knew much of the Bible by heart, instead of talking they were to recite passages of scripture to themselves at all sorts of times, as they did their work, or sat together or went about the monastery. They were required to attend the *syn-*

---

30 Rousseau, *Pachomius*, p. 121.
31 PK, Vol. 1, Greek *Life*, 111; PK, Vol. 2, *Precepts*, 37, 38.
32 PK, Vol. 2, *Precepts*, 79.
33 PK, Vol. 2, *Letter of Ammon*, 21.
34 PK, Vol. 2, *Precepts*, 87.
35 PK, Vol. 1, Bohairic *Life*, 59.
36 PK, Vol. 2, *Regulations of Horseisios*, 17.
37 PK, Vol. 2, *Precepts*, 53, 54, 142; *Letter of Ammon*, 30.
38 PK, Vol. 2, *Precepts*, 60.
39 PK, Vol. 2, *Precepts*, 8, 60, 116, 122; PK, Vol. 1, Bohairic *Life*, 74.

axes and prayers on time, to do whatever work was assigned to them, and to be obedient to the housemaster in all things. They were to refrain from looking at others during worship or meals, to have no possessions of their own in their cells, and to wash their clothes every Saturday. Any breach of these rules led to penalties or punishments imposed by the housemaster, sometimes by removing the monk from his allocated seat or position and putting him lower in the order.

All of this gives the impression of a rigid and uncompromising system, but in fact it did take account of human weaknesses. The brothers were not forced to work excessively.[40] Anyone who returned from outdoor work suffering from excessive heat would not be required to attend the evening prayers,[41] and could eat his food separately. There was thoughtful provision for the sick, and attention was paid to human needs generally: 'Even if all the brothers need a bit of beer or any other food that accords with the law of the Koinonia, the superior of the community will grant this to them generously and gladly.'[42] There was over all a spirit of forgiveness. 'Who is weak and I am not weak?' said Theodore, adding, 'All who weep over their sins shall know they are forgiven.'[43] We read how Pachomius himself, when he had punished a monk excessively by expelling him, had to repent and ask forgiveness, saying, 'If the murderers, the sorcerers, the adulterers, and others, having committed all kinds of evil, flee to the monastery to be saved through penance, who am I to expel a brother?'[44] Another story tells of a monk who fell victim to demons and left the monastery, only to be found, anointed, and sent back to the monastery forgiven.[45]

---

40 PK, Vol. 2, *Precepts and Laws*, 3.

41 Ibid., 11.

42 PK, Vol. 2, *Regulations of Horsiesios*, 49.

43 PK, Vol. 2, *Letter of Ammon*, 21, 28.

44 PK, Vol. 2, *Draguet Fragment I*.

45 PK, Vol. 2, *Draguet Fragment II*.

There seems to have been no arrangement for individual 'spiritual fathers' within this system, but monks were supposed to examine themselves and keep watch over their hearts, and to reveal their thoughts and confess their sins to their house-master. We are not told much about the individual and private prayers of the monks, but this inner watchfulness and the con-tinual recitation of the scriptures must have amounted to a kind of constant prayer; and it can be assumed that the long hours alone in their cells were spent partly in prayer and contempla-tion, especially by those who had lived a long time within the discipline of the monastery.[46]

The question of prayer, however, takes us on to the deeper and more fundamental issue of the inner life of these monks and the spirituality of the Pachomian Koinonia, which we will take up in Chapter 5. But as far as the external and practical aspects of the life of Pachomian Koinonia are concerned, it will be clear that this type of monastic life was very different from the eremitical and semi-eremitical life characteristic of Lower Egypt. There was, of course, much in common between the two systems: the emphasis on complete renunciation, on silence, on the solitude of monks in their cells, on obedience, on manual work, on the asceticism of eating and sleeping, on the recitation of psalms and scripture, on the struggle against demons, and on the discipline of daily and weekly prayers – all this amounted to an attempt by Pachomius to apply the spiritual and ascetic ways of the desert to the corporate life of a coenobium. He recognized that for the coenobitic monk, as for the anchor-ite, 'the ascetic task was an inner one'[47] aimed at guarding the heart and achieving 'the calm self-possession which will open him to the presence of God'.[48] But all this was approached in very different ways in the two systems, the eremitic and the coenobitic. In the one, the individual monk, after a period of

---

46 See Palladius, *Lausiac History*, 32.7.
47 Rousseau, *Pachomius*, p. 141.
48 Ibid., p. 128.

training under an abba, was free to decide his or her own way of life, discipline and movements; in the other most of life was governed by a system of rules, the keeping of which was an essential part of the monastic ascesis.

Links with the desert movement

Nevertheless, the Pachomian Koinonia did not stand alone, but was part of a larger movement that was blossoming at the time. There were monastic communities in existence before Pachomius started his first monastery,[49] and there were hermits or anchorites living locally, as well as others further to the south.[50] The Koinonia also had links with Antony and the movement in Lower Egypt, and the *Life of Pachomius* refers to Antony on several occasions. On one occasion, soon after Pachomius' death, a group of monks led by Theodore, returning from a visit to Alexandria, called in to see Antony at his Outer Mountain and to receive his blessing, at which point Antony praised Pachomius, and wrote a letter to the monks of the Koinonia.[51] We have accounts of a visit to the monastery at Tabennesi by the monk of Lower Egypt, Macarius of Alexandria,[52] and of another monk, Pinufius, who moved between Lower Egypt, Tabennesi and Palestine.[53] We know also that the Pachomian arrangement had an influence on the monasteries that existed in the delta area, and that at some point Pachomian monks were introduced into a monastery near Alexandria by the Patriarch Theophilus.[54] That is to say that, although Pachomius was a significant and influential leader in his own right, what he did was to give powerful new impetus, direction and structure to a movement that was already beginning to develop in a variety of ways and places.

---

49 PK, Vol. 1, Bohairic *Life*, 51; Greek *Life*, 54.
50 PK, Vol. 1, Bohairic *Life*, 10, 31, 67; see also pp. 69ff.
51 PK, Vol. 1, Bohairic *Life*, 126–8, 133; Greek *Life*, 120, 136.
52 Palladius, *Lausiac History*, 17.12ff.
53 Cassian, *Conferences*, 20.1–3.
54 PK, Vol. 2, Introduction, p. 8.

The monasteries of Shenoute

Alongside the Pachomian Koinonia another major monastic development took place in Upper Egypt. This consisted eventually of three monasteries, situated in the neighbourhood of the modern town of Akhmim, on the west side of the Nile, not far distant from the Pachomian ones, but close to the edge of the desert. They were led by a charismatic and controversial figure named Shenoute, whom we know about from a variety of sources. There is a *Life of Shenoute*, a hagiographical work apparently written by a disciple of his named Besa, although modern scholars believe it was probably written considerably after Besa's time. It does, however, give us basic information about Shenoute's life and his rule of the monasteries. Shenoute himself left a large body of written works in the form of 'Canons', or letters, and other communications written in Coptic to the men and women under his guidance. These have been gathered together in nine thick volumes, but are only now being fully edited and translated. So although there is a great deal that is still unknown about him, we do have sufficient information about his character and achievements to know that he was a leader who had a very large following, and who is venerated in the Coptic Church even in our own time.[55]

Shenoute was born probably about the year 348, around the time when Pachomius died and shortly before the death of Antony. Besa's *Life* claims that in his youth he inherited the mantle of Elijah the Tishbite, and indeed that 'the whole of his life and his intention were like [those of] Elijah';[56] and a story tells of him being called 'the new Elijah'.[57] He must have

---

55 The 'St Shenouda the Archimandrite Coptic Society', based in Cairo, is currently engaged in promoting interest in and scholarly study of Shenoute and his works.

56 Besa, *Life of Shenoute*, Chapters 8, 10.

57 Ibid., 19; see also Mekhaiel, 'Shenoute as Reflected in the *Vita* and the *Difnar*', p. 101. This and the other articles noted below are found in a volume on Akhmim and Sohag, the first of a series of publications on *Christianity and Monasticism in Upper Egypt*, edited by Gabra and Takla.

received a good education, since he read and wrote both Greek and Coptic.[58] About the year 385 he became the third head of the White Monastery, which had been founded in about the middle of the fourth century by a man named Peol, believed to be a relative of his. It is likely that the Rule which Peol drew up for the monastery was influenced by the rule of the nearby Pachomian monasteries, but it was probably somewhat harsher.[59] The second monastery, known as the Red Monastery, a smaller establishment situated some three kilometres north-west of the White Monastery, was founded by a man named Pshoi. These two, which still exist today, were situated close to the edge of the desert. The third was a women's monastery, located in a village a short distance to the south, perhaps originally in some kind of private house. Together they formed what has been called a 'federation'[60] under Shenoute's supervision, organized much along the lines of the Pachomian Koinonia of monasteries. Between them they housed several thousand male and female monks.

Shenoute as a person

So what sort of a person was Shenoute? He was often called 'The Prophet' and seems to have regarded himself as in some way similar to the prophets of the Old Testament. He is said to have ruled his federation with an iron hand, pronouncing judgement and administering punishment on any who transgressed the rules. He did not stop short of some quite severe corporal punishment, something that is more understandable within the norms of the society of his time than it is to us today. This, together with the fact that his writings make little reference to the death and resurrection of Christ, has led some modern writers to dismiss him as 'harsh', 'violent' and 'Christ-less'.[61]

58 Emmel, 'Shenoute's Place in the History of Monasticism', p. 41.
59 Goehring, 'Pachomius and the White Monastery', p. 49.
60 Layton, 'The Ancient Rules of Shenoute's Monastic Federation', p. 74.
61 Veilleux, Preface to Besa, *Life of Shenoute*, p. v.

His strict and authoritarian rule was imposed, however, for the sake of leading his monks to purer and more obedient lives, and to encourage repentance. He was also thought to be like an Old Testament prophet in his hatred of paganism. There are two stories of him carrying out violent attacks on pagan buildings to smash their idols,[62] but these can be seen as demonstrating Shenoute's enthusiasm for establishing Christianity in the area.

Although there are controversial and unattractive aspects to Shenoute's character, it is clear that he was a devout man, highly regarded by his contemporaries and remembered by later generations for his holiness. Although he supervised coenobitic monasteries, he was a man of the desert. 'Shenoute himself did not live among his brothers in the monastery, but rather he lived as a hermit somewhere in the surrounding desert ... Under normal circumstances, Shenoute and the other hermits living in the desert near the White Monastery federation entered the main monastery only four times each year.'[63] In Besa's *Life* it is claimed that he 'gave himself up to the anchoretic life with many great labours, many nocturnal vigils, and fasts without number', that he did not eat until after sundown and then only bread and salt,[64] and that on at least one occasion he 'arose and went into the inner desert and spent the whole night there in prayer'.[65] He is also depicted as a very compassionate man, with a particular concern for the poor and the destitute, whom he once relieved by a miraculous supply of bread,[66] and for captives, some of whom he rescued and provided for, once again by a miracle.[67]

---

62 Besa, *Life of Shenoute*, Chapters 83f. and 125.
63 Emmel, 'Shenoute's Place in the History of Monasticism', p. 41; see also Besa, *Life of Shenoute*, Chapter 122.
64 Besa, *Life of Shenoute*, Chapter 10.
65 Ibid., Chapter 31.
66 Ibid., Chapter 138.
67 Ibid., Chapter 89f.

The way of life of Shenoute's monasteries

The organization of the monasteries of the federation was similar to that of the Pachomian Koinonia.[68] Shenoute himself was the supreme leader, or 'father', of the whole federation. Each of the three monasteries had an 'elder' in overall charge, who was assisted and advised by a council of elders. The elder of the women's monastery was for some purposes subordinate to the elder of the White Monastery, but in other respects Shenoute seems to have been keen to ensure equality between the men and the women.[69] The monks in each monastery were grouped in units known as 'houses' each with its own 'housemaster' or 'housemistress'. The monks' day started with an assembly of all the monks of the monastery before dawn for prayer. It continued with times of prayer in each house at intervals through the day, each followed by a time for manual work, and concluded with another assembly of all in the evening. The daily meal was taken at noon. The Eucharist was celebrated at least once a week, on Sundays. 'Instructions', including readings from the rule books, were given at the general assemblies three times a week, and in the houses twice a week, following a pattern very similar to that of the Pachomian monasteries. In addition, two long open letters written by Shenoute to his monks were read in the assemblies four times a year. The housemasters and housemistresses, who were also known as 'Congregational Parents', exercised a kind of spiritual oversight of those in the house, apparently paying attention to the spiritual needs of individual monks in a personal way.

As elsewhere, monastic life involved manual work, and we know that a variety of trades were practised by the monks, including rope-work and basket-making, tailoring, leather-work, baking, writing, carpentry, and building. There was also an infirmary which was separate from the other monastic build-

---

68 Details in Layton, 'Ancient Rules of Shenoute's Monastic Federation', pp. 75ff.

69 Krawiec, 'The Role of the Female Elder in Shenoute's White Monastery'.

ings and served the monks of the whole federation as well as people from outside. Some of the monks were nurses or 'servers of the sick', nursing being classified as one of the monastic trades. The monks in their houses had a responsibility of caring for those of their number who had minor illnesses. Healing was regarded as an important part of the life and ministry of the monasteries.

In Shenoute's writings, which governed the life of the monasteries, there is a great deal about disciplinary matters, but not very much about spirituality.[70] We know little about the spiritual life of the monks and the community, as this aspect of life seems to have been left to the housemaster or housemistress in their relationship with individual monks. Shenoute himself, as we have seen, was regarded as a deeply spiritual man. He was steeped in the Bible, which he read in both Greek and Coptic, and his writings are filled with biblical quotations, chiefly from the prophets. He took a very serious and perhaps severe view of sin, emphasizing that there is no mercy after death for unrepentant sinners; and for this reason he laid a special emphasis on the need for repentance now. Although we find little reference to the common monastic themes of the need to guard the heart against the demons, he does seem to have regarded sin as something inward that emerges and exists within the individual heart, so that no one is impervious to the wiles of the devil. Moreover, during this life repentance is always possible. 'Shenoute was very strict in his view of God's mercy, which he understood to be boundless even for the worst sinner if he truly repents during this life, but woe upon woe unto all eternity for the unrepentant.'[71] There seems little ground, however, for the claim that has been made that Shenoute was 'Christless'. In his writings he strenuously maintained the divinity of Christ,[72] and

70 Boud'hors, 'Some Aspects of Volume 8 of Shenoute's *Canons*', p. 20.

71 Emmel, 'Shenoute's Place in the History of Monasticism', p. 43.

72 Moawad, 'The Relationship of St Shenoute of Atripe with his Contemporary Patriarchs', p. 109.

in a sermon believed to be by him he says that 'Jesus dwells in the man who tries to purify his heart daily', and refers to his monks as those 'who have taken up their Cross and followed the Saviour'.[73] Besa's *Life* portrays him as speaking of 'Christ Jesus, the son of the living God in whom we believe', and says of him that 'He bore Christ'.[74]

This much can be gleaned about the spirituality of Shenoute himself, but this still leaves us with little about the spiritual life of his monks. There is no reason to believe, however, that their spiritual aim and purpose, and the steps they took to pursue it, were much different from those we find in other coenobitic establishments in Egypt and elsewhere, which we will consider in Chapter 5.

Links with the desert movement

Before we leave Shenoute we should note that he and the monasteries of his federation did not exist in isolation from developments elsewhere. In the first place, they had quite close contact with the Pachomian Koinonia. The rule governing their life seems to have been based on Pachomius' rule, the idea of a federation of monasteries was probably also derived from the Koinonia, and the basilica built at the White Monastery was very similar to that at Phbow. The relationship between the two communities is further illustrated by the accounts of two visits by Pachomian monks to the White Monastery, Victor from Tabennesi and Martyrius from Phbow.[75] It is significant that Shenoute referred to Pachomius as 'Pachomius the Great',[76] and seems to have recognized Pachomius as the founder of the coenobitic life. It can be said that the federation and the Koinonia 'had become parallel monastic powerhouses

---

73 Timbie, 'Once More into the Desert of Apa Shenoute', p. 174.

74 Besa, *Life of Shenoute*, Chapters 11 and 59; other references to Christ in Chapters 180 and 188.

75 Ibid., Chapters 17 and 74.

76 Goehring, 'Pachomius and the White Monastery', p. 50.

in Upper Egypt, and while not precluding some form of competition, the two federations continued to recognize and accept one another'.[77]

In addition, Shenoute's federation had connections with developments further afield. There is a story of a visit to the White Monastery by a monk from Sketis, during which Shenoute praised Antony, and of a visit by Shenoute to the famous hermit John in Lycopolis to the north. Shenoute himself had contacts with the wider church. It is said that he was invited to attend the Council of Ephesus in 341, and that he aggressively confronted the 'heretic' Nestorius there. His writings also show that he read the festal letters and other communications of Athanasius and subsequent archbishops of Alexandria, and that he faithfully reflected and supported their theology.

All of which shows that Shenoute's movement was one part of the wider desert movement which was emerging at the time. And it is significant that, in common with other parts of that movement, it was seen as deriving from the biblical tradition of Elijah and John the Baptist. Some of Shenoute's monks are said to have had a vision of him walking with John the Baptist, Elijah the Tishbite and Elisha.[78] Besa's *Life* claims that he had inherited Elijah's mantle, and that 'the whole of his life and his intention were like those of Elijah'.[79]

In spite of all this, however, Shenoute and his monks, unlike the Desert Fathers and Mothers of Lower Egypt, have been ignored by and were almost unknown to the Greek- and Latin-speaking churches. This is largely due to the fact that the Coptic Church to which Shenoute and his monasteries belonged held to the Monophysite view of the nature of Christ, in opposition to the agreement reached at the Council of Chalcedon in 451. Nevertheless, Shenoute's movement continued to flourish, unlike the Pachomian Koinonia which accepted Chalcedon.

---

77 Ibid., p. 51.
78 Besa, *Life of Shenoute*, Chapter 118.
79 Ibid., Chapters 8 and 10.

Indeed, there is no doubt about the importance still attached to Shenoute by the Coptic Orthodox Church, which traces its continuing monastic heritage back to his federation. And there is good reason to regard the federation as an important, if rather neglected, aspect of the desert movement.

The anchorites of Upper Egypt

The desert movement in Upper Egypt was not, however, confined to the monasteries of Pachomius and Shenoute. Hidden away unseen in remote parts of the desert there were hermits or anchorites, living the eremitic life. We have seen that there were some in places not far from the major monasteries, though we know very little about them. But from the *Histories of the Monks of Upper Egypt* and the *Life of Onnophrius*, written by a man named Paphnutius probably at the end of the fourth century and recently translated into English by Tim Vivian, we have a fascinating account of a number of anchorites in the remote desert in the region of Aswan and Philae, some 200 miles south of the monasteries of Pachomius and Shenoute, and further south from there.[80] This is the area of the first cataract of the Nile, and the modern Aswan Dams.

Paphnutius reports that there were Christians living in this area in the first half of the fourth century, some of them in the small island of Philae. Sometime not long after the year 350,[81] the Christian governor of the area, Macedonius, was consecrated as the first Bishop of Philae by Athanasius the Archbishop of Alexandria. He was succeeded by three others named in the account, Mark, Isaiah and Pseleusias, the last of whom died probably towards the end of the century.[82] During that period Paphnutius made a journey into the desert to seek

---

80 Paphnutius, *Histories of the Monks of Upper Egypt, and The Life of Onnophrius*.

81 A date worked out by Vivian, ibid., p. 66.

82 Ibid., pp. 79–85, and Introduction, pp. 52, 114.

out anchorites there. There must have been many of them, for he encountered twelve living in separate places deep in the desert: Pseleusius, Zebulon, John, Anianus, Paul, Zacchaeus, Serapamon, Matthew, Isaac, Aaron, Timothy and Onnophrius. In particular he gives an account of the life of two of them, Aaron and Onnophrius.

Aaron was a soldier who after a frightening experience gave away all he had and joined the monastic community of Sketis in Lower Egypt. Later he moved to a community further south, and then further south still, to settle finally in the remote desert to the east of Philae, living alone and practising great asceticism. He was known as the 'anchorite of Philae'. Aaron, who died 'in very old age' before Paphnutius' account was written, may well have gone off to the desert not long after 350.

Onnophrius was another ascetic whom Paphnutius located deeper still in the desert, having first received directions from another monk, Timothy. Like Aaron, he had been in a monastic community in central Egypt, at Hermopolis Magna, near Antinoe, but inspired by the example of the biblical desert heroes Elijah and John the Baptist[83] he felt a desire for a life of greater asceticism. He travelled, first for six or seven miles, and then, with the help of another monk, for four days to 'a desolate place in the further desert'. He told Paphnutius that he had lived there for 60 years. This may well be an exaggeration, but if it were true he would have gone there perhaps as early as 330.

These accounts, together with the shorter reports Paphnutius gives of the other desert anchorites he met, indicate that a considerable number of monks moved to the deep and remote desert in the very south of Egypt during the course of the fourth century. At a time when large numbers were joining the semi-eremitic communities of Lower Egypt, an eremitic movement was taking place here as well.

---

83 Paphnutius, *Life of Onnophrius*, 11.

The character of this movement

The way of life of these anchorites was in many ways similar to what we find elsewhere, but it also had unique features of its own. As in other places, the monastic life started with renunciation. The first thing that Aaron did on feeling the call was to sell his military equipment and, after buying simple country clothes, to give the proceeds to the poor.[84] Similarly Anianus and Paul, living in Aswan, distributed their excess belongings and went to a monastic community. Giving up all that one depended on was a necessary preliminary to the monastic life. Having done so, many started that life in a monastic community, but eventually moved out into the desert. It is a specially marked feature of the stories recorded here that these monks journeyed far and deep into the desert. Paphnutius had to travel to the 'farthest reaches of the desert' in search of anchorites. He walked for many days before finding Timothy, and travelled deeper still into the desert to find Onnophrius. Each of these monks believed that God had appointed a way of life for him, and a place where he was to go to practise it, and that he had to continue his journeying into the desert until he found the appointed place.[85]

The object of the journey was to get right away from any form of human habitation or contact. The monks sought 'a desolate place in the furthest desert' where one would be able to live by oneself. Paphnutius was told of 'the holy ones in the desert who zealously sought to see no one'.[86] It was a quest for complete solitude, to be able to live a life of 'quiet contemplation' in silence, without interruption by other people. It is true that Aaron, although a desert dweller, apparently lived not very far from human habitation, and performed many miracles to help other people who approached him; but most of the others lived in more complete seclusion. The arrangement

---

84 Paphnutius, *Histories of the Monks*, 88.
85 Paphnutius, *Life of Onnophrius*, 13, 14.
86 Paphnutius, *Histories of the Monks*, 17.

which was common in Nitria, whereby a new monk became the disciple of an abba and lived close to him for many years, is not something we hear of in this desert. When someone came wanting to become a hermit, an experienced monk would take him to a lonely spot by himself and in a few days teach him how to live in the desert, and how to do the 'works of the desert', and then leave him to it. There are also no accounts here of people coming wanting to be given 'a word', as with the well-known monks of Lower Egypt, or of monks visiting one another. More even than Antony, these hermits lived in complete solitude. Nevertheless, in a deeper sense they were not alone, because they had a sense of the mysterious presence with them of all God's saints. 'If they desire to see anyone,' Paphnutius was told, 'they are taken up into the heavenly places where they see all the saints and greet them.'[87] Being so far removed from other Christian people, some of the monks had to travel quite a long distance at weekends to receive the Eucharist; but Onnophrius found that an angel brought it to him every week.[88]

Here as elsewhere the monastic life involved asceticism, sometimes quite harsh self-affliction. All those we are told of severely restricted both their sleep and their food, usually not eating bread at all but living on the palm trees, which in some cases wonderfully produced fruit all the year round. When Paphnutius met him, Onnophrius appeared to be extremely weak from ascetic practices.[89] Aaron is said to have eaten food one day and drunk water the next, and to go in for extreme practices such as hanging a large stone around his neck. 'This way of life', he said, 'is labour and suffering up to the very end.'[90] As with Pachomius and his monks, asceticism was understood to be a way of taking up and carrying the cross.

87 Paphnutius, *Life of Onnophrius*, 17.
88 Ibid., 17.
89 Ibid., 10.
90 Paphnutius, *Histories of the Monks*, 90.

Sitting in their solitary cells, the hermits engaged in manual work, as was done elsewhere. Aaron, it is said, 'would himself do a great deal of work with his hands . . . Sometimes he made grave-clothes and sometimes he plaited rope.'[91] But the 'works of the desert' which a monk needed to learn included more than manual work. An important part of the 'work' was the struggle against demons. In the desert the demons seemed to be physically present, sometimes howling and making fearful noises, sometimes tempting the ascetic by assuming human form, perhaps of a woman[92] or in other ways. A new hermit could only be taken to live in a solitary cell when he had 'understood the hidden and fearful fighting that takes place in the desert'.[93]

And of course an essential part of the work of the desert was prayer. Not much information is given about exactly how the anchorites prayed, but again and again they are said to have prayed. Sometimes a special issue called for prayer, and sometimes they prayed simply in the course of their day-to-day life. Prayer is mentioned on all sorts of occasions. In particular, monks are frequently said to have spent the whole night in prayer.[94] Prayer was an integral part of life and was engaged in naturally at any time. Although some of their prayers were verbal and spoken, the long hours and entire nights of prayer must have included a large element of *hesychia* or 'quiet contemplation'. Indeed, their whole life could be described as 'a life of quiet contemplation'.[95]

These anchorites were men (there is no mention of any women) who took themselves off to very remote places. The Christian communities from which they came belonged to the wider community of the Egyptian church in the archdiocese of Alexandria, but they themselves seem to have little or no direct

---

91 Ibid., 118.
92 Paphnutius, *Life of Onnophrius*, 6.
93 Ibid., 15.
94 Paphnutius, *Histories of the Monks*, 6, 111, 130, 135; *Life of Onnophrius*, 19, 31.
95 Paphnutius, *Life of Onnophrius*, 5, 11, 30.

connection with the desert movement elsewhere. So it is worthwhile asking why they went off to this remote desert in this
way. The question of the spiritual nature and the purpose of
life in the desert is one we will address more fully in Chapter 5;
but some observations about this particular group of anchorites
may be in order here. Why did these men adopt this difficult,
lonely and harsh life? What made them go in for severe ascetic
practices and tests of endurance? With some it was an act of
penitence. The monk Timothy, who had fallen into sin and
repented, said, 'I live in the desert on account of my sins.'[96]
But for others the motive was more expressly Christological,
a way of 'carrying the Cross'.[97] When Aaron was asked about
his self-affliction, he replied, 'When I remember the afflictions
which my good Saviour endured for us . . . I say, "Since God
took upon himself to suffer on our behalf, it is right that we
too should have every kind of affliction until he has mercy on
us."'[98] Asceticism was, in other words, a way of responding to
and sharing in what Christ has done for us. More generally,
these hermits said they went to the desert 'on account of God',
or for the sake of God's holy name, or for 'doing work in the
service of God'. That is to say, the life of the desert was to be
a life given to God, directed totally towards God, and the solitude, the deprivation and asceticism were all seen as a means
of achieving this end.

96 Ibid., 10.
97 Paphnutius, *Histories of the Monks*, 5.
98 Ibid., 94.

3

Judea

The third area brings us to the motherland of the desert movement. The wilderness of Judea was the wilderness of the Bible, the place of Elijah and John the Baptist, the great models and symbols of the desert way, and the inspiration of all the desert monks in every area. Here Jesus spent 40 days and nights in fasting and prayer. Here was the Dead Sea, the region of the Jewish ascetic community of Essenes. Here Christian anchorites had lived in solitude from early days. This was an area close to the Holy City of Jerusalem and the scenes of so many of the great events of the Bible. It was an area where, in all probability, the ascetic life of the desert had always been maintained. As Derwas Chitty has said, 'The wilderness of Judea is in itself a call to such a life. Its memories take us back to Elijah, Elisha and St John the Baptist . . . and to our Lord's own temptations . . . [I]t is difficult to imagine that land remaining for any long period without its ascetics.'[1] Although Antony the Great withdrew to the desert of Egypt probably before any other monk we can name, and although the Desert Fathers of Egypt became better known and more influential than the monks of any other area, it was the wilderness of Judea that provided the background and the inspiration of the whole desert movement.

The Judean desert is different from that in Egypt. Here within a distance of about 15 miles the land slopes away from the high ground of the Judean Hills at Jerusalem and Bethlehem, some 2,500 feet above sea level, down towards the River Jordan and

1 Chitty, *The Desert a City*, p. 14.

the Dead Sea at nearly 700 feet below sea level. This is a long, narrow stretch of barren and largely hilly country. The higher part in the west, sometimes called the 'desert fringe',[2] has moderate rainfall, and can produce crops and fruit. Below it there is the 'desert plateau', a broad and barren stretch of land, intersected by steep-sided ravines or wadis, notably the Wadi Qilt in the north, the Wadi Mukellik in the centre of the area, the Wadi Kidron originating near Jerusalem, and the Wadi Khureitun extending south-eastwards from near Bethlehem. Below and further east again there is the 'fault escarpment', a steep drop down to the dry, hot valley of the Dead Sea in the south, and in the north to the well-watered and more fertile plain of the Jordan near Jericho. Stretching further to the south of the Dead Sea valley there is the 'utter desert', known to the people of the time as the 'Rouba'. Most of this area, even the desert plain, is not without water, mainly from springs found in the cliffs of the wadi ravines, and from the occasional rainfall which can be collected in cisterns.

The Judean desert, then, with varying types of terrain was different from the deserts of Egypt or Arabia, but it had the same basic features of barrenness and solitude, providing the conditions for a life of asceticism and solitude which many were seeking. During the period between the fourth and seventh centuries it became the home of a large number of anchorites and monastic communities of different kinds. Yizhar Hirschfeld, who spent many years exploring and in some cases excavating the remains of them, identified 65 monasteries belonging to that period.[3]

We know about these monasteries and the life of monks who inhabited them partly from a number of 'Lives' of prominent monastic leaders which have come down to us. Seven of these were written by a sixth-century monk named Cyril, from the

---

2 These terms describing the Judean desert are taken from Hirschfeld, *The Judean Desert Monasteries in the Byzantine Period.*

3 Ibid., p. 10.

town of Scythopolis, or Beth Shan, in Palestine, who had stayed in more than one of the monasteries and had gathered stories and information from older monks. After becoming a monk he went first to Jerusalem and then for a short time to Jericho, before living the rest of his life in monasteries in different parts of the Judean desert. Cyril set out to provide a record of the lives of the notable figures who had pioneered the monastic life in Judea. During the course of his short life – he died probably in 558 at the age of about 33 – he conducted a series of interviews with older monks who had known these earlier leaders, on the basis of which he wrote his series of seven 'Lives', of different lengths, focusing particularly on the two outstanding figures of Euthymius and Sabas. Although Cyril lived a long time after the people he was writing about, his careful work has provided us with an amazingly reliable and accurate account of the monks and hermits of Judea during the fifth and sixth centuries.

Some decades later another monk, John Moschos, visited monasteries and monks in Palestine, Syria and Egypt, and collected stories which he published in a work known as the *Spiritual Meadow*. And there are several other 'Lives' of individual monks. The study of these and other written sources undertaken by Derwas Chitty has now been supplemented by the archaeological work of Yizhar Hirschfeld and of Joseph Patrich,[4] with the result that we now have a very full picture of these monasteries and the life of their monks.

Chariton and the origin of the movement in Judea

To understand the monastic life of the Judean desert we should begin with Chariton. We know of him from the *Life of Chariton*, written by an unknown monk in the late sixth century.

---

4 Patrich's book *Sabas, Leader of Palestinian Monasticism* offers an archaeological study especially of the monasteries founded by Sabas.

Although this was penned a long time after Chariton's death and is 'rich in literary hyperbole', 'recent archaeological finds show that the factual descriptions are authentic and based on close acquaintance with real conditions'.[5] Chariton was born towards the end of the third century, and is the first monk of this region to be known to us by name. The desert movement in Palestine did not, however, begin with him: we are told of others before him who were living an anchorite life in the caves of Calamon, near the Dead Sea, in the vicinity of the earlier Jewish monastery of Qumran, where in modern times the Dead Sea Scrolls were found. These were apparently Christians flee-ing from persecution, drawn to this particular place, we must believe, by the powerful biblical associations of the Judean desert. There was also a bishop in Jerusalem, named Narcis-sus, who early in the third century escaped from intrigues and slanders in the city to live for a while as an ascetic in the wilder-ness.[6] None of these, however, had any direct followers, and it was Chariton who established the pattern of monasticism in this area. In the words of his biographer he was, in regard to his way of life, 'ahead of all the holy fathers who came after him', and 'the first fruit of those who embraced the monastic life in all Palestine'.[7]

Chariton belonged to Iconium in Asia Minor, and in the days of persecution was arrested and in danger of being martyred for his faith. After a miraculous escape he fled to Jerusalem on pilgrimage, but soon moved eastwards into the desert, pos-sibly in the early 300s, just about the time when Antony was moving further into the Egyptian desert. Two things appar-ently drew Chariton towards life in the desert. The first was the idea of martyrdom. Having narrowly missed death for his faith in his own country, he was impelled by the idea that monasti-

---

5 Hirschfeld, 'The Life of Chariton in the Light of Archaeological Research', p. 425.

6 Eusebius, *Ecclesiastical History*, VI, 9.1.

7 Hirschfeld, 'Life of Chariton', p. 44.

cism and the practice of rigorous asceticism was another way of becoming a martyr.[8] The second was seclusion. He wanted to live in tranquillity and conversation with God through uninterrupted prayer.[9] So in a cave at Pharan in the Wadi Qilt 'he began to live a life of *hesychia*', of silence and solitude as an ascetic hermit, developing his own ascetic practice of sleeping on the ground, passing much of the night in prayer and psalmody and wearing a garment of hair. It wasn't long, however, before others were drawn to him there, and in this way the monastic community of Pharan came into being, the first such community in the Judean desert. It took the form of a 'laura', a number of cells for individual ascetics, linked together by a system of paths (Greek, *laura*) around a central core consisting of a church and basic service buildings such as a bakery. In Pharan, as in many other places later on, the church took the form of a large cave, which was dedicated by Bishop Macarius of Jerusalem. Life in community, however, did not suit Chariton. He 'saw himself deprived of his beloved tranquillity', and he longed for solitude and silence. So having provided his novice monks with a rule dealing with nutrition, prayer, manual work and the controlling of thoughts through 'assiduous and persistent prayer', and having appointed a leader in his place, he left in search of another secluded spot.

Travelling eastwards he settled himself in a cave in a cliff at Douka above Old Jericho. Here the same thing happened as at Pharan: drawn by his reputation others came to join him, so that a second laura was formed. And, in the words of his biographer, 'here too Chariton and his disciples were most seriously disturbed, as at Pharan, by people flocking to him, and were prevented from devoting themselves to silence.'[10] Eventually, Chariton removed from here also, and went a long

---

8 Ibid., pp. 8, 40.

9 The quotations in this paragraph are from Hirschfeld, 'Life of Chariton', pp. 14, 16.

10 Ibid., p. 22.

way south to a cliff at Souka, in what is now known as the Wadi Khureitun, south of Bethlehem, near the biblical centre of Tekoa. When a laura was formed here also, known later as the Old Laura, he withdrew by himself again to a small cave nearby, high in a precipitous cliff, because he 'set great value on never being diverted from his life of seclusion'.[11] This cave, recently discovered and surveyed by Yizhar Hirschfeld, is little more than an alcove, about 15 metres above ground level, and reached only by means of ladders from two larger caves below it and a narrow vertical passage. It became known as the 'Hanging Cave of Chariton'. Before his death, he returned to Pharan, where according to the *Life of Chariton* he gathered the monks from all his lauras together and addressed them with a long exhortation. He died sometime about the middle of the fourth century, and was buried here at the first desert place he had lived in.

Chariton was known as a holy man who practised rigorous asceticism, with a particular devotion to *hesychia*, to solitude and silence. His 'Hanging Cave' became one of the 'holy sites' of the Judean desert.[12] But his importance lies especially in the fact that he first established the pattern of monastic life in the Judean desert. He was the first to found lauras, which became an important and distinctive feature of Judean monasticism. The laura, with its group of individual cells connected by paths and linked to a core or centre, was in some ways similar to the semi-eremitical system at Nitria and Sketis in Lower Egypt, but in a Judean laura the monks, while living mainly in solitude and silence, were governed or guided by a rule, and supervised by a leader or *hegemon*, in a way that did not apply in Egypt. As we shall see, lauras here were often linked or paired with a coenobium or communal monastery, and there were also opportunities for some to live as hermits in isolation in the

---

11 Ibid., p. 24.

12 See the description in Hirschfeld, *Judean Desert Monasteries in the Byzantine Period*, pp. 228ff.

nearby desert. Together these arrangements made for a balance of communal and individual monasticism that was distinct to this area, and which owed its origin to Chariton.

Chariton can also be credited with demonstrating and establishing the main features of the monastic life as practised here and elsewhere. His rule gave guidelines for monks on living in silence, on restricting food and not eating until sundown, on manual work, on alternating sleep with psalmody, on the fixed hours of prayer, on staying in their cells, and on controlling their thoughts, practices which were much the same as were found throughout the desert movement.

Euthymius

It was nearly half a century after the death of Chariton before the next well-known and influential desert ascetic arrived in Judea: Euthymius, a native of Armenia in Asia Minor. What we know about him comes mainly from the *Life of Euthymius* written by Cyril of Scythopolis. Euthymius was born in 377, into a well-to-do Christian family in Melitene, the principal town of Armenia. He was given a good education, and as a young man was ordained priest and given a position of responsibility; but, not being at ease with it, in 405 he 'went as a fugitive to Jerusalem, out of a desire to inhabit its desert'.[13] It is significant that the first desert place he settled in was Chariton's first laura at Pharan. In the decades since Chariton's death the desert movement in Judea had continued. We do not know whether there were other lauras in existence by then, or other hermit's cells, but the original laura at Pharan had clearly been maintained. Euthymius did not, however, live in the laura itself; because, like Chariton before him, he had a great love of solitude and silence, he preferred to occupy a hermit's cell outside the laura. While he was there he learned how to make

---

13 Cyril, *Life of Euthymius*, 5:14.

cords, the basic craft of the desert monks. He also continued and developed a practice he had begun earlier, of going off to seek greater solitude in the deeper desert for the whole period from the Great Theophany, or Epiphany, until Palm Sunday, accompanied only by Theoctistus, a fellow monk who would become a significant colleague of his.

Once, five years after his arrival at Pharan, while on his way to the utter desert with Theoctistus, he came upon a cave in the cliff of the gorge of Wadi Mukellik, and decided to stay there. Near this spot together they founded a monastery which eventually became the coenobium of Theoctistus, although Euthymius preferred to stay in the cave. But, as happened with Chariton, people heard of him and disturbed his silence, and he missed 'the former peace he had enjoyed when a solitary ascetic'.[14] So leaving Theoctistus he took off with one disciple, Domitian, to the Rouba, the deep desert far in the south near the Dead Sea, spending time first at the ruined fort of Masada, known then as Masda, and then further west in the biblical Wilderness of Ziph, founding a monastery there at a place called Caparbaricha. In the remote desert he survived mainly by eating *maloa*, or 'saltbush', a desert plant whose leaves could be eaten raw or cooked. Eventually he returned to his cliff-face cave in the Wadi Mukellik, near Theoctistus' coenobitic monastery.

On a level spot beside this cave Euthymius now founded the laura which was to bear his name, and where, apart from his annual visits to the remote desert during Lent, he spent the rest of his days. Others came to join him, but, being determined to keep the laura small, he sent many of those who came to him to Theoctistus' coenobium some three miles away. The first disciples he admitted were twelve from various places beyond Palestine – Antioch, Armenia, Cappadocia, and Raithou in the Sinai Peninsula. A group of cells and a small church were built, and consecrated as a laura in 428 by the Bishop of Jeru-

14 Ibid., 11:21.

salem. In spite of Euthymius' love of solitude, however, the laura continued to grow, and according to Cyril the number of monks reached 50. Here Euthymius lived a life of asceticism and prayer, teaching and training his disciples until his death in 473, at the age of 96, having first given instructions that when he was gone the laura should be made into a coenobium. His death was the occasion of great mourning, and for his burial place a special vaulted chamber was built, where his tomb, now empty, can still be seen today. The dimensions of his tomb confirm Cyril's description of him as a 'dwarf-like' man.[15]

Although Euthymius lived a good while after Chariton, the first pioneer of the desert movement in Judea, he was in more than one way a true successor to him. It was the same love of silence and solitude that brought him to the desert. When he found himself surrounded by followers and disciples, he would move on to look for a more secluded and less accessible place, in the way that Chariton did. Unlike others of the desert monks, as we shall see, once he had entered the desert he never returned to Jerusalem. His way of life followed that of Chariton, although he was also influenced to some extent by what he had heard of Arsenius, one of the famous monks of Lower Egypt. About his ascetic practice, those who had known him are reported to have said, 'We never caught him eating or conversing with anyone, without grave necessity, except on Saturday and Sunday. We never knew him to sleep on his side, but sometimes he would snatch a little sleep when seated.'[16] He is said to have resembled Arsenius in his 'hatred of glory and success, his ardour and vigour in prayer, his compassion and powers of discernment'.[17]

As far as we know, Euthymius left no 'rule' for the monks of his laura, but he did teach them and train them in the desert way of life. Cyril reports that, like others in the desert tradition,

15 Ibid., 51:74.
16 Ibid., 21:34.
17 Ibid.

he emphasized the primary importance of 'attending to themselves', and gave his disciples instructions about not admitting evil thoughts, about avoiding acedia or listlessness, and about opposing the 'wiles of the demons'. According to Cyril he advocated a moderate asceticism, emphasizing the spiritual aspect: 'Correct abstinence is to take just enough at meal-times, while guarding the heart and making secret warfare against hidden passions; the weapons of the monk are meditation, discernment, self-control, and godly obedience.'[18]

Euthymius also developed and influenced the pattern of monasticism in the Judean desert. He established a laura of the same kind as Chariton's, but in keeping with his own love of solitude and tranquillity he endeavoured, initially at least, to keep it small, by admitting only twelve carefully selected men. At the same time he seems to have encouraged his partner Theoctistus to found a coenobium close to his own laura, to which he sent others who wanted to join him. Laura and coenobium worked hand in hand in a way that became typical of the movement in Judea. Alongside these, Euthymius maintained the eremitic life by going away at times to live as a hermit in remote cliff caves; and it was he who developed the practice which was continued by others, of retreating to the utter desert for the weeks of Lent. These different aspects of the desert all became characteristic features of the monasticism of the Judean desert.

Sabas

About 50 years after Euthymius first came to the Judean wilderness, another young man who would become a significant figure in Judean monasticism arrived in the desert. Sabas was also from Asia Minor, born in 439 into a Christian family in Cappadocia. From his childhood he aspired to the monastic

---

18 Ibid., 9:18.

life, and in 456, aged 17, he made his way first to Jerusalem and then on into the desert, where he presented himself at Euthymius' laura. As Euthymius did not admit young novices to his laura, he sent him to Theoctistus' coenobium nearby. Here Sabas began his monastic life, undertaking the most humble and menial tasks willingly, and training himself in humility, obedience and manual labour. After spending some 17 years in this coenobium, he withdrew by himself to the deeper desert, first near the Jordan river and then further south to the utter desert of Rouba. Here, we are told, he faced fierce and terrifying attacks by demons similar to those which Antony of Egypt encountered, and overcame them by devoting himself to fasts and ceaseless prayer, 'spending whole days and nights in prayer' and 'making his mind a spotless mirror of God'.[19]

For a period of four years Sabas roamed in the desert, until one day he came to a gorge in the Wadi Kidron, the valley which came down from Jerusalem, in which there was a cave, high in a cliff. An inner voice told him that he should make this his home. After he had lived here alone for five years, 'purifying the eye of his thought' and conquering evil spirits 'by his ceaseless prayers and nearness to God',[20] he felt able to receive others who came to join him. These included some anchorites and 'grazers' – ascetics who roamed about in the desert.[21] Caves in the sides of the gorge were made into cells, a water supply was discovered in the wadi with the help of a wild ass, and Sabas built a small oratory, thus creating a laura, which was known eventually as the Great Laura. A large cave discovered in the gorge was later turned into a church, which became known as 'the Church built by God', above which Sabas built

---

19 Cyril, *Life of Sabas*, 12:95; 16:99. Making the mind or heart a pure or spotless mirror which reflected God was an aspect especially of the spirituality of Ephrem and other Syrians. See Brock, *The Luminous Eye*.

20 Cyril, *Life of Sabas*, 16:99.

21 On 'grazers' see Cyril, *Life of Sabas*, 16:99 and note 18 on p. 211; John Moschos, *The Spiritual Meadow*, 19, and elsewhere (see note on p. 238). Also Binns, *Ascetics and Ambassadors*, p. 108.

himself a secluded tower, reached only by a secret passage from the sacristy of the church.[22]

This then became Sabas' base, but he continued the practice initiated by Euthymius of retreating to the utter desert for the duration of Lent, and he also visited other places in the Judean desert. During one of his travels he came to Castellium, a hill where there were ruins of a fort dating from the Jewish Second Temple period, and here, with the help of other monks, he built a coenobium. Later he went on to found a number of other monasteries, both lauras and coenobia, in the locality of the Great Laura. To one of these, a nearby coenobium, he sent those who came to him as novices, to receive a 'strict monastic formation' before they were given a cell in the laura. Sabas also developed a kind of partnership with a monk named Theodosius who had established another coenobium a few miles further up the Kidron valley. Any 'beardless' young men who wanted to become monks were sent first to Theodosius before being accepted into one of Sabas' monasteries. All did not go smoothly, however, in Sabas' monasteries, as there were some monks who rebelled against his leadership, and withdrew to found a new laura further to the south, not far from the monastery of Chariton. This New Laura would become a source of controversy over a long period.

With a large number of monasteries of different kinds now established in Judea, the church in Jerusalem made arrangements for their supervision. Sabas, who had by now been ordained priest, was appointed archimandrite of the lauras, and Theodosius archimandrite of the coenobia in the whole area, with authority to represent the interests of the monasteries both in Jerusalem and at the Imperial Court in Constantinople. This gave Sabas a different role, and from now on he was involved in frequent visits to these two centres, negotiating with the

---

22 For a detailed description of the Great Laura see Patrich, *Sabas, Leader of Palestinian Monasticism*.

Emperor for financial and other support for the Judean monasteries.

At the same time he became involved in the theological controversies following the decisions of the Council of Chalcedon in 451 about the two natures of Christ. He took part in an important gathering in Jerusalem at which the Patriarch agreed to support the Chalcedonian formula, and afterwards he was sent on a tour round the Judean monasteries to ensure their acceptance of this decision. The controversy, however, divided the monks, and Sabas played an important part in securing the loyalty of the Judean monks to the Chalcedonian side.

All this indicates that in his later years Sabas was something of a public figure, involved in the affairs and the controversies of the church. It was largely through him that Judean monasticism, already closely linked with Jerusalem because of the Holy Places, was more fully integrated into the life of the church than was the case in Egypt. He was also a great builder, who founded and built a total of about nine monasteries, centred on the Great Laura and linked together under his leadership in a loose federation with a common way of life.[23] Although there is some reason to think that he may not have laid quite as much emphasis on *hesychia*, on silence and solitude, as Chariton and Euthymius had done,[24] he did maintain his connection with the solitude of the wilderness, and he was remembered in later times most of all as a saintly man. He practised the monastic way of life through asceticism, obedience, humility, manual labour and constant prayer in the same way as elsewhere, and it was this, together with the miracles he performed, which drew people to his monasteries. When he knew his end was near he returned for a final time to his cave cell in the Great Laura. On his death in December 532, his burial in the Great Laura was attended by Archbishop Peter and other bishops and leading men from Jerusalem. Centuries later, at the time of

---

23 Details of all Sabas' monasteries are given in Patrich, *Sabas*.
24 See Hirschfeld, 'The Founding of the New Laura'.

the Crusades, his remains were transferred to Venice, but were eventually brought back to his own laura in 1965, where his tomb can be seen today.

In Sabas' monasteries a 'tradition', rather than a fixed 'rule', was established which was passed on to his successors, and which influenced the development of monasticism in the Orthodox Church.[25] His Great Laura, regarded as the leading monastery of the area, survived the seventh-century Muslim conquest in which many other monasteries were abandoned and was rebuilt by the Greek Orthodox Patriarchate in the late nineteenth century. Today the Great Laura, generally known as Mar Saba, and the Monastery of St Catherine in Sinai are the two oldest continuously occupied Christian monasteries in the world.[26]

Other monks in Judea

During the fifth and sixth centuries there was a prolific growth of monasticism in Judea. We saw earlier that the sites of no fewer than 65 monasteries have been identified in the desert area. The stories of a few more of the leading figures in this movement, as they have been told by Cyril of Scythopolis and others, will illustrate some aspects of it character.

Theodosius, who became a kind of partner of Sabas, was the founder of a large coenobium situated in the desert fringe area not far from Jerusalem. He was born about 430 in Cappadocia, and as a young man he was drawn, like many others, to the city of Jerusalem. Here he attached himself to a church in the desert fringe area between Jerusalem and Bethlehem. When the founder of the church died he was elected superior, but, not wanting that responsibility, he fled to the desert. He went first to a nearby monastery where the monks were said to have

---

25 See Chitty, *The Desert a City*, p. 117.
26 See the account in Dalrymple, *From the Holy Mountain*, and the detailed description in Patrich, *Sabas*.

been taught their monastic discipline by Euthymius, and then further east to a place in the upper part of the Wadi Kidron, some three or four miles south-east of Jerusalem, where he found a cave to settle in, 'subsisting on plants and devoting himself uniquely to prayer'.[27] When a wealthy visitor secretly left him a large sum of money, he established first a hospice, and then a coenobium.

Having been brought up in Cappadocia, Theodosius had been influenced by Basil of Caesarea, the great Cappadocian bishop and theologian who had himself established monasteries, and developed a way of monastic life which differed from the way of the desert.[28] Basil rejected the idea of the solitary life, and preferred being in community to anchoritism. His monks were involved in the life of the lay community in which the monasteries were located, were willing to be part of the ecclesiastical establishment, and practised only moderate asceticism. Theodosius' monastery was unusual for Judea in that it was similar to a Basilian establishment.[29] It eventually became the largest monastery in Judea, with workshops, hospices and hospitals and four churches, and about 400 monks at its peak time. A present-day monastery built on the site reflects the appearance of the earlier one.[30] Although he had links with Sabas, Theodosius' coenobium developed in different ways from the coenobia established by Sabas. But his leading position was recognized when he was made archimandrite, or supervisor, of the coenobia of Judea, as Sabas was made archimandrite of the lauras. He is said to have remained in his monastery for 50 years, dying in 529.[31] He was succeeded by his prior Sophronius, a

---

27 Cyril, *Life of Theodosius*, 3:238.

28 On Basil, and how his way differed from the way of the desert, see the Additional Note, pp. 226ff.

29 On the connection between Basilian monasticism and Theodosius' coenobium see Patrich, *Sabas*, p. 295; Binns, *Ascetics and Ambassadors of Christ*, p. 45.

30 Hirschfeld, *The Judean Desert Monasteries in the Byzantine Period*, pp. 33, 78.

31 Cyril, *Life of Theodosius*, 4:239.

man from Armenia, who enlarged the monastery even further and built a church to the Mother of God.

Theognius represents a somewhat different approach to monastic life. He too was born in Cappadocia, about the year 425, and is said to have been instructed in the monastic life in his early youth. Like many others, however, he felt drawn to the Holy City, where he joined a monastery founded by Flavia at the Mount of Olives. When eventually he was chosen as superior, he too shrank from this responsibility, and fled to Theodosius, with whom he lived in ascetic seclusion for some years. But when Theodosius established his coenobium, Theognius was troubled by its size and wealth, and 'the turmoil that arises from distraction',[32] and so retreated to the desert: first, it would seem, to a cave at Calamon in the Jordan Valley,[33] where he lived in solitude, 'attending to his quiet contemplation and asceticism',[34] and later to another cave not far from Theodosius' monastery.[35] Others who came to join him eventually persuaded him to build a small coenobium near his cave for a few monks. 'Although many wished to remain with him,' we are told, 'never did he allow himself to mix with a large crowd.'[36] It is therefore perhaps all the more surprising that when he was about 70 years old he was made the bishop of the church in the small town of Bethelia, in the far south-west of Palestine. Thereafter he spent some of his time there and some of it in a cell back at his own monastery, thus combining a great love of solitude with a willingness to accept responsibility in the church.

The monk known as *John the Hesychast* is an example of an opposite kind of move. Born into an eminent Christian family in Armenia in 453 or 454, he entered the monastic life early,

32 Cyril, *Life of Theognius*, 242.
33 Paul of Elusa, *Encomium on the Life of St Theognius*, 8. The accounts given by Cyril and Paul differ on this.
34 Ibid.
35 Cyril, *Life of Theognius*, 242.
36 Paul of Elusa, *Encomium on the Life of St Theognius*, 9.

founding a monastery near his home. At the age of 28 he was made bishop of nearby Colonia, while he still maintained his monastic discipline. When some people stirred up trouble in his diocese he fled to a hospice in Jerusalem; but on finding there 'the hubbub of the world'[37] he moved on, to the desert and to the Great Laura of Sabas, concealing the fact that he was a bishop. Sabas, recognizing his quality, gave him first some responsibility in the laura, then permission to live in solitude in a cell, and eventually the post of steward of the laura. It was only when Sabas tried to have him ordained priest that his true status as bishop was revealed. John lived in his cell in very determined seclusion for six years, until controversies in the laura led him to move away to a cave in the utter desert of Rouba. Here he lived for another six years, eating *melagria*, a desert plant with an edible root, and 'yearning to consort with God in solitude and to purify the eye of the mind by long philosophy so as with unveiled face to behold the glory of God'.[38] Sabas then brought him back to the Great Laura, where he lived in the solitude of his cell for the next 47 years until his death in 557. Here, then, was a man who eschewed ecclesiastical position, and was completely devoted to the solitude of the desert, living mostly in extreme seclusion in a laura cell, but also pioneering life alone in the utter desert for years at a time.

The search for solitude was taken even further by *Cyriacus*, the son of a priest, born in 449 in Corinth. At the age of 18 he went to Jerusalem, and after only a winter there, took himself off to the desert, to the laura of Euthymius. Having clothed him as a monk, Euthymius sent him, because of his youth, to the laura of Gerasimus in the Jordan Valley.[39] Being recognized as a lover of solitude, he was among a small group whom

---

37 Cyril, *Life of John the Hesychast*, 4:204.

38 Cyril, *Life of John the Hesychast*, 11:209. Early writers use the word 'philosophy' to refer to ascetical practice.

39 Cyril, *Life of Cyriacus*, 4:224. It was Euthymius' practice to send young novices to the coenobium of Theoctistus (see above), but Theoctistus had died by this time.

Euthymius took to the utter desert of Rouba for the duration of Lent. On the death of both Euthymius and Gerasimus, Cyriacus returned to Euthymius' laura and took a cell as a solitary. A dispute in the monastery led him to go off to the remote laura of Chariton at Souka, where he stayed for many years. Later he retired entirely by himself, moving by stages further and further into the desert of Rouba, where he lived for five years, surviving on *melagria*. Finally he moved to Sousakim, still further in the south, 'a place that was pure desert and hidden away where none of the anchorites had settled',[40] and where the remains of his cell can still be seen.[41] When plague struck the monastic communities in 537, the monks of Souka brought him back there, to occupy the famous 'Hanging Cave' of Chariton. But later he returned to Sousakim for a further eight years of utter solitude, before being brought back again to Chariton's Hanging Cave at Souka, where he died at a great age. Cyriacus displays in his love of extreme solitude another aspect of Judean monasticism, reminding us of Chariton, its pioneer. Derwas Chitty wrote of him, 'He is the most absolute, and perhaps the most attractive, of all Cyril's heroes. In him we seem to be returning to St Antony.'[42]

The monastery of Choziba, built into a cliff near the road from Jerusalem to Jericho, was an establishment of a different kind. Being on the pilgrim route towards the Jordan, it had the facilities for giving hospitality to both male and female pilgrims. It was a combined coenobium and laura, with a number of cells, known as the Cells of Choziba, close to the main buildings, connected by hazardous paths along the cliff face. The site had first been occupied by five Syrian monks, but the community there was founded by John from Thebes in Egypt sometime before 490. It was here that a famous ascetic, *George of Choziba*, a Cypriot born sometime in the late sixth century,

---

40 Ibid., 10:228.

41 See Hirschfeld, *The Judean Desert Monasteries in the Byzantine Period*, p. 219; Chitty, *The Desert a City*, p. 128.

42 Chitty, *The Desert a City*, p. 131.

spent most of his life. After a spell at Calamon because of his youth, he was accepted at Choziba, and given one of the cells, where he lived a life of extreme asceticism. His cell was a kind of tiny balcony high up the cliff, from which he emerged to collect left-over scraps for his food, to help with menial tasks for the pilgrims, and to attend the Eucharist on Sundays. He had a disciple named Antony, whose ministry was mainly with the 'multitude of guests' coming to the monastery, and who eventually wrote the *Life of George*, our main source of information about him. These were troubled times. Attacks by Saracens and Persians forced George to move temporarily to Jerusalem, but he later returned to live in the coenobium. And there were troubles within the monastery as well. Antony tells of disputes among the monks, which caused George to exhort them on the subject of arrogance and humility. George was a unique figure. He was not a solitary, although he lived in his own inaccessible cell, but his monastic life was one of great simplicity, extreme asceticism, service to others, and humility. The monastery at Choziba survived the Persian and Muslim conquests of the seventh century, and was still standing in the twelfth century. A new monastery, which is still occupied today, was built on its ruins in 1878.

The monasticism of the Judean Desert

During the course of the fifth century, in spite of the prominence of Egypt, the desert of Judea 'became a most important monastic centre for the entire Christian world'.[43] It was, of course, just one of the areas where the desert movement arose, and monasticism there had many features in common with other areas. One thing, however, which differentiated it from other desert areas was its proximity to the Holy City of Jerusalem and other biblical sites. From the early fourth century

43 Patrich, *Sabas*, p. 7.

onwards these became places of pilgrimage, to which people were drawn from far and wide; and in Jerusalem itself there were several large monasteries for women and for men. Most of the monks in the Judean desert, including all those whose lives are described above, had come from beyond Palestine, mostly from Asia Minor but also from Syria and elsewhere. Unlike most of the desert monks of Egypt, who were mainly native Egyptian people of the land and sometimes illiterate,[44] those of Judea were often people from well-to-do, educated, and sometimes aristocratic families, who came to visit the Holy Places in and around Jerusalem and then felt attracted to the ascetic life of the desert. Whereas in Egypt the city of Alexandria was seen by the desert monks as a foreign, pagan and perhaps wicked place, the monks of the Judean wilderness viewed Jerusalem as a holy city, and many of them paid visits to it. Indeed, this desert area was known to the monks as 'the desert of the Holy City' or 'of Jerusalem'.[45]

The proximity to Jerusalem and other holy places associated with Jesus and with other biblical figures linked this desert region in a special way to the desert tradition of the Bible. Throughout the desert movement the monks were conscious that they were following in the wake of the men of the desert in the Bible, in particular Elijah and John the Baptist; but this was true in a special way of the monks of Judea, many of whom had come first to visit some of the biblical holy places. The road down through the desert to the River Jordan where John the Baptist had baptized became a pilgrim route for many who had come from far and wide to Jerusalem. Because of this the Judean desert had a special attraction for those who were drawn to the monastic life. Here they could feel especially close to Elijah and John the Baptist, and indeed to Jesus himself, who had spent 40 days and nights fasting in the Judean wilder-

---

44 PK, Vol. 2, *Precepts*, 139.

45 See the title of Cyril's *Life of Sabas*; and John Moschos, *The Spiritual Meadow*, 92.

ness. In the words of one scholar, 'Great biblical events that had happened in the desert (the exodus, the life of the prophet Elijah, John the Baptist, Christ's forty days of fasting), as well as eschatological promises which made life in the world seem irrelevant, were enough to attract the newly converted to Palestine.'[46] It is interesting, therefore, that the *Life of Chariton* tells us that, at the start, he 'entered the path that leads to the holy city of God, having chosen to imitate Elijah's and John's life in the desert',[47] and ends by reporting that he was 'the first to set a pattern of the eremitical life after the admirable pioneers – I mean Elijah and John the Baptist'.[48] As elsewhere, but even more than in other places, the monks of the Judean desert must have been conscious that they were continuing the biblical tradition.

The twin facts that the Judean movement took its origin from the holy places of pilgrimage, and that it began so early – even before Chariton came there early in the fourth century – together make it clear that it began independently of developments in Egypt.[49] There were, indeed, connections with Egypt later on: there is evidence that some monks came and went between Egypt and Palestine, and that Antony was revered in Judea.[50] Euthymius is said to have modelled his life on that of Arsenius of Egypt. And it is probable that the 'Sayings' of the Egyptian Desert Fathers were first gathered together and noted down here. And because many monks, attracted by the Holy Places, came to Judea from a number of different places, the monastic life of the area was in some ways influenced by that of other monastic centres. Some of the Judean coenobia, particularly that of Theodosius, had a system of organization modelled on Basil's in Cappadocia. The presence of Armenian

---

46 Gribomont, 'Monasticism and Asceticism: Eastern Christianity', p. 91.

47 *Life of Chariton*, 8.

48 Ibid., 43.

49 A point made in Chitty, *The Desert a City*, p. 15; and in Harmless, *Desert Christians*, p. 433.

50 Binns, *Ascetics and Ambassadors*, p. 158.

monks in Sabas' Great Laura influenced liturgical developments there.[51] Nevertheless, the Judean movement was distinct.
It began separately, and was initially an independent part of
the widespread desert movement that was springing up spontaneously in various places.

Another distinctive feature of Judean monasticism was the
variety of different patterns of monastic life developed in it.
This was due in part to the different types of terrain in the area,
and in part to the character and aims of its leading figures.
Yizhar Hirschfeld, in his work of surveying and excavating old
monastic sites, identified four main types of monastic buildings. There were coenobia and laura, and monasteries of each
of these kinds were to be found on level ground and on cliffs.
Within these four types, the establishments varied greatly in
size, from the large coenobium of Theodosius, which at its
height housed about 400 monks, to small lauras with only 20
monks or less. In addition, there were monasteries along the
pilgrim route, such as Choziba, which catered for the needs
of quite large numbers of pilgrims and guests. And apart from
these establishments, many of whose ruins or remains can be
traced today, there was an unknown number of hermits' cells,
some of them deep in the desert, such as the cell of Cyriacus at
Sousakim far in the south, some of them close to a laura, such
as the Hanging Cave of Chariton, and others consisting simply
of caves in the faces of steep cliffs in the wadis and ravines up
and down the area.[52]

This variety of types of monastic establishment reflects the
different approaches to monastic life. We have seen that it
was in Judea that the laura was developed, a form of monastic
organization similar to but not quite the same as the semi-
eremitic pattern in Egypt. We have seen also that lauras and
coenobia often existed close to one another, and worked in
partnership, with younger monks and novices being sent to a

---

51 On these influences see Patrich, *Sabas*, pp. 46 and 178ff.
52 See for example, Cyril, *Life of Sabas*, 24:108.

coenobium before being allowed to live in a cell in a laura. This pattern was a distinctive feature of Judean monasticism.

Another feature was the special importance attached to solitude and silence. The movement in this area started with Chariton, whose main concern was to reach a secluded place where he could be silent with God; and although as time went by many coenobia were established in the area, the pull towards seclusion and tranquillity was to be seen in the 'Lives' of most of the leading figures, especially Euthymius, John the Hesychast, and Cyriacus, and even the more activist Sabas. We are also told of 'grazers',[53] people who roamed about alone in the remote desert, living off *melagria* and *maloa*, in complete solitude. Palladius in his *Lausiac History* tells of a man 'who lived his life with no roof over his head in the vicinity of the Jordan'.[54] Here we find those extraordinary woman anchorites, Syncletica of Palestine and Mary of Egypt, whose stories are told in Chapter 4. And it was here, in Judea, that many experienced ascetics developed the practice of going off to wander in the solitude of the utter desert during the weeks of Lent.

Because we have less written information about the monks of Judea than about those of Lower Egypt, and no one made a collection of their 'sayings', Judea has always been a less publicized area of the desert movement. But we do know that there were ascetics there, especially John the Hesychast and Cyriacus, both of whom 'gained prominence as spiritual fathers and were revered by pilgrims and the faithful', as were the leading figures elsewhere.[55] And archaeology at the Sabaite coenobium of Castellium has discovered wall-paintings of 36 saints, 'almost all of whom are desert monks of Palestine'. About some of them there is virtually no other information, but 'this series of paintings provides us with knowledge of the veneration of saints unique to Palestine'.[56] These facts, together

---

53 See note 21 above.
54 Palladius, *Lausiac History*, 50.
55 Patrich, *Sabas*, p. 169.
56 Ibid., p. 143.

with the sheer number of monastic settlements, make it clear that the desert movement in Judea was of greater magnitude and significance than has sometimes been thought. Moreover, we do not know how many secret hermits may have inhabited the multitude of caves in the rock which can be seen up and down the area. Beneath the corporate life of the coenobia, and the active work of caring for guests in the monasteries on the pilgrim route, the true heart of the Judean movement lay where the solitary monks kept their long hours of silence in the seclusion of the hermits' caves, and the inaccessible laura cells of the remote desert.

These distinctive features, however, should not obscure the fact that the monasticism of the Judean desert had a great deal in common with what was taking place in other parts of the desert movement. Here as elsewhere those who embraced the monastic life abandoned their possessions and 'left the world', spent hours in solitude and silence, practised the asceticism of restricting their food and their sleep, occupied themselves with manual work, guarded their hearts against the demons of evil thoughts, and engaged in constant prayer. Here in Judea we encounter a monasticism which had its own distinctive features but which was part of a wider desert movement.

4

Women in the Desert

It will appear from the foregoing chapters that the desert movement was very much a male affair. We know from various
sources, however, that from very early times there were many
women living an ascetic or monastic life in a variety of ways.[1]
In this chapter we take a brief look at these different ways and
at how women participated in the desert movement.

Varieties of ascetic life

First, there were the well-known monasteries for women established in or near Jerusalem by wealthy and eminent Roman
ladies in the third or fourth centuries. Melania the Elder, a rich
widow, founded a monastery on the Mount of Olives, and 'lived
there twenty-seven years heading a company of fifty virgins'.[2]
Her grand-daughter Melania the Younger also founded monasteries on the Mount of Olives. Paula, a member of a wealthy
aristocratic Roman family, established a monastery in Bethlehem; and Flavia, another Roman lady, built both a church and
a monastery close to the Garden of Gethsemane in Jerusalem.
These monasteries provided opportunities for other women
who came to visit the Holy Places and felt drawn to live the
monastic life there. Melania the Elder had a personal link with
the desert movement in Egypt. She herself visited Lower Egypt

1 See Clark, 'Women and Asceticism in Late Antiquity', p. 40; Elm, *Virgins of God*, Chapter 7.

2 Palladius, *Lausiac History*, 46.

and had conversations with some of the monks there,[3] and her protégé Evagrius became a significant figure in the desert movement, as we shall see.

In addition there were women throughout the Eastern Mediterranean who adopted ascetical practices and lived as virgins, not as anchorites in the desert but in or on the outskirts of towns or villages. The existence of women ascetics and virgins was not a new phenomenon in the fourth century, but is likely to have been a continuation of a tradition begun in New Testament times. St Paul's emphasis on the value of celibacy for both men and women was continued in the Apostolic Fathers,[4] and no doubt encouraged the practice of sexual asceticism. The result was that in the church of the fourth century there were large numbers of 'consecrated women' or 'dedicated virgins' living mainly in the towns.[5] In recently discovered Egyptian papyrus documents they are referred to variously as *apotaktikai* ('renouncers'), *monachai* ('monks') or *parthenai* ('virgins').[6] Some of them were individual ascetics, living on their own or in a cell or hut outside a family home. Examples can be drawn from various sources. Theodoret tells of one woman in Syria who 'set up a small hut in the garden of her mother's house', and adds that there were 'myriad and defeating-enumeration' retreats of this kind, not only in that area but 'throughout the East'.[7] Palladius tells stories of many more women ascetics. Of one he says: 'In a certain village there lives a virgin who has practised asceticism for thirty years. They say she eats nothing except on Saturday and Sunday. But in the whole period of five days she spends between eating, she says seven hundred

---

3 Ibid.

4 1 Corinthians 7.25, 36; Revelation 14.4; Ignatius Ep. of Polycarp 5:2; 1 Clem. 38:2; 48:5; Ep. of Polycarp 5:3 and elsewhere.

5 Terms used by Brown in his full discussion of the topic in *The Body and Society*, pp. 259–84.

6 Elm, *Virgins of God*, pp. 229ff; Goehring, 'Through a Glass Darkly', pp. 63ff.

7 Theodoret of Cyrrhus, *A History of the Monks of Syria*, pp. 186f.

prayers.'[8] John Moschos tells of a woman who lived as a solitary in Jerusalem, but sometimes spent the whole night in the church.[9]

Other women continued to live with their families or at least with their mothers. 'Piamoun was a virgin who lived with her mother spinning flax and eating only every other day at evening.'[10] Another 'had completed sixty years in ascetical practices along with her mother', and 'never went out'.[11] And there were some who lived with their husbands but with a mutual agreement to preserve their virginity.[12]

There were others who lived in communities of various kinds. Some of these seemed to be small, informal groups of women living together, but others were large, well-established institutions, sometimes set up and led by individuals who gathered others around them. Once again, examples can be multiplied. Athanasius writes that when Antony decided to give away his possessions and embrace the monastic life, he placed his sister in a convent 'in the charge of respected and trusted virgins'.[13] Palladius tells of 'Amma Talis, a woman eighty years old in the ascetic life, as her neighbours affirmed', who had sixty young women living with her in the town of Antinoe;[14] also of a man named Elias in Upper Egypt who 'had great concern for the virgins' and built a monastery for them.[15] John Moschos writes of a bishop's sister who was 'hegoumene' of a women's monastery in Armenia, and refers to a 'monastery of virgins housing about forty persons in Lycia'.[16] The central Egyptian town of Oxyrhynchus, in particular, was famous for

---

8 Palladius, *Lausiac History*, 20; other examples in 28, 41, 57, 63, 67; *The Lives of the Desert Fathers*, X:4.

9 John Moschos, *The Spiritual Meadow*, 127.

10 Palladius, *Lausiac History*, 31.

11 Ibid., 60.

12 Ibid., 8, 41:5; 54:4; *The Lives of the Desert Fathers*, XX:1.

13 *Life of Antony*, 3.

14 Palladius, *Lausiac History*, 59.

15 Ibid., 29.

16 John Moschos, *The Spiritual Meadow*, 128, 135.

its very large numbers of both male and female monasteries, which housed, it is alleged, 'ten thousand monks and twenty thousand nuns'.[17]

We don't know much about the details of these women's lives, and no doubt their way of life varied, but it appears that what principally characterized it was, on the one hand, their asceticism – celibacy, limitation of food and abstaining from worldly pleasures – and on the other their commitment to prayer. That is to say, although these women did not live in the desert itself but in or on the outskirts of towns and villages, some elements of their way of life resembled that of the desert, and some of the women, as we shall see, have traditionally been regarded as 'Desert Mothers'.

The women's monasteries of Pachomius and Shenoute were probably something of a special case. We have seen that Pachomius had three monasteries for women in his Koinonia, and Shenoute also included a community of women within his federation. Not much is said about them in the relevant records, but as far as we know these were the only monasteries at that time to be governed by a 'rule', and this rule applied to both men's and women's monasteries. The nuns in the Pachomian monasteries were under the supervision of a 'righteous father', who had to 'guard them in all holiness' according to Pachomius' rules.[18] The arrangement in Shenoute's federation was similar, where a 'female elder' with responsibility for the women's community was subject to a 'male elder' set above her.[19] That is to say, as one would expect in those days, the women monks were supervised by men. With this exception, however, Shenoute himself believed in the equality of men and women, and his rule applied equally to both. Since, as we have seen, Pachomius had incorporated some of the ways of the desert in his monastic rule, the way of life of the women in his

---

17 *The Lives of the Desert Fathers*, V.
18 PK, Vol. 1, Bohairic *Life*, 195.
19 Krawiec, 'The Role of the Female Elder in Shenoute's White Monastery'.

monasteries was probably closer to that of desert anchorites than was the case in other, more informal monastic communities; and something similar was probably true of Shenoute's monasteries.

Anchorites in the desert

None of the women discussed above were truly 'women of the desert' in the literal sense; but there were others who were. The records have a number of stories of male monks who unexpectedly found female anchorites living by themselves in a cell or cave. One is told by a monk from Pharan in Judea named Silas, about Syncletica, the daughter of an imperial senator.[20] Her father had arranged a marriage for her against her wishes, but agreed to let her visit the Holy Places in Jerusalem first. While she was there she slipped away surreptitiously from her entourage and went off to the desert. Going down towards the Jordan, she came to a place called Corpatha, where she found an old anchorite, clothed in sackcloth. At her request, and on being assured that she was genuine, he clothed her in a monastic habit, and gave her a copy of the Bible which he possessed. She left with his blessing, praying 'to be veiled from human sight', and was led by God to a secret cave. 'My inner concern', she later told Silas, 'was to put an end to the deceit of a frivolous life', and to be free of 'the world that had ruled over me'.[21] Silas tells how, on his way to visit and give some food to anchorites near the Jordan, he came across Syncletica's cave. She was clothed in a standard monastic habit and he inwardly wondered if she was a woman. Knowing his thoughts, and being given a promise that he would not tell anyone about her until her death, she told him her story. She had been 18 years

---

20 *A Narrative about Syncletica who Lived in the Jordanian Desert.* This Syncletica should not be confused with Syncletica of Egypt, one of the Desert Mothers, see below.

21 Ibid., pp. 49, 51.

old when she came to the cave, and had lived in it for 28 years without ever seeing anyone. Her face, he reported, still had its youthful beauty. He departed, having been assured by her that she would not leave there till he returned to be blessed. But when he returned a few days later she had disappeared, and he knew nothing more about her.

Elsewhere we read of two 'great old men' who discovered a 'holy old virgin' lying ill and about to die in a cave in the desert of Sketis in Egypt. She told them she had lived there for 37 years, 'surviving on herbs and serving Christ'. She died while they were there, and they buried her.[22] John Moschos tells of two more such women in Palestine. One came knocking at the door of a desert monk who lived in a cave near Jordan, saying she too was an anchorite with a cell not far away, and asking for water.[23] The other had been a nun in a monastery in Jerusalem, who on discovering that a young man had a desire for her had fled to the Judean desert, and had lived there for 17 years before an anchorite met her there.[24] Taken together, these stories suggest that there may have been quite a number of women anchorites hidden and unknown in the deserts of both Judea and Egypt.

Some of these female desert anchorites are of special interest because they lived in the desert disguised as men. Two men returning from Sinai to their monastery in Palestine found a cave in which was the body of monk who had just died. Only on preparing the body for burial did they realize that it was a woman.[25] A similar story is told of Abba Bessarion, who on his way to visit John of Lycopolis found an anchorite living in a cave. Calling again at the cave on his way back he found that the anchorite had died, and when he took the body for burial he discovered it was a woman.[26] Similarly again, some 'seculars'

---

22 *World of the Desert Fathers*, p. 43.
23 John Moschos, *The Spiritual Meadow*, 19.
24 Ibid., 179.
25 Ibid., 170.
26 *Sayings*, Bessarion, 4.

visited an anchorite, who died shortly after speaking to them, and only then did they find out it was a woman.[27] There is also a tale of a woman named Apollinaris, daughter of an Emperor, who fled to the desert of Sketis to escape marriage, took the name of Dorotheus and lived as a man.[28] And there are various accounts of a woman named Anastasia, 'a patrician lady of the highest rank', who fell foul of the Empress Theodora and fled to Sketis. She was given a cell there by Abba Daniel, the 'hegoumen' of Sketis at that time, 'changed her apparel for men's clothing' and lived there in secret.[29] This topic of women disguised as men is a significant one, and we shall return to it later.

Women in the sayings of the Desert Fathers

As we saw earlier, three women are included in the collection of *Sayings of the Desert Fathers*, and regarded as ammas: Sarah, Syncletica and Theodora. Sarah lived somewhere near the River Nile, and the other two on the outskirts of Alexandria. Although this was 'not yet part of the deep desert, they had, however, left the city itself behind'.[30]

Syncletica,[31] whom we encountered briefly in Chapter 1, is known to us through the *Life of Holy Syncletica*, written by a person known as pseudo-Athanasius, probably in the mid-fifth century. This 'biography' is made up largely of teachings attributed to her, with only a minimum of information about her life. The teaching was apparently given to other women ascetics who came to her for instruction, and although it is hard to know to what extent the text we have represents the actual words of Syncletica, the originality of the thought and

---

27 *World of the Desert Fathers*, p. 30.
28 Regnault, *The Day-to-Day Life of the Desert Fathers*, p. 25.
29 *The Life of Daniel of Scetis*, pp. 69ff.
30 Elm, *Virgins of God*, p. 358.
31 Not to be confused with the Syncletica of Judea, described above.

the variety and freshness of the imagery point to a person of great spiritual depth and maturity. The large selection of her sayings included in the collection of *Sayings of the Desert Fathers* has apparently been taken from this *Life*.

Syncletica was born in the later part of the fourth century, the daughter of a wealthy Christian family of Macedonian origin living in Alexandria. Like other subjects of hagiographic writing, she is said to have begun fasting and other ascetic practices at an early age, and to have rejected marriage. When her parents died she sold all her possessions, gave the proceeds to the poor, and went with her blind sister to live in the tomb of a relative outside the city. She cut off her hair as a symbol that she was to be counted as a 'virgin', and began to live as a solitary.[32] 'We close ourselves up in our houses,' she said of herself and her fellow-ascetics.[33] In an interesting sentence which no doubt describes her own situation, she spoke of some who were 'in the city but imagined themselves in the desert'.[34] Solitude and obscurity were important aspects of her life. There were, apparently, some other women ascetics around her, but she must have kept separate from them to some extent, since 'she did not allow anyone to become an observer' of her ascetic life. She wanted to escape the notice of other people and to keep her ascetic practice secret.[35]

Her teaching gives lively expression to other aspects of the way of the desert. Having given away all her possessions herself, she emphasized the value of voluntary poverty and the danger that lies in love of money. 'Our profession', she said, 'is nothing but renunciation of life, the rehearsal of death.'[36] When her fellow-ascetics approached her they were met with silence.[37] She practised asceticism, limiting her eating and sleep-

---

32 That is, she lived a life of *hesychia*. *The Life of Syncletica*, 12.
33 Ibid., 26.
34 Ibid., 97.
35 Ibid., 10, 15, 38.
36 Ibid., 30–7, 73.
37 Ibid., 21.

ing, but not in an extreme way, warning that extreme practices can lead to arrogance, and stressing the importance of temperance and moderation. She laid particular and unusual emphasis on the asceticism of accepting calmly the troubles and ills that come one's way in life, including physical illness. 'This is the great asceticism: to control oneself in illness and to sing hymns of thanksgiving to God,' she said.[38] And the *Life* records how, at the end of her life, she herself endured a long and horrible illness with patience and thanksgiving. Like others she was aware of the need to guard the heart, and to struggle against the demons which try to introduce evil thoughts into it. Her penetrating analysis and discussion of the nature of these 'thoughts' or 'passions', including gluttony, love of pleasure, lust, anger, despair and arrogance, probably owes something to Evagrius, but also bears her own stamp.[39] The struggle against the sinful passions is mainly an internal one. 'The enemy' does battle against us, not only by tempting us to external acts, but 'by means of internal thoughts', so that the ascetic needs constantly to 'be watchful' and to guard against them. Those who have conquered fornication in practice still have to struggle against 'the spirit of fornication'. These 'thoughts' are overcome partly through asceticism and partly through prayer. 'She set aside through fasting and prayer the thorny buds of thought.'[40] Like others she laid special emphasis on humility. 'Just as it is impossible for a ship to be built without nails, just so it is impossible to be saved without humility'[41] – a saying which incidentally illustrates an intriguing aspect of her discourses: her frequent use of imagery to do with ships and the sea.[42]

More than any others, Syncletica provides an example of someone who, without going deep into the physical desert,

---

38 *Sayings*, Syncletica, 8.
39 *The Life of Syncletica*, 49, 54. Evagrius is discussed in Chapter 6.
40 *The Life of Syncletica*, 17.
41 Ibid., 56; *Sayings*, Syncletica, 26.
42 *The Life of Syncletica*, 19, 37, 45, 47, 56, 85, 102.

withdrew from the world into a place of solitude, and pursued the way of the desert through renunciation, silence and secrecy, adopting ascetic practices, including the acceptance of grievous ill health, as part of the ascetic way and struggling against the passions of the demons by means of humility and prayer. Her discourses provide a fine, graphic and personal description of the way of the desert; and she holds a very special place among the desert ammas and abbas.

Of the other two ammas included in the collection of *Sayings* we know much less. *Theodora* was apparently a person of high social position. Palladius reports that she was the wife of a tribune, but 'became so poor that she took alms' and 'finally died in the monastery of Hesychas by the sea'. [43] What is meant by her 'taking alms', how long she lived in this monastery, and where that monastery was, we do not know. She seems to have consulted Theophilus, the Archbishop of Alexandria, and to have been consulted by a number of monks about monastic life; with the result that even though she did not live in the physical desert, ten sayings of hers or stories about her have been included in the collection of *Sayings*.

Like many of the ascetics, she was aware of the effect of evil on both body and mind, and of the importance of bodily discipline and of guarding the heart against evil thoughts. Evil, she said, 'attacks your body through sickness, debility, weakening of the knees, and all its members. It dissipates the strength of soul and body, so that one believes one is ill and no longer able to pray. But if we are vigilant, all these temptations fall away.' [44] Again like others, she emphasized the unique importance of humility in overcoming the demons. She told a story of a monk to whom the demons acknowledged that neither fasting, nor vigils nor withdrawal into the desert could overcome them, but only humility. From the little we know of her

---

43 Palladius, *Lausiac History*, 41.
44 *Sayings*, Theodora, 3.

it seems clear that she had a profound grasp of the essentials of the way of the desert.

The third of the ammas is *Sarah*. What little we know of her is mainly from the nine items under her name in the collection of *Sayings*. She is said to have lived near a river in a cell with a terraced roof, in the district of Pelusium, for 60 years.[45] Just where this was is not clear, but it seems that she had contact with ascetics of the desert, including some monks of Sketis who came to visit her.

She is described as having struggled against the 'spirit of fornication' for 13 years; and she is typical of many of the desert ascetics in regarding this struggle positively, as part of her inner ascesis, so that 'she never prayed that the warfare should cease'. Typically also it was due to a combination of asceticism and prayer that she finally overcame in this struggle, while at the same time attributing her eventual victory to her 'master, Christ'.[46]

Perhaps the most interesting thing about what we know of Sarah was how she saw herself in relation to male monks. When two old men, 'great anchorites', tried to humiliate her, calling her a 'mere woman', she replied, 'According to nature I am a woman, but not according to my thoughts.' And to some other monks she commented, 'It is I who am a man, you who are women.'[47] 'Manliness' was a quality required for engaging in the long and fierce struggle against the demons in the heart, and it could be found as much in women as in men. This again raises important issues about gender in relation to asceticism and the desert way, which we will return to at the end of this chapter.

---

45 *Sayings,* Sarah, 3; Elm, *Virgins of God,* p. 263.
46 *Sayings,* Sarah, 1, 2.
47 Ibid., 4, 9.

'Harlots of the desert'

There are also several stories of prostitutes who were led to repentance and turned to living a life of asceticism. Four of these stories have been translated and gathered together in a book by Sister Benedicta Ward entitled *Harlots of the Desert*. The best known of them is referred to as Mary of Egypt. In the record her story is told by a monk of Judea named Zossima who eventually came across her in the remote desert of Judea across the Jordan. After she had been a prostitute in Alexandria for 17 years, her sexual urge led her to join a boat sailing to Jerusalem, on which there were some pilgrims going to the Holy City to celebrate the Exaltation of the Holy Cross. Once there she got caught up in the crowd going into the church, but found she was mysteriously prevented from going in. She was, however, given a vision of the Virgin Mary, and this led her to confess her sin and offer her life to God. With some coins that a woman gave her she bought three loaves, and then made her way down to the Jordan river and across it into the remote desert, where she began a life of solitude. Years later, when Zossima, making his solitary Lenten sojourn in the desert, came across her naked in the wilderness she had not seen any human person for 47 years. She had survived on the loaves she had brought with her, and had endured a fierce struggle against evil 'thoughts', while the Mother of God helped her to constant repentance. After Zossima and Mary had blessed one another, he left with her instructions to return to the banks of the Jordan the following year, on 'the most holy day of the Lord's Supper', and to bring her 'a portion of the life-giving Body and Blood'. A year later, when he went again on her instructions to the place of their first meeting in 'the huge solitude of the desert', he found her dead, with a message for him written in the sand. He buried her there in a grave dug by a friendly lion.

This is an extraordinary story of a woman who became a desert anchorite. It was a popular tale, probably repeated in various forms, as a very similar story is told by Cyril of Scytho-polis.[48] Just how much historical reality lies behind it is not clear, but there are several points of interest in it. It provides further illustration of the desert ways of solitude, rigorous asceticism, and the struggle against 'thoughts'; and it draws attention to the significance of repentance for the desert monks, a point we shall return to later. And at a different level, it provides an interesting reminder of the link between the Holy Places of Jerusalem and the Judean desert, and of the practice of retreat-ing into the remote desert in solitude for the entire period of Lent, both features of Judean monasticism that we noted in the previous chapter.

The story of Pelagia is rather different. She was an actress and prostitute in the city of Antioch. Once, when decked in her finery and accompanied by her followers she rode past a group of bishops, all but one of them turned their eyes away. But one, Bishop Nonnus, a monk from the Pachomian monastery of Tabennesi, gazed on her and was startled by her beauty. Later she came to a church where he was speaking, and was moved to repentance. He arranged for her baptism, and shortly after-wards she gave away all her goods, dressed herself in a man's clothes and took herself off, not to the desert but to Jerusalem, where she made herself an enclosed cell on the Mount of Olives. Taking the male name Pelagius, she lived as a secluded anchor-ite, spending her life in prayer. Eventually Nonnus' deacon, James, visited her there and managed to speak to her; but on returning a second time he found her dead. Those who buried her were surprised to discover that Pelagius was a woman.

This too is a story of repentance. Unlike Mary of Egypt, however, Pelagia did not retreat to the desert but to a cell near the Holy Places of Jerusalem, in seclusion, solitude and silence, practising prayer and no doubt asceticism, after the manner of the desert. But perhaps the most remarkable feature of the story

---

48 Cyril, *Life of Cyriacus*, 18f.

is the attitude of Bishop Nonnus, who unlike the other bishops – 'more timid men who were aware of their own capacity for lust'[49] – was prepared to look at her, and to acknowledge her God-given feminine beauty. He even compared the attention she gave to adorning herself with their lack of concern to adorn themselves for God. The monks' acute concern over sexual sin did not prevent some of them from recognizing in the human grace of women a gift of the Creator.

The other two stories are in some ways similar to each other. One is a harsh tale of a prostitute in Alexandria named Thaïs, who was visited by Paphnutius, a monk of the Egyptian desert, under the pretence of wanting to 'commit sin' with her. Surprisingly, however, he spoke to her of the judgement of God, with the result that he led her to repent. Taking her off to a women's monastery in the desert, he immured her in a cell, locked it securely so that she could not get out, and told her to pray constantly for God's mercy – an arrangement which seems more like an imprisonment than a voluntary withdrawal to the desert. Three years later, after some monks at Sketis had been told by a vision that she was forgiven, he returned to let her out, but she died after 15 days. The other story is of a woman named Maria, the niece of a monk in Egypt called Abraham. She had lived a life of asceticism for 20 years in a desert cell adjacent to his, but was tempted out of it and seduced by a visiting monk. Filled with despair about herself she fled to the city and entered a brothel. It was two years before her uncle discovered where she was. On doing so he disguised himself as a soldier, and going to the brothel, asked for her. When she recognized him she was filled with compunction, and returned with him to her cell to live out a life of penitence, austerity and prayer.

These are all stories of 'fallen' women who were 'rescued' in one way or another by monks. As Sister Benedicta Ward points

---

49 Ward, *Harlots of the Desert*, p. 59.

out, the theme of repentance runs through them all.[50] In the literature there are other stories of this type. In one, the monk John the Dwarf learned of a young woman who on being left an orphan turned her house into a hospice for monks but finding herself poor she had become a prostitute. The monk visited her, caused her to repent and led her into the desert where, during the first night, she died.[51] Similarly Abba Serapion went to visit a courtesan and read to her at length from scripture. She was filled with compunction and repented, whereupon he took her to a women's monastery to spend the rest of her life in ever more rigorous asceticism.[52] Another story tells how a woman who practised prostitution repented on meeting Abba Timothy.[53]

It is interesting, however, that there are also stories of male monks being rescued by women.[54] One tells of a monk on an errand who saw a woman washing clothes and wanted her. When he asked her to sleep with him she reminded him of how much he would suffer by doing so, and of how much ascetic effort he had made to reach his present state. He was struck with contrition, and returning to his brothers he advised them not to go out from the monastery. Another monk, visiting a secular friend, was struck with desire for his beautiful daughter, and when his friend was out he wanted to lie with her. She managed to put him off the idea by pretending that she gave off a bad smell if anyone came near her; he repented and thanked God for her wisdom that had saved him. A third story tells of a trader whose colleague died leaving a beautiful widow. When he declared his desire for her she persuaded him to fast for several days, whereupon she showed him that he desired food more than he desired her. He was struck with contrition, and took himself to a monastery to become a monk.

---

50 Ibid., Chapter 1.
51 *Sayings*, John the Dwarf, 40.
52 *Sayings*, Serapion, 1.
53 *Sayings*, Timothy, 1.
54 *World of the Desert Fathers*, pp. 13–16.

All these stories illustrate the importance that was attached to sexual sin, for both men and women. But they also demonstrate that while women could endanger their souls by 'falling' into prostitution, the real danger lay in men's sexual urges, and that it was possible for wise women to show men the danger and help them to deal with it.

Women and men in the desert

Nevertheless, it is true that in the literature of the desert movement there are far fewer sayings of female monks or stories about them than there are of male monks. This is partly because, as we have seen, most of the women ascetics lived in or on the outskirts of towns and villages, where they were unknown and undistinguished. Although there were women in the desert itself, they seem to have been few. Why was this? It was partly, no doubt, because the desert was a dangerous place, thought to be not suitable for women. As Susanna Elm says, 'The deep desert itself, it seems, was truly out of bounds for women.'[55] But it is also clear that, generally speaking, the male monks wanted to avoid women and to preserve the desert as a place where they could do that. For this reason, women were not allowed into the main monastic centres of Lower Egypt. Paphnutius, the 'Father of Sketis', said, 'I do not allow the face of a woman to dwell in Sketis.'[56] Sisoes, in his old age, refused the attempt by a disciple to get him to move from the desert to 'inhabited country', saying that he wanted to be in a place 'where there are no women'.[57] And John of Lycopolis in later life could say, 'Forty years have I been in this cell, never beholding a woman's face.'[58] But it is important to recognize that this was not because they regarded women as wicked or

55 Elm, *Virgins of God*, p. 356.
56 *Sayings*, Eudemon, 1.
57 *Sayings*, Sisoes, 3.
58 Palladius, *Lausiac History*, 35:13.

evil. The accounts of women ascetics and anchorites, and in particular the stories of women who rescued monks by reminding them of their vocation, show that it was just as possible for women as for men to be holy. The reason for wanting to avoid women was that male monks were afraid that women would arouse the sexual desires which they were struggling to keep in control. The danger lay not in women, but in the men's own desires which could be aroused through women. It was not the women themselves, but the 'demon of fornication' working in their own thoughts and imaginations which they had to guard against. Arsenius, who had known the world of high society, commented that 'it is through women that the enemy wars against the saints'.[59] For this reason monks visiting the city had to be particularly careful not to let themselves be tempted by women. Women were excluded from the desert in order to help men with the control of sexual desire, which was an aspect of monastic asceticism.

Underlying these stories, however, there are important questions about gender and sexuality. A superficial reading of the sayings and stories of the desert might lead one to think that the desert ascetics despised human bodies, and were especially concerned about sexual sin. A closer study shows that, on the contrary, they attached special importance to the body. They believed that at the resurrection their bodies would be restored to the angelic purity which Adam and Eve possessed, and that by controlling the body, and ridding it of the desires and appetites that tend to govern it now, they could bring about the transformation of their bodies into the heavenly state.[60] 'Christian ascetics,' says Gillian Clark, 'far from wishing to negate the body . . . as being hostile to the soul, took embodiment with complete seriousness . . . [T]hey thought it possible to transform the body together with the soul, freeing it from the constraints of life after the Fall and causing it to function

---

59 *Sayings*, Arsenius, 28.
60 See Brown, *Body and Society*, pp. 222f.

differently.'[61] The body was not to be rejected, but rather carefully 'tuned' by ascetic practice so as to enable the real struggle to take place, the struggle to subdue one's own will, to overcome pride, and to reach purity of heart. While it was necessary to be on one's guard against it, sexual sin was not the worst of sins, but rather an indication of an unsurrendered heart and will.

If desert life involved aspiring to the heavenly life of angels it followed that, since there were no male and female angels, there was no fundamental difference between men and women ascetics. Those who truly lived the desert life had moved beyond gender. This was illustrated by the fact that in the desert men and women wore the same monastic habit. That was why it was possible for women anchorites to go unrecognized as women until the time of their burial. We may recall, for example, that when the monk Silas met the Palestinian Syncletica, who had been clothed with the monastic habit, he did not know from her habit whether she was a woman or a man.[62] The monastic habit was not a man's habit, but one which was worn equally by both men and women, demonstrating their unity in the heavenly life.

The desert movement, then, was made up not only of men: a great many women were part of it, most of whom entered the desert emptiness without withdrawing deeply into the physical desert, and were largely unseen and unknown. There were not many women living the solitary life in the desert clothed in the monastic habit. This was partly because men felt that they needed to escape from women so that they could deal with their own sexual urges, but quite largely simply because the sheer physical rigours and difficulties of living in a desert cell demanded physical strength and stamina which was beyond many women. To live in the desert one needed to be 'manly', to have certain masculine characteristics. As we saw earlier,

---

61 Clark, 'Women and Asceticism in Late Antiquity', p. 39.
62 See above, p. 103.

Amma Sarah said to some male monks (who must have seemed weak to her), 'It is I who am a man, you who are women.'[63] Syncletica of Egypt was known for her 'manliness' and her 'manly deeds'.[64] But conversely (although this is nowhere said in the texts) one can regard the male monks as having something of the 'feminine' qualities of meekness and gentleness. That is to say, the desert life involved reaching for a way of life which transformed the body and transcended the differences between the sexes.

---

63 *Sayings*, Sarah, 9.
64 *Life of Syncletica*, 15, 111.

5

The Way of the Desert

Long before Chariton founded his Judean lauras, or Antony retreated into the Egyptian desert, or Pachomius gathered men and women into his monasteries, perhaps even from New Testament times, there were ascetics who had begun to live a monastic life in Palestine and in Egypt. Now in the third, fourth and fifth centuries there was a further development. Out of the soil of the desert tradition of the Bible, the desert movement burst apparently spontaneously into life, as thousands of people of all kinds began to withdraw into the deserts of Egypt and Palestine to embrace the way of the desert. In the previous four chapters we have seen that these desert Christians developed new kinds of monastic life in a variety of ways.

At the one extreme there were the desert hermits or anchorites, such as Syncletica or Cyriacus in Palestine, or Onnophrius or Aaron in the remote desert of Aswan, who withdrew by themselves completely into the deep desert, sometimes hiding themselves away in remote cells with no human contact, or wandering as 'grazers' living on roots and herbs, and perhaps not seeing another human face for many years. Others were anchorites living in the solitude of individual cells in the desert, but as part of a *laura* or a semi-eremitic community, where there were other monks not too far away with whom they came together for worship, and sometimes a meal, on Saturdays and Sundays, as in the lauras of Euthymius or Sabas in Judea, or the loose communities of Nitria and Sketis. Others entered monastic communities of various kinds in or on the edge of the desert: communities such as those of Pachomius or Shenoute, the coenobia of Judea, or the small informal gatherings of women in Egypt. There were also some, particularly women such as Amma Syncletica of Egypt, who moved to the edge of towns or villages and secluded themselves in cells, living a life of rigorous asceticism, solitude and prayer, not very different from the life of those who went off into the desert. All of these can be said to have embraced what we may call the 'way of the desert'.

In the foregoing chapters we have been looking at the external and practical aspects of the way of the desert as we have encountered it in different places – who the principal leaders of the movement were, and how the monks and ascetics lived. In this chapter our main concern is to look beyond these external details to the inner and spiritual aspects of the desert way, to the monks' purpose in engaging in this harsh life, to their inner struggles and temptations, and the qualities of mind and heart and spirit that they aimed to achieve. But before we do that it will be useful to gather together and summarize the main practical and external features of this desert way of life, which we outlined first in our discussion of Lower Egypt but can now illustrate from elsewhere also. We can identify seven such features, which are summarized on page 120. All of these had significant implications for the inner and spiritual life of the person concerned.

Practical features of the desert way

The first feature of the way of the desert was *withdrawal*, or *anachoresis*. Whether it was to a cave in the remote recesses of the desert or to the enclosed seclusion of a small house on the desert edge of a town, the desert Christians withdrew from the world and ordinary human society. This withdrawal involved giving up one's worldly possessions. Famously, Antony heard the Gospel: 'Sell what you have and give to the poor', and

The way of the desert: summary

The practical features

1 Withdrawal. Giving up possessions.
2 Solitude. Staying in one's cell.
3 Silence.
4 Obedience to spiritual director.
5 Ascetic practice: food and sleep.
6 Manual work.
7 Unceasing prayer and psalmody.

The inner features

1 Facing one's inner self:
    Repentance.
    Detachment. Renunciation of will.
    Attention to oneself. Discernment.
    Guarding the heart: passions, thoughts, demons.
    Calling for God's help.
2 Seeing oneself in relation to others:
    Self as sinner, not better than others.
    Not judging.
3 Bearing insults.

The inner disposition

Humility.
Stillness.
Purity of heart.

The ultimate aim: to be with God

Desire for God.
Keeping God before one's eyes.
Living the heavenly life.
Judgement and heaven.

proceeded to dispose of all his possessions; and the same is said of many others, such as Syncletica of Palestine, Aaron of Aswan, and Syncletica of Egypt. In Pachomius' monasteries any new entrant was required to 'spurn his own possessions'.[1] Then, having embraced the monastic life, the desert Christians continued to live a life of renunciation, not possessing anything apart from the bare necessities of life. Pachomius and his brother John, it is said, 'lived in great renunciation, for they gave away everything they earned through their manual work except what they absolutely needed'.[2]

The second feature, *solitude*, was an aspect of this withdrawal. The degree of solitude adopted by the desert Christians varied considerably. Those who withdrew to the extreme desert as hermits sought a complete isolation from other people. Antony retreated first to his 'Outer Mountain' and then further into the desert to his 'Inner Mountain' in search of solitude. Chariton's desire for solitude led him deeper into the Judean desert and eventually to an almost inaccessible 'hanging cave'; and a similar desire impelled, among others, Euthymius and Cyriacus in Judea and all the hermits of Aswan and Philae in the far south of Egypt. A necessary aspect of the way of the desert was the discipline of staying in one's cell. For the hermits of the desert this meant sitting alone in their cell for long hours of the day and night, without going out to satisfy their curiosity or to relieve boredom. The monks of Nitria and Sketis and of the lauras of Judea, even though they had some contact with others, lived mainly in the solitude of their individual cells. Those in coenobia, whether in Egypt or in Judea, necessarily experienced less solitude, but in most cases they occupied individual cells. Solitude also implied secrecy. The desert discipline involved keeping one's ascetic practices hidden, something that could only be done in solitude. Amma Syncletica, living on the edge of town and in contact with some others, 'did not allow

---

1 PK, Vol. 2, *Precepts*, 49.
2 PK, Vol. 1, Bohairic *Life*, 19; First Greek *Life*, 14.

anyone to become an observer' of her ascetic life.[3] Some monks are said to have relaxed their ascetic rule when others visited them so as not to have their ways known.[4] Solitude meant being open and visible to God and to God alone. Abba Alonius said, enigmatically, 'If a man does not say in his heart, in the world there is only myself and God, he will not find peace.'[5] As we shall see, however, the quest for solitude arose not from a desire to escape from relationships with other people but because it provided a means of dealing with the things within themselves which obstructed such relationships.

Third, along with solitude went *silence* or *hesychia*. The desert way involved living in a silent place, away from surrounding noise and the voices of other people. Of the Cellia of Lower Egypt Rufinus wrote that 'there is a huge silence and a great quiet there'.[6] Perhaps more important than the surrounding silence was the monks' discipline of keeping silence when with others, of restricting their speech, of holding their tongue even if provoked. John Moschos tells of a monk who refused to converse with visitors, saying, 'I left the world to learn how to keep silent.'[7] Abba Moses kept silent when he was abused and misunderstood by his fellow monks.[8] Bessarion advised a brother who lived with others, 'Keep silence and do not compare yourself with others.'[9] Of Isaac the priest it was said that 'what he did he did in silence',[10] and of Zeno that he 'worked in silence'.[11] Arsenius was told in a vision, 'Be silent, pray always, for these are the source of sinlessness'; and he said of himself, 'I have often repented of having spoken, but never of having been

---

3 *Life of Syncletica*, 15.
4 *Sayings*, Eulogius, 1, Sisoes, 15.
5 *Sayings*, Alonius, 1.
6 *The Lives of the Desert Fathers*, Rufinus' Additions, XX:8, p. 149.
7 John Moschos, *The Spiritual Meadow*, 222.
8 *Sayings*, Moses, 3.
9 *Sayings*, Bessarion, 10.
10 *Sayings*, Isaac, 2.
11 *Sayings*, Zeno, 8.

silent.'[12] Chariton and his disciples in Judea 'devoted themselves to silence'.[13]Abba Daniel of Sketis said that the whole of monastic life depended on poverty and silence.[14] Even in the coenobia there was a need for silence. Pachomius ruled that during their work monks should not speak unless it was of holy things; and he was particularly distressed that monks working in the bakery conversed with one another.[15] 'Let us put on silence,' he said, 'for to it many owe their salvation.'[16]

The fourth feature was *obedience*. This was, of course, an inner virtue, based on an attitude of submissiveness to God; but it found expression in an outward and practical willingness to obey one's spiritual director or monastic superior without question or delay. A new monk was often placed under an elder or spiritual father partly in order to teach submissiveness and obedience. As we saw in Chapter 1, some abbas gave their disciples extraordinary and apparently unreasonable commands in order to test their obedience. In the coenobia of Pachomius and Shenoute, monks were required to obey the housemaster or head of their monastery in a way described as 'unquestioning obedience unto death'.[17] In Judea Euthymius' rules meant that his monks were trained in obedience.[18] 'Obedience', said Amma Syncletica, 'is preferable to asceticism',[19] because obedience led to the supreme virtue of humility.

A fifth feature of the desert way was *ascetic practice*. In every area and in all forms of monastic life the monks controlled and limited their intake of food; but how and to what extent they did so varied considerably. We read of some who went without food for unimaginably long periods, even fasting totally for the

---

12 *Sayings*, Arsenius, 2, 40.
13 *Life of Chariton*, 22.
14 *The Life of Daniel of Scetis*, p. 48.
15 PK, Vol. 1, Bohairic *Life*, 74; Vol. 2, *Pachomius' Rules*, 60, 116.
16 PK, Vol. 3, *Pachomius' Instructions*, 1.40.
17 PK, Vol. 1, Bohairic *Life*, 30.
18 Cyril, *Life of Euthymius*, 9.13.
19 *Sayings*, Syncletica, 16.

whole of Lent.[20] Macarius of Egypt took food once a week,[21] and Aaron took food every second day.[22] Probably Shenoute's practice of eating once a day at sundown or the ninth hour was the most common one.[23] Poemen said that the Fathers 'found it preferable to eat every day, but just a small amount'.[24] Some apparently carried fasting to an extreme, and were advised by wiser people to moderate their ascetic practice.[25] In addition, most monks limited the kinds of food they would eat, often taking only bread, or bread and raw or cooked vegetables. The hermits in the extreme desert of Upper Egypt lived on dates from the palm trees,[26] while the 'grazers' of Judea and those who withdrew to the utter desert for the duration of Lent lived on roots and desert plants.[27] In the Pachomian coenobia, where some monks did hard, physical work, there were two meals a day, but individual monks were free to adopt their own practice. Everywhere the question of what one should eat was a matter of concern, over which individual monks often sought advice. Something similar may be said about sleep. All monks were committed to restricting their sleep and keeping vigil, and some, such as Chariton in Judea, apparently did so to an extraordinary extent, staying awake and reciting psalms for most or all of the night.[28] It seems to have been common practice to divide the night into a period of sleep and a period of vigil and psalmody.[29] Pachomius' monks were required to spend the night in a kind of chair to prevent them from sleeping

---

20 See Regnault, *The Day-to-Day Life of the Desert Fathers,* p. 61. Some apparently did so to excess, see *Sayings*, Phocas, 1.

21 *Sayings*, Macarius the Great, 21.

22 Paphnutius, *Histories of the Monks of Upper Egypt*, 95.

23 Besa, *Life of Shenoute*, 10.

24 *Sayings*, Poemen, 31.

25 Palladius, *Lausiac History*, 53.

26 Paphnutius, *Histories of the Monks of Upper Egypt*, 24.

27 Cyril, *Life of Sabas*, 99; *Life of Cyriacus*, 228; Binns, *Ascetics and Ambassadors of Christ*, p. 108.

28 *Life of Chariton*, 15. See also *The Lives of the Desert Fathers*, XX.17.

29 PK, Vol. 1, Bohairic *Life*, 59.

too deeply,[30] and others too are said to have remained seated for sleep.[31] Some of the anchorites in the Judean caves slept on the ground or on a short stone bunk. Generally, however, there is little evidence of attempts to inflict extreme hardship on the body such as we find among some of the monks of Syria.[32]

A sixth feature was *manual work*. In both Egypt and Palestine, as the monks sat in their cells they worked with their hands. This usually took the form of weaving or plaiting of mats or baskets, and making ropes or cords. John the Dwarf in Lower Egypt and the monks of the lauras of Judea did basketry for which they gathered reeds or palm branches.[33] Euthymius made cords,[34] and Aaron made grave-clothes and plaited rope.[35] The produce of their labour was sold, either in the towns or through passing tradesmen, in order to buy food for themselves. Some of the Pachomian monks made mats out of rushes gathered from the Nile, and others were employed in several kinds of manual work, including agriculture and various crafts, to support the life of their monasteries.[36] But manual labour had a deeper purpose as well. Working with one's hands at simple routine tasks kept one occupied, while allowing the mind to be free for the inner work of prayer and guarding the heart. Abba Lucius said, 'While doing my manual work I pray without interruption. I sit down with God, soaking my reeds and plaiting my ropes, and I say "God, have mercy on me".'[37]

The seventh and final feature of the desert way was *prayer and psalmody*. All the 'practical' features of the monk's life were, of course, not only practical. They were undertaken not

---

30 PK, Vol. 2, *Rules of Saint Pachomius*, 87.

31 Palladius, *Lausiac History*, 33; Cyril, *Life of Euthymius*, 21.

32 See Theodoret of Cyrrhus, *History of the Monks of Syria*; and the Additional Note, pp. 226ff.

33 *Sayings*, John the Dwarf, 19; Hirschfeld, *Judean Desert Monasteries in the Byzantine Period*, p. 18.

34 Cyril, *Life of Euthymius*, 6, 14.

35 Paphnutius, *Histories of the Monks*, 118.

36 PK, Vol. 2, *Letter of Ammon*, 19; Jerome's *Preface*, 6.

37 *Sayings*, Lucius, 1.

for their own sakes but to enable the inner and spiritual work of the monk. But this was true in a special way of prayer and psalmody. It was a practical activity but also an inner and spiritual one. All the ascetics, whether in individual cells or in coenobia, observed offices of prayer of various kinds; but in addition they devoted much of their time to private prayer and to the recitation of the biblical Psalms, which they knew by heart. This recitation was done in a gentle, murmuring way which amounted to a kind of meditation. As this was similar to the way of meditation referred to in the Hebrew Psalms and practised by some of the ancient Israelites, it provides another link with the biblical tradition. Much of the night, sometimes the whole night, was spent in prayer and psalmody: Shenoute is one of many who are said to have spent whole nights in prayer.[38] 'Pray without ceasing,' said Abba Benjamin, echoing the words of St Paul.[39] 'The true monk', said Abba Epiphanius, 'should have prayer and psalmody constantly in his heart.'[40] Theognius of Judea could be described as a 'model of unceasing prayer'.[41] Solitude, silence, routine manual work and the other features of the way of the desert all contributed to achieving uninterrupted or constant prayer, which was one of the aims of the desert way.

The inner way

These practical aspects of the way of the desert, taken together, show what a radical and uncompromising way it was, demanding stamina, determination, courage and commitment. They were important, however, not for their own sake but because

---

38 Besa, *Life of Shenoute*; See also Cyril, *Life of Euthymius*, 21; PK, Vol. 1, Bohairic *Life*, 190; Vol. 2, *Regulations of Horsiesios*, 6; Paphnutius, *Life of Onnophrius*, 33.

39 *Sayings*, Benjamin, 4.

40 *Sayings*, Epiphanius, 3; see also Cyrus, 1; *Life of Chariton*, 16; Cyril, *Life of Theodosius*, 3.

41 Paul of Elusa, *Encomium on the life of St Theognius*, p. 138.

they provided the basis for the inner and spiritual qualities which it was the object of the monastic life to achieve.

When we turn from the external features to the inner way, the qualities of heart and mind to which the desert monks aspired, we see even more clearly what a revolutionary way it was – a way in which commonly accepted assumptions about behaviour and how life should be lived were overturned, and the radical, apparently extreme demands of the gospel of Jesus Christ were taken seriously and uncompromisingly implemented. Although they may be listed and discussed separately, all these inner qualities overlap and are part of one total attitude or way of inner being. Examples of them can be drawn from every area and every type of monastic life that we have looked at, illustrating again the unity of the desert movement.

The inner way of the desert may be said to have consisted of two main tasks, which opened the way to a particular state of being. The first task was to recognize and face one's true inner self. In order truly to do this several steps were necessary, the first of which was *repentance*. This was a key feature of the desert way. For some it was a sudden realization of their sin and need for repentance that drove them to the desert. The powerful surge of sorrow and regret for the way their life had been, and the vital desire for forgiveness and a new life, made them flee to the wilderness to find the grace and mercy of God. This was true most notably of the 'harlots of the desert', all of whom experienced sudden repentance and took themselves off to the solitude of the desert.

Repentance was not just a single act, however, but a process. The desert way involved continually remembering one's sins and weeping over them in penitence. No one ever fully escaped from the subtle and powerful snares and entanglements of sin, so there was always a need to recognize how one was entrapped in them, and to repent. 'We all fall very often,' Pachomius reminded one of his brothers.[42] 'I live in the desert

---

42 PK, Vol. 1, Bohairic *Life*, 68.

on account of my sins,' said Timothy, one of the anchorites of Upper Egypt.[43] Even Shenoute, who sometimes appears very harsh, placed great emphasis on the perpetual need to repent and on the possibility of forgiveness.[44] The desert way was a way of constant repentance.

Repentance, of course, was itself a gift of God, for which they had constantly to ask. 'If the soul gives itself to God wholeheartedly, God has mercy upon it and gives it the spirit of repentance,' wrote Antony in one of his letters.[45] God 'grants us repentance after our failings,' said Theodore.[46] Repentance arose from faith in and dependence on the mercy of God. And the forgiveness and deliverance from evil which the monks sought came not from their tears of penitence but from the grace of God. To repent in the biblical sense means not only to lament over one's sins and turn away from them, but to turn to God; and in their penitence the desert monks turned to God. They wept over their sins not in despair but in the confidence that the God before whom they wept would indeed forgive. 'God receives those who truly return to him,' says the Letter of Ammon.[47] God's gift of repentance led to the richer gift of forgiveness and the grace of being received into the fellowship of God.

Another basic aspect of facing oneself was *detachment* or *inner renunciation*. The practical renunciation of material goods had to be accompanied by what St Augustine called a 'secret renunciation'. For the desert monks this meant allowing themselves to be stripped of all they were attached to, possessing nothing, and standing naked and exposed before God. Material possessions were 'the first bond with the world'

---

43 Paphnutius, *Life of Onnophrius*, 10.

44 Emmel, 'Shenoute's Place in the History of Monasticism', p. 43; Timbie, 'Once More into the Desert of Apa Shenoute', p. 174.

45 *Letters of Antony*, 1.

46 PK, Vol. 3, *Theodore's Instructions*, 18.

47 PK, Vol. 3, *Letter of Ammon*, 17.

which had to be cut,[48] but this had to be followed by the cutting of other bonds: the inner emotional attachment not only to material things but to their habits and way of life, and to whatever gave security and comfort. According to the story of Mary of Egypt, the monks of the desert had to 'die to everything in the world'.[49] In accordance with the words of Jesus, they had to 'lose their lives' in order to find new life in him.[50] They were to live as people who had no rights – no right to be heard, understood, or respected, or to possess anything. It was this attitude that enabled Macarius the Great, on returning to his cell and finding a thief removing his goods, to help him load them onto his beast.[51] An 'old man' told an enquirer that the monk had to be 'denuded of all things of this world . . . naked and stripped of all things'.[52] 'Our profession', said Amma Syncletica, 'is nothing but the renunciation of life, the rehearsal of death.'[53]

Such renunciation included the *overcoming of one's desires* and the *abandonment of one's own will*. This was directly connected with the practice of asceticism, because part of the purpose of the training (*ascesis*) of their bodies through restricting and controlling their diet and their sleep was in order to reduce the intensity of bodily desires. In addition, the monks' aim was to give up their own wishes of whatever kind, to let go of what they personally wanted or liked, to overcome their will by handing over absolutely everything to God, and be totally pliable in God's hands. Learning to abandon one's own will was an essential part of the desert way of drawing near to God, because acting according to one's own will hindered a true, submissive obedience to God. 'The will of a man',

---

48 Ward, *Harlots of the Desert*, p. 87.
49 Ibid., p. 39.
50 Mark 8.35 and parallels.
51 *Sayings*, Macarius the Great, 18.
52 *Wisdom of the Desert Fathers*, 11.
53 *Life of Syncletica*, 73.

said Abba Poemen, 'is a brass wall between him and God.'[54] 'Cast your will behind you,' said Abba Sisoes.[55] For some this was achieved partly through submitting themselves to a senior abba, undertaking to do everything that was asked of them no matter how apparently unreasonable, without demur and without delay. Years of submitting to another person was a training in the abandonment of one's will to God. As Christ himself even in his time of agony prayed, 'Not my will but yours be done,' so the monk had to surrender his own will to God. 'When a man gives up his own will,' said Abba Moses, 'then God is reconciled with him.'[56]

How this was to be done can be seen from a short phrase, which was used frequently in all parts of the desert movement and provides another little window into the inner way of the desert. Time and again monks were advised to *pay attention to yourself*. According to St Luke's Gospel, Jesus used the phrase twice (Luke 17.3; 21.34) when speaking to his disciples, and the desert monks took it over and applied it to themselves. We find it, for example, in Athanasius' description of Antony, in several of the *Sayings of the Desert Fathers*, in Pachomius' advice to a young monk, in the 'Instructions' of both Pachomius and of Theodore, in Paphnutius' account of the anchorites of Upper Egypt, in the *Life of Syncletica*, and a number of times in the *Life of Euthymius* of Judea. To pay attention to oneself was not to be selfish or self-centred; it was to take a hard, honest, searching look at one's inner self to see what its state was and what was in it; to search out the hidden, secret sins, to recognize the subtle, twisted motives, and to see the lurking danger in the form of evil thoughts and intentions. The desert monks realized that all one's outward behaviour and ways of acting are the product of what goes on within; that, as Christ himself said, both evil thoughts and all sorts of evil deeds come 'out of

---

54 *Sayings*, Poemen, 54.
55 *Sayings*, Sisoes, 43; see also Paphnutius, 2; Syncletica, 17.
56 *Sayings*, Moses, Instructions, 4.

the heart' (Mark 7.21); and that it is useless to try to correct one's outward behaviour without first paying attention to what goes on within. This deep, rigorous examination of one's inner self, carried out in the long hours of silence in one's cell and perhaps with the help of an abba or spiritual father, was a key element in the way of the desert. What the monks had to face in the desert was not only the hardship of physical austerity but also the hard and sometimes painful work of uncovering their inner self, and acknowledging the unwelcome things hidden there. To do this was to 'pay attention to oneself'.

Having looked deeply into their inner self and seen what was there, they needed also to be able to distinguish the good from the bad, to know where evil was lurking, to recognize where they were in danger of being led astray; that is to say, they needed *discernment*. Pachomius and others were credited with the gift of being able to discern the hidden thoughts and sins of others. But discernment was important primarily in relation to oneself. Without it one could be deceived about one's inner state. Discernment brought about the true knowledge of oneself which Antony repeatedly urged on his followers, and which Ammonas prayed would be given to his disciples.[57] One 'old man' went so far as to say, 'Discernment is better than all the virtues.'[58]

It was when one saw oneself clearly that one was able to engage in what Paphnutius called 'the work of the desert', the task of *guarding the heart* from the attacks of the *demons* and the infiltration of evil thoughts. This task was central to the way of the desert. The desert monks lived in a world where demons were felt to be an ever-present reality. These were the minions and agents of the enemy, the devil, whose aim was to lead humankind away from God, and to subvert and overcome the monks' commitment to the desert way. Demons were understood to be of many kinds, to be capable of assuming

---

57 *Letters of Ammonas*, IV.
58 *World of the Desert Fathers*, p. 37.

various forms, and to operate in different ways. Often they worked by enticement and deception, but sometimes through fear. At times they were experienced as physical beings, or at least as having material form, capable of attacking monks bodily. Antony, when he had shut himself in a tomb in the desert, found himself having to fight a fierce battle against the physical onslaught of demons, whose object was to terrify him into abandoning his monastic vocation.[59] Shenoute is said to have fought physically with the devil and his demons.[60] Aaron and Isaac, deep in the desert of southern Egypt, encountered demons who 'took on phantastic shapes and were crying out . . . with the voices of roaring lions'.[61] The lady Anastasia, who fled Rome and lived in secret at Sketis, endured 'the attacks of the demons and the hand-to-hand combat with them'.[62] When Pachomius was in the desert the demons afflicted him to the point where he was about to lose heart.[63] Demons were generally understood to be essentially invisible,[64] but they tried to deceive and mislead monks by assuming one of a great many different forms. Sometimes they appeared as angels giving spurious advice or information, sometimes as an attractive and enticing woman, sometimes as a fearsome beast or reptile. The monk had to be constantly on his guard, to be ready to recognize the demons behind the appearances, and to resist their enticements or suggestions.[65]

The demons, however, were not always thought of as beings external to oneself, but were identified with the evil 'thoughts' which arose in one's mind. The demons' 'stumbling blocks', said Antony, 'consist of evil thoughts'.[66] These 'thoughts', or

---

59 *Life of Antony*, 8, 9.
60 Besa, *Life of Shenoute*, 73.
61 Paphnutius, *Histories of the Monks*, 95.
62 *Life of Daniel of Scetis*, p. 75.
63 PK, Vol. 3, *Pachomius' Instructions*, 1.11.
64 *Letters of Antony*, 6.
65 See Brakke, *Demons and the Making of the Monk* for a full study of the significance of demons.
66 *Life of Antony*, 23.

logismoi, were not rational concepts or the ordinary workings of one's mind, but states or movements of mind or feeling that entered unawares and tended to linger and take one over, and so affect one's attitudes, intentions and possibly behaviour. They were often identified with particular demons, so that one could talk of 'the demon of fornication',[67] meaning lustful thoughts or images which would not go away, or of the demons of avarice, gluttony and pride. At a later period they were more usually called 'passions', and were in due course investigated and analysed by Evagrius, as we shall see in the next chapter. But even without Evagrius' analysis, the monks in all parts of the desert were aware of the danger arising from the passions, and of the need to 'guard the heart' against them. This guarding of the heart against the intrusion of 'thoughts' which tended to enter it and take it over required constant vigilance, constant paying attention to oneself, constant discernment. This was the great struggle which the desert monks engaged in, the great inner 'work of the desert' which Paphnutius referred to. This was 'the hidden and fearful fighting that takes place in the desert',[68] the battle the monks fought as they sat weaving their baskets or chanting their psalms in the solitude of their cells, or keeping vigil through the dark hours of the night.

It was not, however, a battle which they could win on their own. Certainly it required constant effort on their part, including prayer and fasting, but that was not enough. Sometimes they needed the advice and support of a spiritual father or abba, and there are many stories of monks seeking out a senior abba because they are troubled by 'thoughts'. But most of all they needed God's help and grace. 'We must at all times be on our guard and oppose the mind to the wiles of the demons,' said Euthymius of Judea; but, he added, 'Everywhere we need protection by God's help.'[69] 'If the conflict grows fiercer,' said

---

67 Cyril, *Life of Euthymius*, 24:37; *Sayings*, Sarah, 1.
68 Paphnutius, *Life of Onnophrius*, 15.
69 Cyril, *Life of Euthymius*, 19:30.

Macarius the Great, 'say, "Lord, help!" He knows very well what we need, and he shows us his mercy.'[70] 'Call on God,' said one 'old man', 'and he will deliver you from every temptation.'[71] 'Cast your weakness before God and you will find rest,' said Abba Agathon.[72] Prayer, said Amma Syncletica, 'chases away foul thought'.[73] It was important to remember that the demons did not possess the ultimate power, but were ultimately subject to God. So demons could be dismissed by invoking the name of Christ or making the sign of the cross, or sometimes simply by treating them with contempt and refusing to fear them.[74]

If the first main task of the inner way of the desert was to face one's own inner self, the second was to adopt a radically different way of seeing oneself in relation to other people. Through the process of repentance, of paying attention to themselves and struggling against their inner demons, the monks came to see themselves in a new way, and this affected their way of relating to others. They realized that they were flawed and sinful people, constantly in need of repentance, and so they had to abandon and root out the tendency inherent in most people to regard themselves as in some way better than others. Against all the conventions of society they had to look on *all* other people as better than themselves. Their task was to blame themselves, to weep for their own sins, and to remember always that they stood in need of the forgiveness of God. When they did this they could not stand above others in superiority. They had to be careful not to despise or be scornful of others,[75] but to look up to them no matter what they were like on the outside, and to regard them as inwardly superior to themselves. Thus Abba Poemen said, 'When a man is watchful about himself, and has

---

70 *Sayings*, Macarius the Great, 19.
71 *World of the Desert Fathers*, p. 33.
72 *Sayings*, Agathon, 21.
73 *Life of Syncletica*, 80.
74 *Life of Antony*, 23; *Wisdom of the Desert Fathers*, 32.
75 *Sayings*, Poemen, 70; Theodore of Pherne, 13; *Life of George of Choziba*, 38.

to reproach himself, in his heart he thinks his brother better than he'; on another occasion he added that if someone sees a man committing a murder he should say, 'He has only committed this one sin but I commit sins every day.'[76]

From this it followed that one should not mentally sit in judgement over other people. The desert monks took very seriously the Gospel command not to judge or condemn another person. This is a very common theme in the desert literature. Pachomius said in his Instructions, 'Never condemn anyone.' 'We have it in writing to abstain from judging.'[77] 'In all circumstances,' said Abba Joseph, 'say, "Who am I?" and do not judge anyone.'[78] A fascinating story about Isaac the Theban makes the point very vividly. One day, we are told, when he was visiting a monastery, 'he saw a brother committing a sin and he condemned him. When he returned to the desert, an angel of the Lord came and stood in front of the door of his cell and said . . . "God has sent me to ask where you want to throw the guilty brother whom you have condemned." Immediately he repented and said, "I have sinned, forgive me." Then the angel said, "Get up, God has forgiven you. But from now on, be careful not to judge someone before God has done so."'[79] In order to avoid judging or condemning it was important not to pay any attention to other people's failings. An elder once said to a brother monk, 'Someone who knows himself does not see the shortcomings of his brothers.'[80] It was said of Macarius the Great that 'just as God protects the world, so Abba Macarius would cover the faults which he saw, as though he did not see them; and those which he heard, as though he did not hear them'.[81] This total obliviousness of the faults of others was the way to avoid judging and condemning them.

---

76 *Sayings*, Poemen, 148, 97.
77 PK, Vol. 3, *Pachomius' Instructions*, 1.12, 44.
78 *Sayings*, Joseph of Panephysis, 2.
79 *Sayings*, Isaac the Theban, 1.
80 John Moschos, *The Spiritual Meadow*, 144.
81 *Sayings*, Macarius the Great, 32; see also Poemen, 64.

The way of the desert involved not only overlooking the faults of other people but also being willing to endure insults and even false accusations. In accordance with Jesus' instruction to 'turn the other cheek', the desert monks had to accept blame and insults without retaliation. Once again it is Macarius the Great who provides the most remarkable example of this. When he was falsely accused of making a young girl pregnant he did not counter the accusation, but accepted responsibility for the girl and the child, until eventually the truth emerged and he was exonerated.[82] The advice to accept insults and abuse without retaliation and without self-justification is repeated again and again.[83] Abba Nisterus told himself: 'You and the donkey are the same. The donkey is beaten but he does not speak, and when ill-treated he does not reply; now you must do the same.'[84] Moreover, insults were to be seen as useful for the spiritual life: 'Nothing is so useful to the beginner as insults,' said Abba Isaiah;[85] and Amma Syncletica commented, 'Reproach and insult lead [the soul] to the greatness of virtue.'[86] When monks were maltreated or abused they were to see the cause of it as lying in themselves, and to use it to learn of their own sins. One old man said, 'In all trials do not blame others but only yourself, saying "it is because of my sins that this had happened."'[87] The monk should, indeed, be impervious to both praise and blame, paying no attention to either of them. Macarius once sent a brother to the cemetery first to shout curses at the dead and then to praise them. 'Like the dead,' he then advised him, 'take no account of either the scorn of men or their praises.'[88]

---

82 *Sayings*, Macarius the Great, 1.

83 See *Sayings*, Antony, 15, 19; PK, Vol. 3, *Pachomius' Instructions*, 1.22, 24, 28, 44; *Theodore's Instructions*, 30, 32; *Wisdom of the Desert Fathers*, 193, 203.

84 *Sayings*, Nisterus the Cenobite, 2.

85 *Sayings*, Isaiah, 1.

86 *Life of Syncletica*, 39.

87 *Wisdom of the Desert Fathers*, 172.

88 *Sayings*, Macarius the Great, 23.

These admonitions, however, were not concerned in the first place with how the monks behaved towards their neighbours, but with how they saw themselves. It is not that relationships with neighbours were unimportant – quite the opposite. As a famous saying of Antony has it, 'Our life and our death is with our neighbour.'[89] Recent studies have demonstrated that the desert monks were not isolationist, and that their love of solitude did not mean that they were unconcerned about their neighbour.[90] The *Sayings of the Desert Fathers* repeatedly reflect the monks' concern over how to live with others in community. But the desert monks saw that right relationships with neighbours were brought about not by trying to control one's external behaviour but only by reaching a true understanding of oneself as a sinful person, who needed to stand before others with humility and penitence, and not with superiority or judgement. It was from this humble stance that one could view others with compassion and love. Moreover, it would be a mistake to think that by living in solitude they could do no good for others. By the depth of their prayers of intercession and self-oblation, and by their inner wrestling with the demons and forces of evil in the world, they could have a deeper togetherness with other people than the togetherness of physical presence, and could do more for the true good of others and for the life of the world than could be done simply by practical action. This was the way of the desert.

These two difficult and demanding tasks – facing one's true self, and changing how one saw oneself in relation to other people – were the desert monks' main inner occupations. By engaging in them they were aiming to reach beyond them to a certain inner state or disposition, a mode of being which was characterized by a triad of qualities, which were the principal objectives of their ascetic life: humility, stillness and purity of

89 *Sayings*, Antony, 9.
90 See especially Gould, *The Desert Fathers on Monastic Community*; Williams, *Silence and Honey Cakes*.

heart. These three belonged together, and it is not possible to say which comes first. Each one produced and was produced by the others. They were gifts of God, not human achievements, but they were given only to those who had worked hard and faithfully at the tasks of the inner way.

Humility is emphasized over and over again in the desert literature. It is referred to in every area of the desert movement and in every kind of monastic life; and everywhere the leading figures are commended for being humble. Antony and Pachomius and other leading monks were known for their humility. Amma Syncletica, Pachomius, Euthymius and George of Choziba all gave teaching on the subject. The way of the desert was, more than anything else, a way of humility. To be humble was to be ready to be seen as small and insignificant in the eyes of the world. It was to be willing to live in obscurity, unknown to the world. It was to see all others as better than oneself. All the desert monks' ascetic practices of fasting and keeping vigil were done to open the way for humility. All their work of facing their inner selves and closing their eyes to the faults of others was aimed at attaining it. It was prized above all else. It was 'the crown of the monk' (Abba Or), 'the most beautiful of all virtues' (Syncletica), 'the rampart of all virtues' (Pachomius). Indeed, the whole of the way of the desert could be summed up by the word 'humility'.

Ascetic practices could, of course, be of help in the quest for humility, but they could also be a source of pride, especially if they were carried to excess. Humility, on the other hand, was the most effective weapon against attacks by demons and infiltrating thoughts. In one story the devil told Macarius the Great that there was only one thing that made him powerless: 'Your humility. Because of that I can do nothing against you.'[91] Similarly, a voice told Antony that humility was the only way to overcome the 'snares of the enemy'.[92] 'Nothing so weakens

---

91 *Sayings*, Macarius, 11.
92 *Sayings*, Antony, 7.

the demon', said Pachomius, 'as humility.'[93] Amma Theodora said, 'Neither asceticism, nor vigils nor any kind of suffering are able to save, only humility can do that.'[94]

The desert monks, however, knew that humility was not an ordinary human virtue, but a divine quality. 'Humility', said Pachomius, 'is that great holy strength with which God clothed himself when he came into the world.'[95] It was the gift of God given to those who sought to follow the example of Christ, who 'humbled himself and became obedient unto death' (Phil. 2.8). 'It is Christ's own example of humility – his *kenosis* or self-emptying (Phil. 1.2) – whose shadow falls most dramatically across the *Sayings*.'[96] The 'sinews of humility', said Syncletica, come from imitating him who 'took the form of a slave' and who said 'I am gentle and humble in heart'. [97] Humility was supremely a Christian quality. It was attained through turning to God, and following in the way of Christ.

The second of the three features of the inner disposition was *stillness* or tranquillity. This represents principally two Greek words: *anapausis* or rest, and *hesychia* or silence and stillness. To obtain tranquillity is to live with a calm and quiet mind, without inner disturbance. In the Bible 'rest' is one of the gifts of God to his people, a gift which Jesus offered to those who came to him (Matt. 11.28). *Hesychia*, as we have seen, can refer to external silence, but it also refers to an inner state of quiet and peace. In the stories and sayings of the desert we read frequently of monks who, after being disturbed by 'thoughts', found a way to this inner tranquillity or peace. It was said of Antony that 'he was never troubled, his soul being calm'.[98] Abba Chariton of Judea advised his disciples to 'adhere with

---

93 PK, Vol. 2, *Paralipomena*, 4.

94 *Sayings*, Theodora, 6.

95 PK, Vol. 3, *Pachomius' Instructions*, 1.47.

96 Burton-Christie, *The Word in the Desert*, p. 240; and see his whole chapter on 'The Humble Way of Christ'.

97 *Life of Syncletica*, 57, 58.

98 *Life of Antony*, 67.

all their might to tranquillity, the mother of all virtues'.[99] Abba Onnophrius of Upper Egypt described how monks lived a life of *hesychia*.[100] The life of the desert could be likened to water poured into a bowl which was disturbed at first but after a while became so still that it reflected the onlooker's face.[101]

The person who had attained stillness was able to accept everything that happened, whether inwardly or in the world outside, whether comforting or troublesome, without inner disturbance but with equanimity and peace. Theodore in his *Instructions* urges his followers towards 'a true quietness' in the face of troubles and provocations of all kinds.[102] In particular, tranquillity involved being able to be patient and to give thanks to God during times of illness. Theodosius of Judea was 'stricken by bodily illness', but preserved 'a spirit of thankfulness'.[103] More than any other, Amma Syncletica regarded the enduring of illness, even terrible and painful illness, with thanksgiving and patience as an important part of the ascetic life.[104] Such tranquillity or serenity was a by-product of purity of heart.

Like humility and stillness, *purity of heart*, the third feature of the inner disposition, is emphasized throughout the literature of the desert movement. The phrase comes from the Bible: Psalm 24 says that anyone who wants to stand in God's holy place must have a pure heart; and Jesus said, 'Blessed are the pure in heart for they shall see God' (Matt. 5.8). In the teaching of Jesus a pure heart goes along with having a 'single' or 'simple' eye (Matt. 6.22). Attaining this purity of heart and eye was seen by many as the purpose of the way of the desert. Pachomius, it is said, 'paid great attention to the Beatitudes,

99 *Life of Chariton*, 17.
100 Paphnutius, *Life of Onnophrius*, 5; see also Vivian's Introduction, p. 39.
101 *Wisdom of the Desert Fathers*, 2.
102 PK, Vol. 3, *Theodore's Instructions*, 31.
103 Cyril, *Life of Theodosius*, 4.
104 *Life of Syncletica*, 99.

striving especially to be found pure in heart'.[105] According to Philip Rousseau, the phrase purity of heart 'comes closest to Pachomius' spiritual ambition'.[106]

Purity of heart is a quality of inner clarity and simplicity, of wholeheartedness. A pure heart is an undivided heart, one which is wholly and simply given to God, and is single in its devotion to God. Theodore in his *Instructions* speaks of 'tasting the simplicity of a pure heart'.[107] Ammonas in his *Letters* laments the fact that there are people who come to God 'not with their whole heart but in two minds'.[108] Prayers should be offered, said Macarius of Alexandria, with 'simplicity of heart'.[109]

For the desert monks the way to purity of heart was partly through repentance, which according to Antony led to purity of both body and heart,[110] or more generally through what John Binns has called 'the unrelenting practice of the ascetical life'.[111] Most of all, the way to purity of heart was through the constant work of guarding the heart against 'thoughts', of resisting the demons' attempts to take over one's mind with *logismoi* or compulsive 'passions'. An impure heart was one which was overcrowded, cluttered up with unnecessary things, and dominated by *logismoi*. A pure heart was one which had reached a state of passion-less-ness, or *apatheia*,[112] a term meaning not ruled by passions or compulsive thoughts. It was only by preventing the entry of such 'thoughts' into one's mind that one could achieve purity of heart.

Above all, a pure heart was one that was open to God. The fundamental reason why the desert monks sought to attain to

---

105 PK, Vol. 1, Greek *Life*, 18.
106 Rousseau, *Pachomius*, p. 142.
107 PK, Vol. 3, *Theodore's Instructions*, 9.
108 Ammonas, *Letters*, III.
109 Palladius, *Lausiac History*, 20:3.
110 Antony, *Letters*, I.
111 Binns, *Ascetics and Ambassadors of Christ*, p. 233.
112 The term *apatheia* is especially associated with the spiritual theologian Evagrius. See Chapter 6.

purity of heart was so that they could come nearer to God. In keeping with what the Psalm says, they believed that without a pure heart it was impossible to approach God, or 'stand in his holy place'. 'If you do not first purify your thoughts you may not approach the grace of God,' said a priest-monk named Eulogius.[113] 'We shall be like him in so far as we have been purified,' said Abba Zossima to Mary of Egypt.[114] By purifying the heart one becomes like God and so can draw near to him.

The desert monks also believed the words of the Beatitude, that the pure in heart shall see God. When the heart is pure and clear, freed from all sullying thoughts, it becomes like a mirror in which the reflection of God can be seen. The image of the heart as a mirror in which God can be seen by the 'luminous' or clear eye was much used by the Syriac Fathers,[115] but is also found here among the monks of Judea and Egypt. It was said of Pachomius that 'because of the purity of his heart he was, as it were, seeing the invisible God as in a mirror'.[116] When Sabas withdrew by himself to Rouba, the remote desert of Judea, 'he devoted himself to solitude, fasts and ceaseless prayer, making his mind a spotless mirror of God'.[117] To purify the heart was also to purify the eye of the mind so that one could 'see God'. Like Sabas, John the Hesychast withdrew to the Rouba, 'yearning to consort with God in solitude and to purify the eye of the mind . . . so as with unveiled face to behold the glory of God'.[118]

---

113 *The Lives of the Desert Fathers*, XVI.2.
114 Ward, *Harlots of the Desert*, p. 53.
115 See Brock, *The Luminous Eye*.
116 PK, Vol. 1, Greek *Life*, 22.
117 Cyril, *Life of Sabas*, 12:95.
118 Cyril, *Life of John the Hesychast*, 11:209.

Towards God

'God requires nothing but a pure heart,' said one young monk of Sketis.[119] Purity of heart and all that went with it was the fruit of the unrelenting practice of the ascetical life; to reach it was the object of the way of the desert. It was not, however, the final and ultimate end, but only the means of attaining this end. The ultimate end was simply God himself, and being with God. All the hardship of the practical life of the desert, all the long days and nights of loneliness, hunger and thirst, all the fierce battles against the demons, all the diligent guarding of the heart, all the weeping over their sins and the humbling of themselves before their neighbour, all the quest of purity of heart and eye; all this was undertaken because of an irrepressible yearning for God and God alone, an unquenchable thirst for the living God, in comparison with which all hardship pales in significance, all suffering is worth enduring and all effort is infinitely worthwhile. The monks of the desert were not much given to expressing this openly. Their advice to those who sought 'a word' and the description of their way of life by those who wrote their 'Lives' were mainly concerned with the question of how to follow the desert way. Their yearning for God was largely kept secret within the depths their hearts. Their relationship with God was deeply personal and was not lightly to be spoken of to enquirers and disciples, or exhibited to visitors. But it was this yearning, and only this, which both lies behind and explains and justifies the radical, unconventional and uncompromisingly demanding way of the desert.

This ultimate end was in some measure attainable during this present life. The more the desert monks followed the desert way the more their hearts and minds were turned towards God, so that they lived in close relationship with God. It was said of Macarius the Great that 'he occupied himself much more with

---

119 John Moschos, *The Spiritual Meadow*, 194.

God than with earthly things';[120] and of the other Macarius that he wanted to keep his mind 'fixed on God without any distractions'.[121] John of Lycopolis 'kept himself in the presence of God by a perfect desire'.[122] Abba Phortas spoke of 'those who are consecrated to God and look only to him'.[123] According to Onnophrius, to live in the desert was to live 'for the sake of God'.[124] It was a relationship of intimacy and freedom, in which God could be approached with *parresia*, or boldness. This relationship is spoken of throughout the desert literature in a variety of ways: 'being mindful of God', 'contemplating God', 'being attached to God', 'standing before God', 'advancing towards God', 'having one's mind fixed on God', 'knowing God'. These and many other phrases describe how God was the main focus of the monks' lives. The knowledge of God always breeds a desire and a longing for a fuller and deeper knowledge; and so the yearning and desire for a greater closeness to God was always there. Pachomius, it was said, had 'a great desire for God';[125] and Euthymius went off into the deeper desert during Lent 'yearning to consort with God in solitude'.[126]

By their life of rigorous physical asceticism and careful discipline of the mind, the monks were understood to have begun even now to live the life of heaven. The monastic life was itself a kind of death. Poemen was advised by Abba Ammonas to 'engrave it on your heart that you have been in the tomb for a year already'.[127] A monk was to 'think in his heart that he is already three days dead and in the tomb'.[128] For the monks of the desert, 'there was only one aim to which all were hastening: to be in the body as a corpse, to die completely to the

---

120 Palladius, *Lausiac History*, Macarius of Egypt, 5.
121 Palladius, *Lausiac History*, Macarius of Alexandria, 17.
122 *The Lives of the Desert Fathers*, I.45.
123 *Sayings*, Phortas, 1.
124 Paphnutius, *Life of Onnophrius*, 14.
125 PK, Vol. 1, Greek *Life*, 52.
126 Cyril, *Life of Euthymius*, 7.
127 *Sayings*, Poemen, 2.
128 *Sayings*, Moses, 12.

world and everything in it'.[129] Both Pachomius and his successor Theodore laid great emphasis on bearing the cross and so
sharing in Christ's death, as part of the monks' way of life.
When Christians were no longer persecuted and martyred for
their faith, the monks of the desert became the new martyrs.
Chariton, who narrowly escaped death during the persecu-
tions, was called a martyr because of his struggle against the
unseen powers of evil.[130] Having passed through death the
monks now entered the heavenly or angelic life. In the words
of Peter Brown, 'Only in the desert . . . could a few great ascetics bring back, through long penance and hard labour on their
own bodies, a touch of the angelic glory which Adam enjoyed
in the Garden of Eden.'[131]

At the same time, the desert monks looked beyond this life to
the life of heaven. Their aim and hope was to be given entrance
to God's kingdom in heaven, but they were also very conscious
that before that there would be the great judgement, and they
would be judged on their earthly life. Antony's advice was:
'Always have the fear of God before your eyes . . . Remember
what you have promised, for it will be required of you on the
day of judgement.'[132] Preparation for the day of judgement was
a constant part of their life. But beyond the judgement, for those
who were found faithful there would be the joy and peace of
God's heavenly kingdom. The longing for heaven was always
in their hearts, and the hope of it before their eyes. Antony, in
withdrawing to his cell, was 'reflecting on' and 'longing for'
'the dwellings of heaven'.[133] Their 'great afflictions', said Abba
John the Persian, were borne 'for the sake of the kingdom of
heaven'.[134] Amma Theodora taught that through many trials
and temptations 'we can obtain an inheritance in the kingdom

---

129 Ward, *Harlots of the Desert*, 'Mary of Egypt', 4.
130 *Life of Chariton*, 40.
131 Brown, *The Rise of Western Christendom*, p. 174.
132 *Sayings*, Antony, 33.
133 *Life of Antony*, 45.
134 *Sayings*, John the Persian, 4.

of heaven'.[135] Their great hope was that following this earthly life, their years of toil, of asceticism and prayer, and their ceaseless quest for humility and purity of heart would culminate in the joy of heaven, where they would see God face to face. This was the ultimate aim of the desert way – to go through the low door of humility, along the narrow path of purity of heart, towards God.

* * *

The desert movement of these early centuries emerged apparently spontaneously in a number of places: in the lauras and coenobia of Judean wadis, the Jordan Valley and the caves of the utter desert of Rouba; in Nitria, Cellia, Sketis and the isolated hermitages of Lower Egypt; in the coenobitic monasteries of Pachomius and Shenoute and the remote cells of desert anchorites of Upper Egypt.

These places differed from one another in their geography and their history, and the types of monasticism varied also. There were monks who lived in coenobitic monasteries, in semi-eremitic communities, in scattered lauras, in houses on the desert edge of towns, in the solitude of hidden cells and caves, and even as wanderers in the open desert. But all of them adopted in one way or another what we have called the way of the desert – renouncing the life of society, living in solitude and silence, restricting their food and their sleep, engaging in manual work and in constant prayer; facing their inner selves, struggling with the demons of pernicious thoughts, learning to humble themselves, seeking purity of heart; and through all this, seeking to live always in the presence of God and to draw ever nearer to God, aiming to live the life of heaven now, and hoping finally to be found worthy of God's heavenly kingdom. And they were conscious that in pursuing the way of the desert they were continuing the ancient biblical desert tradition. In

---

135 *Sayings*, Theodora, 2.

their various places and different ways they were all part of the one, extraordinary, God-given desert movement.

Following these early developments there were others who developed this desert way in places beyond the desert itself; who adapted it in different ways to suit other patterns of monastic life, and who expounded and interpreted the convictions, ideas and values of the first desert monks to make them applicable to people in other situations. To these developments we now turn in Part Two.

Developing the Way of the Desert

6

Evagrius and Cassian

As time went on, the way of the desert, which had been pioneered, developed and exemplified in the three principal areas
of the desert movement, came to be further developed, interpreted, and extended by others, not all of whom were directly
people of the desert. In Part Two we turn our attention to three
groups of people through whom this happened: first, Evagrius
and Cassian, then the monks of Gaza, and finally John Climacus
and the monasteries of Sinai. We shall not attempt to give an
overall account of their writings and thought, as this would be
a major undertaking well beyond the scope of this book, but
only to consider their relationship to the desert movement, and
how they took forward and developed both the practical way
and the inner way of the desert monks, as we have described
it in the previous chapters. We begin with two men, Evagrius
and Cassian, each of whom had come to Lower Egypt from
elsewhere and spent time with the monks of the desert. They
were both able, intelligent, educated men and theologians of
stature, who thought deeply about the ascetic and monastic
life, and how the desert way could be understood theologically
and applied in practice.

Evagrius Ponticus

Evagrius was born about 345 CE in a small town in Pontus in
north-east Asia Minor, where his father was a *chorepiscopos*,
or local country bishop. We know the details of Evagrius' early

life mainly from Palladius, who devotes a number of pages of his *Lausiac History* to him.[1] Living in Pontus, Evagrius was influenced at an early age by Basil of Caesarea and Gregory of Nazianzus, two of the great church fathers in nearby Cappadocia. When Gregory was made Bishop of Constantinople sometime in the 370s, he took Evagrius with him and ordained him deacon. Along with Gregory he played an important part in the Council of Constantinople in 381, helping to defend the Nicene faith.

Evagrius stayed on in Constantinople after Gregory resigned as bishop later in 381, and became a prominent figure in the society of the city. Soon afterwards, however, he fell in love with the wife of a high official in the city, and in order to avoid scandal he fled to Jersualem. Here he came under the influence of Melania and Rufinus and their monastic community at the Mount of Olives, and became active in the intellectual life of the city. But while he was there he was taken seriously ill and his life was in danger. Melania offered to pray for him if he agreed to adopt the monastic life once he was healed. When he recovered he was clothed as a monk, and went off to Egypt to the semi-eremitic monastic community at Nitria, which Melania had herself visited previously.

Evagrius arrived in Egypt about the year 383 and remained there as one of the desert monks until his death in 399. He spent two years in Nitria and then moved to the more remote Cellia where he lived for the rest of his life, devoting himself to severe asceticism and prayer in the manner of the eremitic monks, including refusing cooked food and undertaking feats of endurance. He was trained in the way of the desert by Macarius the Alexandrian, by the priest at Cellia, and by Macarius the Great, to whom he became particularly attached, referring to him as 'Our holy and most ascetic master' and a 'vessel of election'. Macarius had been the first to move to the even more

---

1 Palladius, *Lausiac History*, 38.

inaccessibly remote region of Sketis, and Evagrius must have visited him there.

Evagrius thus became one of the monks of Lower Egypt, and there are six 'sayings' of his and one story about him included in the *Sayings of the Desert Fathers*. But he was no ordinary desert monk. He brought with him a lively and able mind and great theological learning, and had been considerably influenced by the controversial spiritual and philosophical writings of Origen. Unlike most Egyptian monks he did not undertake the manual labour of weaving baskets or ropes, but earned his living as a calligrapher. He attracted a considerable following among his fellow monks, but there were apparently some who disapproved of his setting himself up as a teacher. On one occasion a priest reproved him saying, 'Abba, we know that if you were living in your own country you would probably be a bishop and a great leader; but at present you sit here as a stranger.'[2]

Evagrius' importance lies mainly in his many written works of different kinds, which display a deep theological learning and a profound knowledge of the working of the human heart. As his teaching is based on and arises from his experience as a desert monk, he can be regarded as the first great theorist and psychologist of the way of the desert. His debt to the desert tradition can be seen in his references to Macarius the Egyptian[3] and Macarius the Alexandrian,[4] in the way he illustrates his teaching from the oral tradition of the desert monks of Egypt by referring to 'the brothers', and in his inclusion of ten sayings of the desert monks at the end of his *Praktikos*.[5]

In some of his works, however, he was also indebted to the writings of Origen, which had been declared heretical because they leaned towards Greek neoplatonic thought. Because of

---

2 *Sayings*, Evagrius, 7.

3 Evagrius, *Praktikos*, 29, 93; *On Thoughts*, 33.

4 *Praktikos*, 94; *On Thoughts*, 37.

5 For example *To Eulogius*, 4, 7, 29; *Praktikos*, 91–100.

this Evagrius himself was viewed with suspicion by orthodox church people, and much of his work was ignored or attributed to others, and relatively unknown until modern times. Even in fairly recent times some have looked askance at him.[6] Some of his works have to do with mystical theology or philosophy, including cosmology, but many of them deal with the inner aspects of the monastic and ascetical life, and it is these which concern us here. They include *The Foundations of the Monastic Life* and *To Eulogius*, dealing with the beginnings of the monastic life; *On the Vices*, *On the Eight Thoughts*, and *Praktikos*, dealing in greater detail with the passions; *To Monks*, *To a Virgin*, and *On Thoughts*, which explore the inner life further; *Antirrhetikos*, offering biblical texts to be used in spiritual warfare; *Chapters on Prayer*, focusing largely on the nature of 'pure prayer'; and other shorter works.[7] In a number of them he made use of a unique way of expressing his thoughts, in the form of 'Chapters' – brief, pithy and sometimes enigmatic sentences, often similar to proverbs. This can sometimes make his thought seem fragmented, but taken together his works present a coherent, systematic vision of the inner life of the ascetic, based on the experience of the desert monks.

In his writings he sets out an understanding of the ascetic life as 'a progression of stages that the monk must pass through in order to attain the ultimate goal of knowledge of God'.[8] The first stage, which he calls *praktikê*, involves cleansing the soul of passions so as to bring about a state of *apatheia*, passion-less-ness or impassibility. The second stage, that of *gnostikê* or mystical knowledge, involves pure prayer and the contemplation, first of created beings and then of God, through which one reaches *gnosis*, or knowledge of God.

In the first stage of the ascetic life, the *praktikê*, Evagrius includes not only what in the previous chapter we have termed

---

6 John Meyendorff, *St Gregory Palamas and Orthodox Spirituality*, pp. 23f.

7 Translations of most of these are in the Sinkewicz edition of Evagrius' works.

8 Sinkewicz, Introduction, p. xxi.

the 'external or practical' aspects of the desert way, such as solitude, manual work and ascetic practices, but also all the elements, both outer and inner, of the ascetic life. He pays relatively little attention to the external or practical aspects, not because he regarded them as unimportant but probably because they were well known and accepted in the desert tradition, and needed little elaboration by him. In his treatise on *Foundations*, however, he briefly 'presents the common teaching of the desert tradition'[9] on these matters. He outlines how a monk must give up wealth, separate himself from family, and go into what he calls 'voluntary exile'. He must adopt a frugal diet, not stay outside his cell for a prolonged period, limit his sleep, labour with his hands, and practise *hesychia* or stillness. Scattered throughout the *Praktikos* there are similar injunctions, advising monks to flee from worldly pleasures, not to abandon their cell at times of temptation, to practise vigils, and to have a 'dry and regular diet'. In *To Eulogius* he recommends the habit of manual work, 'the ascesis of renunciation' and the practice of obeying a spiritual father. He also emphasizes the importance, at the start of the ascetic life, of having relationships of love and patience with others, bearing offences, refusing to take vengeance, not returning evil for evil, not passing judgement on others, not listening to those who find fault with them, and showing hospitality.[10] For Evagrius the desert monk, the inner or spiritual ascesis of the monk was built on the foundation of these practical ways of the desert.

The larger part of Evagrius' ascetical works has to do with the inner aspects of the ascetic life. His main concern was with ascetics' struggle to guard against and overcome the *logismoi* or thoughts which arouse the passions of the soul, something with which all the desert monks were concerned. In his work *On the Eight Thoughts*, written probably for those in the early stages of the ascetic life, he identifies and briefly describes the

---

9 *Foundations of the Monastic Life*, Sinkewicz, Introduction, p. 3.
10 See especially *To Eulogius*, 4, 5, 16, 17.

eight evil thoughts which the ascetic needs to guard against; these eight are also discussed elsewhere, especially in the *Praktikos*. They can be described briefly as follows: (1) *Gluttony*, or the desire for food, is dangerous because 'much food arouses desire', prevents prayer, and darkens the mind. It is overcome only by abstinence, which quells desire and helps towards *apatheia*. (2) *Fornication* refers not only to sexual acts but to mental or imagined sexual activity. It can be aroused not only by satiety of food but by the presence and sight of women, so that it is important to keep away from women, and not to allow fantasies of women into one's mind. (3) *Avarice*, the love of money or of possessions, is insatiable: the more one gets the more one wants. Because it leads one into other evils it is described as 'the root of all evil' (1 Timothy 6.10), and so makes one bound and heavy-laden. These three – gluttony, fornication and avarice – are thoughts that afflict the 'concupiscible' part of the soul, that part which has to do with bodily desires. (4) *Anger* refers not only to rage and bad temper but to the resentment that lingers when anger is suppressed. This is disturbing and hard to control, and the only answer to it is patience and gentleness or meekness. (5) *Sadness* refers not to godly sadness, which arises from knowledge of one's sins, but to 'worldly sadness', which arises from loss of things that one is attached to, or frustration at not achieving one's desires. (6) *Acedia*, sometimes translated as sloth, or listlessness, is called by Evagrius 'a relaxation of the soul'.[11] It is a state of mind in which one 'can't be bothered', and longs for change and variety. A particularly well-known and vivid description of it is given in *Praktikos*.[12] It is overcome only by perseverance. These three thoughts – anger, sadness and acedia – can afflict the 'irascible' part of the soul, that part which has to do with mental desires. Finally there are (7) *vainglory* and (8) *pride*, two related thoughts which can affect the 'rational' part of the

11 *On the Eight Thoughts*, 'Acedia', Sinkewicz, p. 83.
12 *Praktikos*, 12; Sinkewicz, p. 99; Bamberger, p. 18.

soul. Vainglory is the love of human esteem and the desire for praise, which can subtly and secretly affect and play havoc with the spiritual life: even, or perhaps especially, of someone who is doing well at resisting the other thoughts. It is 'an underwater rock; if you run against it you lose your cargo'.[13] Pride is the ascribing of one's accomplishments to one's own strength, feeling that one has no need of God, forgetting one's weakness and rejecting God's help, and so despising other people. Like vainglory, pride is a very insidious thought: even ascetic work itself can lead to pride.

In Evagrius' view these thoughts were suggested by the demons in order to arouse the passions. The demons, the thoughts and the passions were all interrelated. As David Brakke explains, 'The thoughts are synonymous with the demons and, at times, synonymous with the passions. And so Evagrius can speak of "the demon of vainglory", "the thought of vainglory", and simply "vainglory" interchangeably – they all refer to the same thing.'[14] In some of his writings Evagrius analyses very closely just how these demons operate, how they use subtle devices to trick and deceive the monk into entertaining the thoughts. It was the task of the monk to learn how to discern the operation of the demons and so resist the thoughts, or overcome the passions. The treatise *On Thoughts*, in particular, is 'an advanced tactical manual designed to assist the monk in developing his faculty of discernment'.[15]

All the desert monks were well versed in the Bible,[16] and Evagrius was no exception. In his *Antirrheticus* he provided an array of biblical verses which could be used as weapons to counter the demons and resist each of the passionate thoughts. For example, in the struggle against avarice or love of possessions one should remember the words: 'Keep your mind free from the love of money, and be content with what you

---

13 *On the Eight Thoughts*, 'Vainglory', Sinkewicz, p. 85.
14 Brakke, *Demons and the Making of the Monk*, p. 54.
15 *On Thoughts*, Sinkewicz, Introduction, p. 137.
16 See especially Burton-Christie, *The Word in the Desert*.

have; for he has said "I will never leave you or forsake you"' (Heb. 13.5). Or to deal with the anger that arises from being wronged one should recall St Paul's words: 'Why not rather suffer wrong? Why not rather be defrauded?' (Rom. 12.15).[17] That is to say, Evagrius developed the practice of the desert monks by suggesting how they could use their knowledge of the Bible in their struggle with the passions.

The object of all this struggle was to reach the state of *apatheia*, or passion-less-ness. This was a concept developed by the Greek stoics, but used by Christian writers before Evagrius, including Ignatius, Athanasius and Clement of Alexandria. We have seen how for the monks of the desert achieving purity of heart was the aim of the ascetic life. A pure heart was a mirror by which the eye could gaze upon God – a concept which Evagrius himself adopted: 'The mind will not be able to see the Lord as in a mirror without having purified the soul.'[18] Evagrius uses the term *apatheia* to express something similar to what others called purity of heart. For him, as for the other desert monks, *apatheia* or purity of heart is a state of deep calm, tranquillity and *hesychia*, reached by those who through long ascetic practice had overcome the passions. 'Perfect *apatheia*', he says, 'emerges in the soul after the victory over all the demons that oppose the practical life.'[19] It is 'the blossom of the practical life'.[20] When a monk reaches this state he is 'undisturbed by passions', and has 'no more need of abstinence and perseverance'. Because he has established the virtues within himself, 'he no longer remembers the law or the commandments or punishment'.[21] This victory over the passions, however, and the ability to cross over the threshold into the state of *apatheia*, comes not simply from the ascetic's own efforts: *apatheia* is a gift of Christ. 'Remember', says Evagrius, 'how when you were

17 Evagrius, *Antirrheticus*, Philargyria, 52; Orge, 43.
18 Evagrius, *Exhortation To Monks*, 5.
19 Evagrius, *Praktikos*, 60.
20 Ibid., 81.
21 Ibid., 67, 68, 70.

caught in the passions, you made the transition to *apatheia* by the mercy of Christ.'[22]

Apatheia, however, is not an end in itself: it is the gateway to the *gnostic* life and to knowledge of God. The *gnostikê* follows the *praktikê*. For Evagrius this 'knowledge' is not only something cognitive, it refers to what we might call a relationship with God. This comes about because *apatheia* gives birth to love, or *agape*, and it is love that leads us into spiritual knowledge of God: 'The one who loves God is ever communing with him as with a father.'[23] The gnostic life is characterized by pure prayer and contemplation – contemplation first of beings or created things, and then of God. In his discussion of the gnostic life and contemplation Evagrius moves into realms of theology and philosophy which lie beyond what we find in the sayings and lives of the desert monks; but what he says about prayer, found largely in his *Chapters on Prayer*, follows on from what we know of the practice of the desert.

We have seen that the way of the desert culminated in the practice of prayer. But the monks tended to be reticent about their own inner life; they said little about their experience of prayer, and did not develop a theory or theology of prayer. Evagrius, however, reflects on the subject at length. His well-known definition of prayer as 'the ascent of the mind to God',[24] which is reminiscent of neoplatonist thought, may seem rather abstract and impersonal, but some of his other statements make it clear that for him prayer was part of a personal relationship with God. Prayer is 'the continual converse (or "communion") of the mind with God';[25] it is 'standing before God the Almighty, the Creator, and Provider of the universe',[26] and 'standing before [God] with reverence and fear'.[27] Like the

---

22 Ibid., 33.
23 Evagrius, *Chapters on Prayer*, 54.
24 Ibid., 35.
25 Ibid., 3.
26 Ibid., 100.
27 Ibid., 90.

other desert monks,[28] Evagrius is concerned with unceasing prayer. 'The law of unceasing prayer has been handed down to us', he says,[29] no doubt with 1 Thessalonians 5.17 in mind. And like others he recommends 'short intense prayers' at times of inner struggle.[30] He is also aware that prayer is not simply something that we ourselves do, but is the gift of God. 'If you want to pray, you have need of God, who bestows prayer on the one who prays.'[31]

Evagrius' principal concern, however, is with what he calls 'pure prayer'. By this term he refers to a state of being still before God, without words and without mental images. Pure prayer is the fruit of *apatheia*, which itself is the result of long perseverance in the asceticism of guarding the heart against the intrusion of the thoughts. It can be described as a state of habitual *apatheia*:[32] requiring complete purity of heart. For pure prayer one's mind needs to be free of all concepts or mental images of God. In Evagrius' understanding it is image-less prayer. 'Stand on your guard,' he says, 'keeping your mind free of mental representations during the time of prayer, so that it may stand firm in its proper tranquillity; as a result . . . you may receive the most glorious gift of prayer.'[33]

It has been said that there is a danger that Evagrius' pure prayer may be regarded as 'some sort of intellectualized blankness'.[34] But this would be a misunderstanding, because Evagrius makes it clear that pure prayer, while excluding mental concepts and images, nevertheless involves a relationship of desire and love for God. *Apatheia* gives birth to love, and love is at the heart of prayer. 'The one who loves God is ever com-

---

28 For example *Life of Antony*, 3, 4; *Sayings*, Epiphanius, 3, Benjamin, 4; Palladius, *Lausiac History*, Paul, 1; *The Lives of the Desert Fathers*, I.63; Cyril, *Life of Sabas*, 16; Paul of Elusa, *Encomium on the Life of St Theognius*, p. 138.

29 Evagrius, *Praktikos*, 49.

30 *Chapters on Prayer*, 98; see also *Sayings*, Macarius the Great, 19.

31 *Chapters on Prayer*, 58.

32 Ibid., 52.

33 Ibid., 69.

34 Stewart, *Cassian the Monk*, p. 96.

muning with him as with a father.'[35] When one prays without distraction one 'acquires an ever greater longing for God'.[36] In prayer one becomes like the angels, 'longing to see the face of the Father who is in heaven'.[37] For Evagrius, therefore, pure prayer was not an impersonal or merely intellectual activity, but a deeply personal engagement with God.

All that Evagrius wrote about the ascetical life, his penetrating analysis of the 'thoughts' and the activity of the demons, his explanation of *apatheia* or purity of heart, and his deep exploration of prayer, although influenced in some degree by neoplatonism and the teaching of Origen, nevertheless had deep roots in his experience of living with the desert monks. As a result of this desert experience Evagrius' approach to the ascetic life was very different from that of Basil of Caesarea, whose disciple he had been when he was a young man in Pontus.[38] He took the desert monks' understanding of the ascetical life, analysed, developed and expanded it, and produced an account of the ascetical life which is both intellectual and practical, and has had a deep and lasting influence on later Christian spirituality. And although he was influenced by Greek philosophic thought, he was deeply rooted in the biblical tradition. Through Evagrius the way of the desert eventually reached out into the life of the Church.

John Cassian

John Cassian was born a few years after Evagrius, in about 360, probably in the area known as Scythia, between the Danube and the Black Sea, in what is now Romania. It seems that he came from a well-to-do family, and received a good education.

---

35 *Chapters on Prayer*, 54.
36 Ibid., 118.
37 Ibid., 113.
38 See Augustine Holmes, *A Life Pleasing to God*, p. 64, on Evagrius' relationship to Basil.

About the year 380 he moved with his friend Germanus to Bethlehem, where they both entered the monastic life. Having heard stories of the desert monks of Egypt they made their way there in around 385, promising to return shortly. They visited a number of monastic sites in the delta area, and then went on to the great monastic site of Sketis, where they settled down to live the life of desert monks. They seem to have visited and had conversations with some of the monks whose fame they had heard of while in Palestine. We don't know how widely they travelled in Egypt: in his writings Cassian appears to use the word Sketis to refer to other places as well. We know that they visited monks at Cellia, but it is unlikely that they went any further south than Sketis. The two friends stayed in Egypt for about 15 years, leaving it only once to return briefly to Bethlehem, to explain why they had failed to keep their promise to return there after a brief visit to Egypt.

About the year 400 they left Egypt, probably because of events connected with the controversy over Origen's teaching, and sometime before 403 they were in Constantinople, where they were attached to the circle of the patriarch John Chrysostom. After Chrysostom's downfall and exile in 404 Cassian was part of a delegation sent to Rome on his behalf, but we know nothing more of his movements until he went to southern Gaul. The fact that he spoke and wrote both Greek and Latin enabled him to move easily between the Greek-speaking east and the Latin-speaking west. By 415 he had settled in Massilia (Marseilles), where he founded two monasteries, one for men and one for women, probably with the encouragement of local bishops and leading laymen. As far as we know he lived there until his death, probably about 435.

Cassian is known mainly for his two major works, written in Latin: *The Institutes* and *The Conferences*. In them he sets out to portray the way of life of the monks of Egypt so as to provide a pattern for his monks in Gaul. For him, Egyptian monasticism was a model which could be transferred elsewhere to form the basis of monastic life in other places. In *The Institutes* he discusses in twelve 'books' some basic aspects of monastic practice and spirituality as it existed in Egypt. The first four deal with practical issues such as the monastic garb and the arrangements for prayer, and the next eight discuss the eight 'thoughts' or vices which had been identified by Evagrius. *The Conferences* consists of 24 books, purporting to be a record of conversations or 'conferences' which he and Germanus had had with a total of fifteen leading monks in Egypt, mainly on questions of the inner and spiritual life of the monk, but sometimes on more theological issues. Each Conference begins with a request from the visitors for instruction, usually on a particular topic. It is generally recognized that although these conversations no doubt reflect the thought and theology of the desert monks, they are written in Cassian's own words and have been adapted to suit the situation and needs of the monks in Gaul. Cassian was a prolific writer, and it is not possible here to discuss his works and his thought as a whole, but simply to illustrate how he carried forward and expanded the way of life of the desert.

We should note, first, that Cassian was deeply influenced by Evagrius. But although his analysis of the eight thoughts, and much of what he wrote on other matters, bears the stamp of Evagrius, he does not anywhere mention him by name, no doubt because of Evagrius' association with Origen. Cassian adopted Evagrius' distinction between *praktikê* and *theoretikê*, the practical and contemplative aspects of the monastic life.[39] The former, 'which reaches its fulfilment in correction of behaviour and in cleansing of vice', is discussed mainly in *The Institutes*, and the latter in *The Conferences*. Cassian discusses both aspects, however, with a greater amount of reference to the Bible, and in a more down-to-earth way than Evagrius does.

---

39 John Cassian, *Conferences*, 14.1.3.

Cassian was also more conscious than Evagrius seems to have been of the biblical and Jewish origins of monasticism, as opposed to its debt to Greek or Platonic influences. He refers in a number of places to Elijah and to John the Baptist, telling how the anchorites of Egypt 'were not afraid to penetrate the vast recesses of the desert in imitation of John the Baptist . . . and of Elijah and Elisha'.[40] He also believed, on the basis of the account in the book of Acts of how the first Christians gave away all they possessed and held all things in common, that the Christian monastic tradition was established by the apostles. He claimed that 'monasteries founded by holy and spiritual fathers at the time when the apostles started preaching remain even to our own day'.[41] 'The discipline of the coenobites', he says, 'took its rise at the time of the apostolic preaching.'[42] Cassian, that is to say, saw his monasteries as continuing the biblical desert tradition and perpetuating a monastic movement which was begun by the apostles of Christ.

In describing the purpose or aim of the monastic life Cassian uses the Greek terms *skopos*, to refer to its current object or goal, and *telos*, to refer to its ultimate end. 'The end (*telos*) of our profession', he says, 'is the kingdom of God or the kingdom of heaven; but the goal (*skopos*) is purity of heart.'[43] It is by pursuing the goal or object that one can attain the end. Much of what he writes in both *The Institutes* and *The Conferences* deals with the way to pursue the object. His works do not constitute a monastic 'rule' like that of Benedict; and Cassian, like Evagrius, does not give a great deal of attention to some of the practical or external aspects of the monastic life. But in the first four books of *The Institutes*, he does describe some of the practical details of monastic life in Egypt – the symbolic meaning of the monastic garb and the arrangements and hours

---

40 Ibid., 18.6.2; see also 14.4.1; 24.4.2; *Institutes*, 1.1.2.
41 *Institutes,* Preface, 8.
42 *Conferences*, 18.5.1 (referring to Acts 4).
43 Ibid., 1.4.3.

for prayer, and the way 'renunciants' or novices were received and trained – and instructions on some other practical matters are to be found in various parts of *The Conferences*. Thus he emphasizes the importance of staying in one's cell (*Conf.* 6.15 and 7.23.3), and the value of solitude (*Conf.* 9.35.1; 10.6.2). Manual work, he says, helps one to 'acquire a loftier insight into spiritual contemplation' (*Inst.* 2.12.2). Fasting and the practice of eating only selected and cheap food are important in order to arrive at purity of heart (*Inst.* 5.22–23); but fasting and ascetic practice should not be taken to excess, nor allowed to interfere with the practice of hospitality. Moreover, 'a uniform rule concerning the manner of fasting cannot easily be kept because not all bodies have the same strength,' and so 'each individual must calculate for himself the degree of frugality that his bodily struggle and combat require' (*Inst.* 5.5.1; 5.9.1). And in the second and third books of *The Institutes* he describes the practical arrangements for prayer in Egypt in some detail. In general, he assumes that the day-to-day monastic life in Gaul should be based on the practice in Egypt, with some adjustments to take account of different climatic conditions.

As with Evagrius, however, Cassian's concept of *praktikê* covered not only the practical or external arrangements but also the inner aspects of the ascetic life, and it is to these that he pays most attention. In *The Conferences*, and to a lesser extent in *The Institutes*, he has something to say about most of the inner aspects of the ascetic life identified in Chapter 5. He develops the theme of *renunciation* or detachment in the third Conference, following ideas put forward by Evagrius.[44] It is, he indicates, both a practical and an inner thing, involving three stages: first, renouncing worldly goods, then renouncing one's previous patterns of behaving and thinking, and finally renouncing all visible reality and desiring things that are

---

44 Evagrius, *On Thoughts*, 26.

invisible (*Conf.* 3.6.1). This inner renunciation, he argues else-where, 'is nothing else than a manifestation of the cross and of a dying' (*Inst.* 4.34; 12.25). *Repentance*, another fundamental theme of the desert monks, is discussed in the twentieth Con-ference. To repent is to weep with compunction over one's sins, and it should lead to reparation through works of asceticism and almsgiving.[45]

Like all the monks of the desert movement, Cassian pays a great deal of attention to the need to guard the heart from the passions or 'thoughts'. He adopts Evagrius' taxonomy of the eight principal vices or 'thoughts', and discusses them in detail in books 5–12 of *The Institutes* and again in the fifth book of *The Conferences*, in something of the way that Evagrius had done. He shows how each of the passions takes various forms, and affects people in different ways (*Conf.* 6). The passions, he says, lie 'concealed in our heart' (*Conf.* 5.27.2), so resisting them is not so much a practical as an inner matter to do with the heart. In order to overcome gluttony one's 'superfluous appetite for food' must 'be trampled on by the contempla-tion of virtue' (*Inst.* 5.14.3). Dealing with fornication requires abstinence, but is mainly an inward struggle (*Inst.* book 6). Avarice attacks us from outside ourselves, but it lodges within us, so overcoming it requires not only giving up money and possessions but the inner disposition towards them (*Inst.* book 7). Similarly, anger is something in the heart, and sadness arises from inner desires not being achieved and inner hopes failing. Acedia is described as 'a wearied and anxious heart' (*Inst.* 10.1). Vainglory 'strikes the monk not only in his carnal part ... but also in his spiritual part'. Pride has both a carnal and a spiritual part, but the spiritual part is 'more pernicious' (*Conf.* 5.12.4). Each of these is not a sin which is committed, but a state of the mind or heart. Cassian illustrates the danger of the passions by extensive quotations from the Bible to demonstrate that victory over them does not lie in our own strength: we

---

45 *Conferences*, 20.8. See also Stewart, *Cassian the Monk*, pp. 123f.

learn 'from innumerable scriptural texts that we cannot conquer such great enemies by our own strength but only with
God's help, and that every day we must attribute to him the
sum of our victory' (*Conf.* 5.15.2).

As we have seen, the monks of every part of the desert movement attached great importance to *humility*; and in his writings
Cassian does the same. 'Humility is the teacher of all the virtues; it is the most firm foundation of the heavenly edifice; it is
the Saviour's own magnificent gift' (*Conf.* 15.7.2). Works of
inner asceticism, important as they are, are not of any value
unless they are done with humility. 'A person cannot attain
the end of perfection and purity except by true humility' (*Inst.*
12.23). 'True patience and tranquillity are not acquired or held
onto without profound humility of heart. If they proceed from
this source they will stand in need of neither the benefit of a cell
nor the refuge of solitude' (*Conf.* 18.13.1). 'The more a person
is purified in mind, the filthier he sees himself and the more he
finds reason for humility rather than pride' (*Conf.* 23.19.3).

As these quotations imply, the goal or *skopos* of the whole
ascetic life, both its practical and its inner aspects, is *purity
of heart*. This was true, as we have seen, of the monks who
followed the way of the desert, and it was certainly true for
Cassian. Purity of heart is a theme that runs through all his writings. Although it seems clear that in his use of this idea he was
influenced by Evagrius, he replaced Evagrius' term *apatheia*,
drawn from Greek philosophic writing, with 'purity of heart'.
This is a biblical phrase, found in the Psalms and on the lips
of Jesus himself, and also one used by the desert monks.[46] As
was stated above, Cassian uses this term at the start of *The
Conferences* to define the monks' goal. 'The end (*telos*) of our
profession', he says, 'is the kingdom of God or the kingdom of
heaven; but the goal (*skopos*) is purity of heart' (*Conf.* 1.4.3).
He goes on to explain how important it is: 'Whatever, therefore, can direct us to this *skopos*, which is purity of heart, is to

---

46 See page 140.

be pursued with all our strength, but whatever deters us from this is to be avoided as dangerous and harmful' (*Conf.* 1.5.3). Purity of heart means having a heart untouched by the passions, and the ascetic labours are undertaken in order to achieve this. 'For the sake of this everything is to be done and desired. For its sake solitude is to be pursued; for its sake we know that we must undertake fasts, vigils, labours, bodily deprivation, readings and other virtuous things, so that by them we may be able to acquire and keep a heart untouched by any harmful passion, and so that by taking these steps we may be able to ascend to the perfection of love' (*Conf.* 1.7). 'It is for its sake that we do and endure everything, for its sake that family, homeland, honours, wealth, the pleasures of this world, and every enjoyment are disdained – so that perpetual purity of heart may be kept' (*Conf.* 1.5.3). 'Purity of heart', says Columba Stewart, 'is the centrepiece of Cassian's monastic theology, the term he uses to describe monastic perfection.'[47]

Prayer was at the heart of the way of the desert, and Cassian, like Evagrius, gave a lot of attention to it. It is the only topic to which he devotes two Conferences. But whereas Evagrius expressed his thoughts on the subject in short pithy 'chapters', Cassian is more discursive. And whereas Evagrius presents an analysis of the nature of prayer, in particular of what he called 'pure prayer', Cassian, using the device of questions put to Abba Isaac in Egypt, deals with some more practical issues. In Conference Nine he discusses the four kinds of prayer mentioned by St Paul – supplications, prayers, intercessions and thanksgivings – and then turns to the Lord's Prayer, discussing its petitions one by one. Later, in Conference Ten, in response to a question from Cassian's friend Germanus about how to deal with distractions in prayer, Abba Isaac recommends the use of a brief 'formula' as a method of reaching the ideal of unceasing prayer. He claims that a formula consisting of the opening words of Psalm 70, 'O God be pleased to deliver me;

---

47 Stewart, *Cassian the Monk,* pp. 41f.

O Lord, make haste to help me,' had been 'handed down to us by a few of the oldest fathers', and that its use was 'absolutely necessary for possessing the perpetual awareness of God' (*Conf.* 10.10.2). He then goes on, in a famous passage, to describe all kinds of circumstances, from bodily troubles to assaults by the passions, in which this brief prayer can be used. This seems to be the first reference to the use of a kind of rhythm prayer which eventually led to the use of the Jesus Prayer in the Orthodox Church.

All of this is very practical advice; but Cassian moves beyond this to discuss a purer form of prayer for which he can use the language of ecstasy. Use of the Lord's Prayer, he says, can lead to a higher form of prayer, to 'that fiery and, indeed, more properly speaking, wordless prayer which is known and experienced by very few' (*Conf.* 9.25.3). Use of the prayer formula he recommends can lead to 'an unspeakable ecstasy of heart' in which the mind transcends 'all feelings and visible matter' (*Conf.* 10.11.6). Cassian uses language reminiscent of Evagrius when he describes this higher kind of prayer as 'that purest form of prayer which will not only mix no representation of the Godhead or bodily contour into its supplication . . . but will indeed permit itself neither the memory of any word whatsoever nor the likeness of any deed nor a shape of any kind' (*Conf.* 10.5.3). But Cassian's language of ecstasy is in fact closer to that of the desert tradition than to that of Evagrius.[48] This is illustrated by his quoting an otherwise unknown saying of Antony the Great: 'That is not perfect prayer wherein the monk understands himself or what he is praying' (*Conf.* 9.31). The goal of the monk is that 'one's whole way of life and all the yearnings of one's heart become a single and continuous prayer' (*Conf.* 10.7.3).

This kind of prayer, arising from a heart made pure by ascetic practice and the struggle against the passions, leads the monks beyond the *skopos* or object of the ascetic life towards

---

48 Ibid., p. 122.

the *telos*, its ultimate end or purpose. The *telos*, he says, is the kingdom of God. The aim is to enter the life of heaven. According to Cassian, 'the purpose of the monastic life was to prepare for citizenship in heaven'.[49] This preparation is done not only by purity of heart but by loving God – loving him 'for no other reason than sheer love of him', and because in Christ he loved us first (*Conf.* 11.7.6). The love of the Lord alone should be our 'unchanging and fixed centre' (*Conf.* 24.6.3). A person can begin even now to live 'the blessed way of life of the holy in the future' if he 'desires only one thing, thirsts for one thing, and always directs not only every deed but even every thought to this one thing . . . that God may be all in all' (*Conf.* 7.6.4). In this, as in other ways, Cassian's thought was profoundly Christological. He believed that Jesus' prayer in St John's Gospel for all to be one in him and the Father would be fulfilled. He summed up this vision of the heavenly life in famous words in which he longs for the time 'when every love, every desire, every effort, every understanding, every thought of ours, everything that we live, that we speak, that we breathe, will be God' (*Conf.* 10.7.2).

In these various ways, Cassian carried forward, developed, interpreted and transposed the way of the desert. After writing briefly of some of the practical aspects of this way, he enlarged on the desert monks' concern over the passions and their way of guarding the heart. His main importance, however, lies in his development of three themes which were fundamental to the desert way, but about which the 'sayings' and 'lives' of the desert monks say relatively little: the importance of purity of heart as the goal or *skopos* of the ascetic life; the nature and practice of the prayer which underlies all the ascetic life; and the mystery and wonder of the life of heaven and the kingdom of God which was the ultimate end or aim of the ascetic life. Cassian took these themes from the way of the desert and applied them to a different context in such a way that they

---

49 Ibid., p. 40a.

have had a permanent influence on monastic and spiritual life, especially in the West. This influence can be summed up in the words of two modern scholars: '[I]n Cassian's work, the lives of the Fathers are made into a new and different text that provides the basis for a theology and discipline of medieval Western monasticism. There is continuity, but a profound change from the restless wanderings of the Fathers to the ideal of "stability" within the walls of the monastery, and a life formed upon static contemplation and focussed on the church and sanctuary rather than the boundless horizons of the desert . . . As Owen Chadwick puts it: "Thus the Egyptian ideal as interpreted by Cassian received a frame by which it was modified and in which it was bequeathed to the Middle Ages."'[50]

---

50 Jasper, *The Sacred Desert*, p. 36, quoting Chadwick, *Cassian*, p. 13.

7

Gaza

In the fifth and sixth centuries the region of Gaza on the coastal strip in the south-west of Palestine became an important monastic centre. The town of Gaza and surrounding villages were not in the desert, although there was desert to the east, but in rural agricultural country, with fertile soil and a number of streams. It was not a remote, inaccessible area, as main routes connecting Egypt with Palestine, Syria and Asia Minor ran through it. People from far and wide passed through Gaza. Although this was not a desert place, some of the monks of this area were among those who preserved and interpreted the tradition of the desert, and applied it to the monastic life elsewhere.

Its monastic history goes back to Hilarion, the story of whose life is told in the hagiographic *Life of Hilarion* written by Jerome. He was born in Thavatha about five miles south of Gaza town probably towards the end of the third century. After studying in Alexandria he paid a visit to Antony the Great, and then returned to Gaza to build a hermitage close to the sea near the port of Maiuma. Later he left and travelled widely in the eastern Mediterranean, and died in Cyprus, from where his body is said to have been brought for burial at his old monastery in Maiuma. Hilarion had no immediate successors, but before long others established monasteries or hermitages in the area. One of these was Silvanus, a native of Palestine, who was for a while in Egypt living with a group of twelve disciples in Sketis. Twelve of his 'sayings' are recorded in the *Sayings of the Desert Fathers*. In 380 Silvanus moved with his followers to

Sinai, and later to Gaza where he established a monastery. This was probably a semi-eremitic community similar to those in Egypt. Archaeologists have discovered the remains of what was probably the community church.[1] One of Silvanus' disciples, a monk named Zeno, built a hermitage in the locality, at a site where a cistern and potsherds have recently been found. In the fifth century Peter the Iberian, a leading and controversial figure in Palestinian monasticism, spent some years in a monastery in Gaza near the port of Maiuma. Peter, who was from a royal family in Iberia in present-day Georgia, became a leader of the Monophysite group in Palestine. His story is told in an anonymous *Life*. He was active in ecclesiastical politics and travelled widely, but finally returned to his monastery in Gaza and died there in 489. One of his colleagues, Severus from Pisidia in Asia Minor, who was also a leading figure in the church and later patriarch of Antioch, made himself a hermitage nearby, and later a monastery for his disciples.

Abba Isaiah of Sketis

On the evidence mainly of Sozomen's *Ecclesiastical History*,[2] it is believed that several monasteries had been built at different times during the fourth and fifth centuries in a fairly small area near the town of Gaza, and there were others further afield. Gaza was therefore a place to which from early days people had come from far and wide to live the monastic life, but none of these left significant writings. The first to do so was Abba Isaiah of Sketis. He was brought up in Egypt and was trained as a monk in an Egyptian coenobium before withdrawing to the desert, probably in Sketis. But when he became well known as an ascetic and attracted many followers, he moved to Palestine, first to Jerusalem to visit the Holy Places, and then to the desert

1 For details of the remains of hermitages and monasteries in Gaza see Hirschfeld, 'The Monasteries of Gaza: An Archaeological Review'.

2 Sozomen, *Ecclesiastical History*, Book VI, Chapter 32.

near Eleutheropolis in southern Palestine. Finally, sometime before 485 he settled at Beit Daltha near Gaza, close to the monastery of Peter the Iberian, who was a friend of his. Isaiah lived there as a recluse, but was closely connected with a coenobium which he controlled through a disciple of his, also named Peter. It must have been there that he wrote his *Asceticon*, a series of 29 *Discourses* for the instruction and guidance of the monks of the coenobium.

The *Discourses* of Abba Isaiah represent the first known example of something like spiritual guidance through the written word, a form which became very significant in Gaza, and later throughout Christian history. The discourses vary in their length and subject matter, and to some extent in their style, and it has been claimed that some may not be the work of Isaiah himself. He was apparently sympathetic to the Monophysite cause, but his writings show little interest in theological argument, and were accepted by Christians of all persuasions. Some of them, especially Discourses 1, 3–5 and 9, contain down-to-earth practical advice about day-to-day living in the monastery. Isaiah does not give us a systematic presentation or a rounded account of the ascetic life: his writings are more piecemeal, and sometimes repetitive. So rather than attempting to give an overall account of his thought, it will be worth rehearsing the main features of the way of the desert to see to what extent they are to be found in his writing.

If we look first at what we have called the practical features, we find that as he is writing for professed monks he assumes that they will have adopted the first of them: *withdrawal from the world and renunciation of worldly goods*. 'The first struggle', he says, 'is exile'. The struggle is 'to leave your own and move to another place' (D17, p. 131).[3] Elsewhere he spells out the practical implications of this withdrawal: 'If you have

---

3 References in this form are to the number of the Discourse and the page number in the Chryssavgis and Penkett edition of *Ascetic Discourses*.

renounced the world, do not allow yourself to keep anything' (D4, p. 58).

Isaiah also assumes that the monks, although living in a coenobium, will spend a great deal of time in *solitude* in their cells. Discourse 4 is addressed to 'Those who Stay in their Cells' (D4, p. 53); in it he repeatedly gives instructions about what to do while 'living silently in your cell' (p. 57), 'working inside your cell' (p. 69) or 'sitting in your cell' (p. 96). 'We stay', he says elsewhere, 'well withdrawn in the cell' (D28, p. 231).

With the solitude of the cell goes *silence*. Discourse 6 is addressed to 'Those who Desire to Lead a Life of Good Silence'. Sitting alone in one's cell obviously involves silence, but there is also a need at times to be silent in company. Silence is described as one of the virtues which 'purify the soul' (D7, p. 81). 'Force yourself', he says, 'to practise silence' (D27, p. 225).

The monks he was addressing were apparently under the *direction of a spiritual father* or 'elder' in the same way as the semi-eremitic monks of Egypt. He advises them, 'Do not conceal any of your thoughts, sorrows or desires, but confess them openly and freely to your elder, and try faithfully to carry out whatever you hear from him' (D1, p. 41). He urges them also to 'take care in your heart that you do not upset your teacher according to God' (D8, p. 94). Elsewhere he stresses the need for obedience to one's elder or spiritual father: 'Let us be obedient to our fathers in everything' (D25, p. 201).

Isaiah also emphasizes the importance of the *ascetic practices* of eating and sleeping, but he discourages excess. 'Place a limit for yourself so far as eating goes,' he says. 'Eat only once a day, and give your body what it needs so that you will continue to want to arise from sleep. Keep your vigil modestly, and do not deprive your body of its needs, but perform your duties leniently and sensibly, lest your soul is darkened by the degree of sleeplessness and gives up the struggle' (D4, p. 57). He recommended, as Pachomius had done,[4] that the night should be

4 PK, Vol. 1, Bohairic *Life*, 59.

divided equally between sleep and prayer: 'Half the night is sufficient for your duties and the other half for your physical rest' (D4, p. 57).

He believed also, as all the desert monks did, in the importance of *manual work*, and of how it was carried out. 'Force yourself', he said, 'to perform your manual work' (D9, p. 96). 'When you are carrying out your manual labour, do not despise it but perform it carefully and in godly fear' (D3, p. 49).

And, of course, he emphasized *prayer*. He not only wanted his monks to 'repeat many prayers, for prayer is the light of your soul' (D4, p. 53), but continued the desert monks' insistence on the importance of practising unceasing prayer: 'Love continual prayer, in order that your heart may be illumined' (D16, p. 121).

As well as the practical features, we find that the inner features of the way of the desert were no less important for Isaiah. Like the monks of the desert he understood that the monastic life must begin with *repentance*. In keeping with the biblical understanding of the word, he says that 'Repentance is to turn away from all sin' (D21, p. 151). Monks are described as those who have already 'offered yourselves to God for repentance' (D9, p. 95). But this is not something which takes place only once: it is perpetuated in a life of continuous compunction or weeping over one's sins. He describes himself humbly as one who 'has not begun the work of repentance', and so he invites his readers to 'Weep with me, all my brothers' (D14, p. 113).

Similarly, the *inner renunciation of one's own will* and detachment from worldly desires must be practised day by day in the ordinary relationships of living. Monks are instructed to 'surrender their will' to their neighbour. They must be detached from worldly desires, 'for freedom does not come while your heart desires something worldly' (D15, p. 115). To surrender one's will as Jesus did in Gethsemane is to 'ascend the Cross with him' (D13, p. 106). This is one of Isaiah's distinctive phrases, which is repeated frequently throughout the

Discourses. It is not typical of the literature of the desert, but is found in some of the letters of Barsanuphius and John who followed Isaiah in Gaza.[5]

To do this one must *attend to oneself*. Discourse 7 is devoted entirely to ways in which monks should 'attend diligently' to aspects of their inner life. And elsewhere he repeatedly urges his readers to 'examine yourselves'. 'Examine yourself, therefore, you who have been baptized in Jesus' name' (D22, p. 168). 'Examine yourself, then, dear brother. What more can you do?' (D22, p. 169). 'Let us examine ourselves, brothers, and consider our own behaviour before we meet with him' (D25, p. 207). The purpose of such self-examination was to discover and reveal the passionate thoughts that are affecting the soul, and for this one needs *discernment*. 'Therefore, my brother, a person has great need of discernment, which removes all carnal lust, and an attentive vigilance in all his ways to avoid going astray' (D25, p. 202). But discernment is a gift which only comes when one prepares the way for it by one's ascetic discipline: 'All things are abolished by discernment . . . but it is impossible for discernment to come to you, unless you cultivate its ground, beginning with silence' (D16, p. 126).

Attending to oneself involves *guarding the heart* against the incursions of passionate thoughts and the attacks of the demons. The ascetic life is a constant struggle against such thoughts. Like all the monks of the desert Isaiah attributes these attacks to the activity of the *demons*, and he recognizes that the demons can operate in subtle and devious ways, for example by persuading a monk to undertake some ascetic discipline that is beyond his capacity (D4, p. 57). As with other ascetic writers, Isaiah speaks of 'demons', 'passions' and 'thoughts' interchangeably. All of these refer to the way in which our minds can be dominated and controlled by thoughts and feelings which draw us

5 See, for example, the *Letters* of Barsanuphius and John, nos 45, 48, 185, 351, 567. The idea of 'bearing the Cross', but not of 'ascending the Cross', was common among the monks of different kinds in Upper Egypt; see pp. 50, 67, 72, 74, 145.

away from God; and the principal task of the ascetic monk is to recognize and resist them.

Victory in the struggle against the passions cannot, however, be achieved simply by one's own strength, but only by *calling for God's help*. Isaiah speaks of 'surrendering oneself before God with one's whole heart', for 'he will save you from all the attacks of the enemy' (D4, p. 61). 'If you are struggling against a passion,' he says, 'do not lose heart, but surrender yourself to God, saying, "I cannot do this; help me, the wretched one"' (D4, p. 59).

What goes on in one's heart, however, has a bearing on how one relates to other people. When one discerns the evil thoughts that are within oneself, one knows oneself to be a sinner and no better than one's neighbour. One must therefore be careful not to despise or pass judgement on others. This theme, found so frequently in the *Sayings* of the Egyptian monks, is repeated again and again by Abba Isaiah. 'Do not scorn your neighbour,' he counsels (D9, p. 96). 'Your duty is not to feel contempt' (D4, p. 62). Even if a monk sees someone 'entirely in sin or carelessness' he should not show contempt towards that person (D8, p. 92). 'Guard yourself against blaming anyone' (D10, p. 99). 'Do not judge someone whom you know in your heart' (D26, p. 212). Along with this goes a determination to bear the wrongs done to one, and to refuse to return evil for evil. 'If you hear that some evil was done against you by someone, hold up your good will in order not to return the evil in your heart' (D18, p. 140).

All of this leads to what we have called an inner disposition, characterized by three main qualities, the first of which is *humility*. The theme of humility occurs in the *Discourses* probably more than any other. The word is found on almost every page. To aspire to it is seen as part of the object of the ascetic life. Isaiah begins his second Discourse addressed to beginners by telling them: 'Above all we require humility ... Through humility the enemy is entirely destroyed' (D2, p. 47). Humility is nowhere defined in any precise way. It is a state of heart, and a way of regarding oneself and other people, which characterizes the whole way of the monk. The various attempts to live the ascetic life 'are all found in humility' (D5, p. 70). After giving advice of all kinds about living the ascetic life he concludes: 'If you keep these things you will acquire humility' (D5, p. 76). 'Ascetic discipline, poverty, detachment, suffering and silence give birth to humility' (D9, p. 97). 'Love humility,' he concludes, 'and it will protect you from your sin' (D9, p. 96).

Along with humility goes *stillness* or tranquillity, to which Isaiah devotes Discourse 24, his shortest but one that is full of rich expression. In a passage that is unusually reminiscent of Evagrius' concept of *apatheia* he says, 'Tranquillity lacks nothing because it dwells in God and God in it. It no longer knows enmity, nor fall, nor unbelief, nor the effort to guard oneself, nor fear of the passions, nor any desire, nor pain caused through enmity. Its glories are great and innumerable' (D24, p. 181).

The third main characteristic of the inner disposition is *purity of heart*, and this too is emphasized by Abba Isaiah. Unlike Evagrius and Cassian, he does not explore or analyse the concept of *apatheia* or purity of heart, nor does he characterize it as freedom from the passions, but writes of it in a very general way. 'Let us purify our heart and body from sinful desire,' he urges (D16, p. 120). And in a short sentence that offers a simply summary of the ascetic life he says, 'Purity consists of praying to God' (D22, p. 170).

We have seen earlier that for the desert monks the purpose or goal of their life of asceticism was to lead them towards God; and here again Abba Isaiah was no different. For him the final end of the ascetic life is to be with God, and find rest in God's kingdom. He attaches great importance to the desire for God. It is this that impels and motivates the genuine monks: 'The eager desire for God dwells in his heart' (D21, p. 160). 'Without desire for God there is no love' (D2, p. 44). 'Remember the kingdom of heaven, in order that your desire for it may very gradually attract you' (D16, p. 121). To stimulate this desire monks should live 'always in front of God', with their thought 'concentrated on God'. 'Hold God before your eyes in whatever work you are doing,' he counsels (D5, p. 75).

It is safe to say, then, that all of the principal aspects of the desert way, both the practical and the inner ones, are to be found in Isaiah. Clearly his background and training in Egypt was the principal influence on his approach. There is little evidence of the influence of other monastic traditions such as that of the Cappadocian Basil of Caesarea.[6] The significant thing for us, however, is that Isaiah was writing in Gaza, not for desert anchorites in Egypt but for monks in a very different place living in a coenobium. In doing so he took the various features of the way of life of the eremitic monks in Egypt, and interpreted and adapted them for a different context.

Generally, although Isaiah's writings do not display much deep theological thought or penetrating new insights into the nature of the ascetic life, there are plenty of helpful thoughts and advice about living the Christian life. It is obvious that he was a man of deep and sincere conviction, with no lack of fervent and heartfelt sentiments. He is very conscious throughout of his own sins and weaknesses, and of the need which everyone has of the mercy and help of God. 'Abandon yourself before God with all your heart, and he will help you, for he has compassion on human weakness' (D4, p. 56). 'What is important is to wait upon God with all your heart and all your strength' (D8, p. 90). 'Become, in purity, an altar of God, continually having the inner priest making sacrifices' (D5, p. 72). Because 'if the place of the heart is undefiled and pure, the divine gifts come of themselves' (D6, p. 78).

---

6 Chryssavgis and Penkett, Introduction, p. 23.

Barsanuphius and John

Isaiah had a considerable influence on the next two important figures of Gaza monasticism, Barsanuphius and John. These two, known respectively as the 'Great Old Man' and the 'Other Old Man', lived as recluses in cells outside a monastery of which a monk named Seridos was the abbot. This was located a few miles south of Isaiah's monastery, in Thavatha where Hilarion was born and had his first hermitage. The monastery itself was a large establishment. Archaeological excavations have uncovered the remains of a large and splendid coenobium, with a courtyard, halls, many rooms, a bathhouse, a hospice and a church with a crypt below it.[7] It was apparently something of a mixed establishment, where some monks lived together in the coenobium and others lived separately as anchorites nearby.

Barsanuphius was an Egyptian whose native language was Coptic. He was probably trained in one of the monastic communities of Lower Egypt, and so would be familiar with the way of the desert. He seems to have come to Gaza in the early part of the sixth century, and he was joined there by John sometime between 525 and 527. Barsanuphius and John occupied separate cells, and lived in complete isolation, seeing no one except for Seridos, who acted as a mediator between them and other people who wished to consult them. Over a period of years Seridos made a practice of conveying to one or other of the 'Old Men' questions or problems raised by a wide variety of people – monks or anchorites of the monastery, clergy and even bishops from the nearby churches, and lay people in different walks of life. Among them were some high-ranking officials such as the 'governor', and ecclesiastical leaders including, on one occasion, the Patriarch of Jerusalem.

The issues about which they wanted advice and help were of various kinds: questions about the inner life and the struggle against evil thoughts, about ascetic discipline, about prayer

---

7 Hirschfeld, 'The Monasteries of Gaza', p. 76.

and psalmody, about behaviour towards other people, about church practice and procedure, and questions raised by the abbot about how he should manage the monastery. All these enquiries were brought to the Old Men either in writing or orally by Seridos, who then wrote down the answers they gave. Some are single responses to one question; others form part of a long series of answers to questions from the same person. All these questions and answers, totalling nearly 850, were preserved and collected to form a large corpus of spiritual and practical advice on all sorts of issues. The *Letters* of Barsanuphius and John, recently translated into English for the first time by John Chryssavgis, are therefore different from any other early monastic literature. Here we do not have the enigmatic sayings of the *Apophthegmata*, the pithy 'Chapters' of Evagrius, the systematic teaching of Cassian or Basil of Caesarea, or the Discourses on the spiritual life by Isaiah or others who came later. The Old Men of Gaza do not give systematic instruction or theological teaching. There are indications in the correspondence that Barsanuphius was conscious of the theological controversies of the time, but he has little to say about them and discourages theological speculation. Instead we have guidance and advice relating to particular questions and day-to-day issues raised by a variety of people who were looking for help. The correspondence thus gives us a unique insight into the spiritual and practical lives of monks and of some clergy and Christian laymen, which is not to be found in any other early monastic literature.

The *Letters* also illustrate in fascinating detail how two senior and respected figures went about the business of spiritual direction. Both the Old Men, but especially Barsanuphius, dealt with people and issues of various kinds with discernment, tenderness, humility and authority. They have no hesitation in giving, on some occasions, quite specific advice, instructions and commands on matters on which they have been consulted, and on other occasions rebuking those who have not fulfilled their instructions. A monk wrote saying that he was a sinner but had critical feelings about his abbot. Barsanuphius responded, 'I shall rebuke you. For you called yourself a sinner, but in your deeds you do not consider yourself in this way' (L.17).[8] But all this is done with great flexibility, gentleness and understanding. Their counsel is based on a quite remarkable discernment, and the ability to read people's thoughts and to see into the hidden motives and attitudes underlying a person's words. To a monk who came to him saying that he wanted to be the servant of all people, Barsanuphius replied, 'This does not come from humility . . . When did you come to this measure of humility? You do not know what you have said, brother. May the Lord forgive you' (L.97). But there is deep affection, gentle caring and humility in all that they wrote. Quite often they referred to their correspondents as 'soul-mates' (e.g. L.57, 96, 99, 105), and they constantly assured them of their prayers for them. 'Take heart, my brother', wrote Barsanuphius; 'unless you were my soul-mate for the sake of the love that is according to Christ, I could not give you any response' (L.64). They also insisted that they themselves had no ability or wisdom, but that any valid counsel they gave came only from God; and they asked their correspondents to pray for them. Perhaps the most remarkable aspect of their spiritual direction, however, was their willingness to take responsibility for those who consulted them, even to the point of bearing their sins before God. 'I bear half your sins,' said Barsanuphius to one person; 'I have made you my partner' (L.73). To others he said: 'If you so hold to my commandment, or rather God's, I confess that I shall give account for you on that day when "God shall judge the secret thoughts of all"' (L.58). 'I bear your burdens and transgressions . . . I am giving you a commandment for salvation. If you keep this, I shall bear the indictment against you' (L.239). Barsanuphius and John obviously took their work of spiritual direction very

---

8 This refers to the number of the Letter in the Chryssavgis edition.

seriously, accepting a deep personal responsibility within themselves for caring for and praying for their correspondents. In the words of Simon Tugwell, this correspondence gives us 'a unique picture of the way in which spiritual fatherhood could operate during this period'.[9]

There is no doubt that the two Old Men, like the other Gazan leaders, continued and interpreted the way of the desert. This was largely through the influence of the traditions of Lower Egypt where Barsanuphius had been trained. They followed in the footsteps of Isaiah who came to Gaza from Sketis. The great figures of the Egyptian desert were never far from their minds: in the questions and the answers there are references by name to more than twenty of them, including Evagrius, and there are also frequent references to the *Sayings*. Egyptian practice is commended, as when John, the 'Other Old Man', describes the way the 'Scetiotes' recite the Psalms (L.143). While there are a few references to Euthymius of the Judean desert, and the influence of Basil of Caesarea may be detected in places,[10] there is no suggestion that the 'Old Men' were influenced to any great extent by other monastic traditions. According to Bitton-Askelony and Kofsky, although the Gaza monastic community had its own local and rural character, and was not a direct offshoot of Egyptian monasticism, it 'adhered primarily to the Egyptian ascetic tradition'.[11]

Their dependence on this tradition is apparent, first, in the extent to which the monastic life in Gaza reflected the practical features of way of the desert. As in the Egyptian desert, *solitude, silence and staying in one's cell* were important aspects of the monastic life. The writers assumed that their monastic correspondents, both those living in the coenobium and those in nearby hermitages, would each have an individual cell, and they emphasized the importance of staying or spending time in

---

9 Tugwell, *Ways of Imperfection*, p. 83. Tugwell offers an extended discussion of their approach to spiritual direction.

10 Chryssavgis, Introduction, p. 14.

11 Bitton-Ashkelony and Kofsky, *The Monastic School of Gaza*, p. 223.

one's cell. To one correspondent, John writes, 'Do your best to see that unimportant matters do not take you out of your cell prematurely' (L.269). The monks' cells were not just living quarters but places of solitude and silence, which they should 'enter with God as your guide' (L.36). Sitting in the cell should be done 'according to God' (L.211, 543), and with a purpose. 'Entering into the cell', writes Barsanuphius, 'is a matter of the soul' (L.237). 'Furthermore,' he adds, 'as you sit or pace around in your cell, blame yourself in all things, brother, and cast your weakness before God' (L.260). It is also clear from many references that the monks in their cells engaged in *manual labour*, and that this normally took the form of basket-weaving, as in the deserts of Egypt and Judea (L.143).

The Old Men also attached considerable importance to *obedience*; but whereas in the semi-eremitic communities of Lower Egypt the emphasis was largely on obedience to one's personal abba or elder, here it was usually referred to as a general virtue, involving submission to the will of God, the will of other people, or the will of the abbot who was head of the monastery. 'Become obedient, especially to your abbot' (L.242). Dependence on the abbot was one of the distinctive features of life in this monastery. Monks were expected to reveal their thoughts and sins to him, to take to him any problems to do with personal relationships or life in the monastery, and to be unquestioningly submissive to him in everything.

Correspondents frequently asked for advice about the *asceticism of food*. Here as elsewhere the norm was apparently for monks 'to eat nothing until the ninth hour' or three in the afternoon (L.522); but decisions about how much to eat were left to the individual, even in the coenobium. A measure of fasting was necessary in order to discipline the body, but it should not be overdone, because 'God does not require of us anything beyond our strength' (L.78). Also those who were ill or weak in body should treat their body more leniently. They should take care of the body, because it is 'the tool of the soul' (L.518).

With regard to *sleep*, the generally accepted principle was one which 'the fathers ordained': that monks should sleep for half the night and keep vigil for the other half (L.158). But just how the time should be divided between spells of sleeping and waking was left to the individual. John recommended prayer for two hours, followed by six hours of sleep and then vigil for a further four hours (L.146). Alternatively one could 'sleep a little during the day . . . and stay up in prayer for the entire night' (L.147). But generally one should act 'according to capacity . . . whether in terms of food or sleep' (L.158). 'Do not bind yourself with strict rules,' he said elsewhere, 'but do whatever the Lord gives you strength to do' (L.85, see also L.503).

The Old Men do not discuss the *practice of prayer* at length in the way that Evagrius and Cassian do, but they advocated a practice similar to what is found elsewhere. During the day monks in their cells should alternate standing for prayer and sitting for manual labour; but even while working they should engage in unceasing prayer (L.143, 212). It is interesting that, in contrast to the practice advocated by Cassian, the use specifically of the Jesus Prayer – 'Lord Jesus Christ, have mercy on me' – seems to have been an established custom for achieving unceasing prayer (L.175, 446), although other brief forms could be used for the same purpose (L.255). Bitton-Ashkelony and Kofsky conclude: 'Adopting the Jesus Prayer and developing various formulas illustrates the distinctively practical nature of the spiritual exercises of the community in Gaza.'[12]

If we turn to the inner features of the way of the desert, we find that Barsanuphius and John stress the importance of the inner self, echoing what we find in the desert communities. 'We should first think in terms of the inner self,' said John (L.383). To do this one has to begin with *repentance*. Monks should constantly repent and weep for their sins with compunction

---

12 Bitton-Ashkelony and Kofsky, *The Monastic School of Gaza*, p. 182.

and tears. 'To sit in one's cell means to remember one's own sins and to weep and mourn for these' (L.172). Similarly *renunciation* is seen as essentially an inner thing. The Old Men usually speak of it in terms of 'cutting off one's own will'. This involves submitting to the wishes of other people (L.61) and of God (L.40), but it is essentially something that one has to do inwardly, in the secrecy of one's heart. 'Be sure', says John, 'that you are cutting off your will while sitting in your cell' (L.173).

Cutting off one's own will is the way to *discernment* (L.266). To live the monastic life one should 'do everything with discernment' (L.681). It was important to 'strive hard to acquire discernment from the holy fathers' (L.416); but ultimately discernment was a gift which should be asked of God (L.570c). It is a necessary quality if one is going to *guard the heart.* As we have seen, guarding the heart against the incursions of evil thoughts or passions was a fundamental part of the ascetic life, and it is stressed by Barsanuphius and John as it was by the desert monks (L.166). 'True spiritual work', said Barsanuphius, 'is to struggle against the thoughts that disturb us' (L.103). It is taken for granted that the 'thoughts' are suggested by *demons*, but there is no indication here that the demons have bodily form or can attack monks physically, as in the case of Antony and others; nor is there any detailed discussion of their methods and operations as in the writings of Evagrius. Individual passions can, however, be identified with particular demons, such as 'the demon of fornication' (L.166). Because the demons work largely by deception (L.414–15), the monk needs discernment to be able to recognize which thoughts or intentions are of demonic origin. The two Old Men do not offer a systematic analysis of the 'thoughts' or passions after the manner of Evagrius or Cassian, but in the course of the correspondence they do make mention of each of Evagrius' eight 'thoughts', and in one place Barsanuphius lists them all along with some others (L.137b). There is particularly frequent mention of the danger of anger and of vainglory, both of which can come upon one unawares. The task of guarding one's heart, discerning one's thoughts, and recognizing and resisting the subtle temptations of the demons was central to the monastic life here as in all the desert tradition.

The two Old Men also attach importance to a monk's attitude to their fellows and to other people. Here again, the emphasis of the desert monks on refusing to *judge one's neighbour* is repeated. 'Do not judge or scorn anyone,' said Barsanuphius, 'for through this the heart is rendered blunt' (L.498). Moreover, when people are led astray it is the work of the devil, so 'we cannot blame them but only their passion' (L.151). Along with this their readers are encouraged 'to endure insults, rebukes and everything else that our teacher Jesus suffered' (L.150).

We have seen that the object of the desert ascetic life was to attain an inner state or disposition characterized by humility, tranquillity and purity of heart. As in the Discourses of Abba Isaiah, *humility* plays a large part in the correspondence of the two Old Men. It is seen as the principal virtue, and should be constantly sought after. 'Let us seek to attain humility in all things' (L.70). Humility is essentially an inner thing, a way of thinking of oneself. It means regarding oneself as 'earth and ashes' (L.100); it 'means not reckoning oneself as anything in every situation' (L.278). It is this inner attitude that forms the basis of all other virtues. By reaching towards humility one can hope to enter a state of tranquillity, stillness or *hesychia*. As we have seen, the Greek word can refer to external silence and peace or to the state of inner stillness and tranquillity which comes from excluding compelling thoughts or invading passions. The Old Men write frequently about this inner stillness. A monk, they say, is 'perfected in stillness' (L.90). This does not come easily: one needs to wait and pray for it (L.208). But 'if you reach the point of stillness, then you shall find rest with grace' (L.789). This state of inner stillness is closely related to *purity of heart*. The Old Men do not use this term often, but in one place Barsanuphius seems to follow Evagrius when he says that purification is the sign of someone who is saved from all the passions (L.137b; see also L.93). For him, as for the other exponents of the way of the desert, this triad of humility, inner tranquillity and purity forms the object of the ascetic life.

Beyond this, however, there is the *ultimate* end, to the attainment of which all the monastic life is directed. The end itself is beyond our experience in this life, and so it cannot be described in detail. But from time to time Barsanuphius and John point to that something beyond this present life which the monk can hope to reach. A long letter describing the ascetic way and the gift of God to one who follows it describes the end as 'the joy, gladness and reward of the kingdom of heaven' (L.187). Reaching this end requires constant remembrance and naming of God (L.329, 424, 454) and doing everything 'for God alone' (L.401). More significantly, perhaps, living in this way leads to deification. In Jesus, says Barsanuphius, we have 'a God who deifies us' (L.109). The end of the process of purification through overcoming the passions is not only to be made like God, but to become God, or a god. Deification or *theosis* is a concept which is rarely found in the earlier monastic writing, even in Evagrius and Cassian, but was to have an immensely important part in the theology and spirituality of the Orthodox Church. In a rare exposition of Christology, Barsanuphius gives succinct expression to this doctrine: 'The Son of God became human for your sake; you, too, should become god through him.'[13] And in a beautiful passage which gathers together what the ascetic life is about, and shows how humility, tranquillity and purity go together and lead to deification, he writes:

---

13 Barsanuphius' words echo the well-known sentence of Athanasius, 'He was made man that we might become god.' Both Evagrius and Cassian describe the life of heaven not principally in terms of 'deification' but of 'beatitude' (Stewart, *Cassian the Monk*, pp. 55–60). See Russell, *The Doctrine of Deification in the Greek Patristic Tradition*, where, however, Barsanuphius is not mentioned.

Inner work with labour of heart brings purity, and purity brings true stillness of heart, and such stillness brings humility, and humility renders a person the dwelling-place of God, and from this dwelling-place the demons are banished . . . as well as their shameful passions. Then that person is found to be a temple of God, sanctified, illumined, purified, endowed with every grace, filled with every fragrance and goodness and gladness; and that person is found to be a God-bearer, or rather is even found to be a god. (L.119)

It will be clear from all this that Barsanuphius and John adhered closely to the way of the desert as they had learned it from the monks of Egypt. The close parallel which can be seen between their teaching and that of Abba Isaiah shows how they all followed the same tradition. But we can also see, especially from the letters of the two Old Men, how they adapted it to suit monks living not in the desert but in a rural setting, in a coenobium with attached hermitages, all under the authority of an abbot.

There are, however, two particular emphases, found throughout their writings, which if not unique to their approach are specially characteristic of it. One is their concern over what they term '*pretence to rights*', a phrase used very frequently in the letters. A monk is seen as someone who, by renouncing and leaving the world, possesses no rights in this world. According to John Chryssavgis, the translator of the *Letters*, 'Pretence to rights is a phrase derived – albeit implicitly – from the Desert Fathers, and is used by Barsanuphius to signify self-justification, self-trust, and self-deceit.'[14] Assuming that one has rights of one kind or another is, however, an insidious temptation. In their life in the monastery and in their relationships with others, monks were continually in danger of behaving as if they had rights, and the two Old Men had frequently to draw this to their attention. Barsanuphius knew that he himself

---

14 Footnote to L.56.

was in danger of it, and asked his respected old correspondent Euthymius to 'pray that I may avoid the pitfall of pretending to have rights' (L.67). Having no 'pretence to rights' is a powerful and expressive way of describing that attitude of total denial of self which is inherent in the way of the desert.

Second, there is a particularly strong emphasis on the need for *patience and endurance* with thanksgiving. The recipients of their letters often faced kinds of difficulties not frequently mentioned in the sayings and stories of the desert monks. Many of the letters written to the Old Men were from people who were suffering illness. Like others before them, especially Amma Syncletica (see Chapter 4), Barsanuphius and John believed that illness should be the occasion for patience and thanksgiving. 'Illness', said Barsanuphius, 'is greater than mere discipline, being reckoned as a substitute for the regular way' (L.78). And they repeatedly urged their readers in all circumstances to endure difficulty and hardship with patience. Among their most quoted texts are Matthew 10.22 and Acts 14.22, both dealing with endurance, and 1 Thessalonians 5.18, dealing with thanksgiving in all circumstances. This was the way to be saved, because in this way they were sharing in the sufferings of Christ. Using a phrase probably inherited from Abba Isaiah, Barsanuphius wrote: 'You ought to ascend the cross with Christ, and to be nailed with the nails and pierced with the spear' (L.45). 'Anyone who wishes to ascend with Christ on the cross must become a partaker of his sufferings' (L.351; see also L.48, 185, 351, 567). Not only by undertaking the rigours of the ascetic life in the desert, but also by enduring with thanksgiving all the ordinary and unavoidable hardships, illnesses and sufferings of life in the monastery, they were 'ascending the cross' with Christ. This particular emphasis on endurance and patience, and its association with the cross, is a special feature of the writings of Barsanuphius and John, and a development of the way of the desert to suit the life of the monks in their monastery.

Dorotheus

Before we leave Gaza we should take a look at one more figure there, a man known as Dorotheus of Gaza. He was born in Antioch in Syria about the year 507, of a fairly wealthy and probably Christian family. He studied for some years, possibly in Alexandria but more probably in Gaza where there were institutions of learning. He then joined the monastery at Thavatha, where he became, first, the disciple of Seridos, the abbot, and then the personal assistant and mouthpiece of John, the 'Other Old Man'. Over the next nine years he was in correspondence with both the Old Men, seeking their advice on the ascetic life and on decisions he should make – a correspondence, totalling 87 questions and answers, which is recorded in numbers 252 to 338 of the *Letters* of Barsanuphius and John. During this time, and on the direction of Barsanuphius, he accepted the charge first of the infirmary and then of care of the guests in the monastery. Dorotheus suffered from poor health, and both these responsibilities bore heavily on him. Eventually he retired from the coenobium and moved to one of the hermit's cells. It seems that many monks came to him there for spiritual direction, and it was probably there that he wrote the series of homilies known as his *Discourses*. He died sometime after 560.

The *Discourses* of Dorotheus of Gaza became popular and influential sources of instruction and exhortation on the ascetic life. These fourteen homilies do not offer a systematic account of the ascetic life, nor do they give practical details of life in the monastery. Dorotheus selects certain topics to do with personal spiritual life and writes about them thoughtfully and imaginatively. In the course of them he discusses some but not all of the aspects of the way of the desert which we have identified.

He refers to withdrawal from the world (D1, p. 81),[15] to the

---

15 This refers to the number of the Discourse and the page in Wheeler's edition of the *Discourses and Sayings*.

importance of bodily labour (D2, p. 102), and the necessity of having a spiritual director, because being one's own director is 'grievous' (D5, p. 126). In one place he summarizes the 'good customs' which formed part of the basis of the desert way – fasting, keeping vigil, keeping silence, and obedience (D5, p. 122). Once he mentions the practice of 'praying unceasingly' (D2, p.101) and there are several passing references to vigils. But generally he says little about the practical features of the way of the desert.

There is more emphasis on the inner life of the monk. Like Barsanuphius he urges the need to cut off one's own will (D1, p. 88; D5, p. 124); and like all the desert monks he stresses the importance of paying attention to or examining oneself (D8, p. 152; D10, p. 170; D11, p. 173), or, as it is put, 'groping about in one's heart' (D4, p. 115; D10, p. 169). This is necessary in order to check and uproot the passions. There is no detailed discussion of the various passions, as in Evagrius or Cassian, but anger and vainglory are mentioned frequently, and one whole discourse (D11) is devoted to 'Cutting off passionate desires immediately before they become rooted habits of mind'. He sees the passions as coming from the devil, but he makes no mention of the demons which are so universally found in the writings of the desert. He warns against judging one's neighbours and particularly against despising them secretly in one's heart (D6, p. 132), and he urges the need to blame oneself and not even to see the faults of others (D8, p. 151). All of this leads to the supreme virtue which is humility. 'Humility protects the soul from all the passions', and for doing this 'nothing is more powerful' (D2, p. 96). Dorotheus does not emphasize purity of heart or *apatheia*, nor does he give a clear picture of the ultimate end of the ascetic life; but he writes frequently of the state of tranquillity, which is reached by cutting off one's own will and resisting the passions.

All of this echoes some if not all of the aspects of the way of the desert, and it is clear throughout that Dorotheus was strongly influenced by the desert monks of Egypt. He refers by name to a number of them – Antony, Agathon, Macarius and several others including Evagrius – and also to 'the Fathers' in general and to the 'Book of the Elders', in such a way that it is sometimes thought that it was Dorotheus himself who collected together the *Apophthegmata*, or *Sayings of the Desert Fathers* of Egypt.

But it is significant that Dorotheus goes beyond this in more than one way. In the first place, he clearly follows his mentor Barsanuphius in his emphasis on the importance within the ascetic life of enduring temptation, hardship and affliction with patience and thanksgiving. Discourse 13 is largely devoted to this subject. He concludes that if a person 'bears the yoke of his trial and affliction with thanksgiving, and puts up a little fight, the help of God will deliver him' (D13, p. 196). This, as we have seen, seems to have been something that was specially emphasized in the Gaza monastery.

Second, and even more significant, Dorotheus refers to and sometimes quotes from not only the sayings of the recognized desert monks but also the writings of Evagrius, of the Cappadocians Basil of Caesarea and Gregory Nazianzen, and once of John Chrysostom.[16] It is clear, therefore, that although he was influenced most by the desert monks of Egypt he had also read and learned from the work of other writers, some of whom were not a part of the desert tradition. Basil is mentioned quite frequently. In particular, he refers specifically to Basil's concern that monks should live a life 'pleasing to God' (D4, p. 110), and discusses this at some length in Discourse 14. This represents an approach to monastic spirituality which differs from that of the way of the desert (see the Additional Note). We may recall that Dorotheus belonged originally not to Egypt but to Antioch in Syria, and may have been particularly aware of the teachings of Basil and others on the communal life. In Dorotheus,

---

16 On Evagrius, pp. 87, 102, 154, 187, 205; on the Cappadocians, pp. 97, 105, 110, 165, 187; on Chrysostom, p. 185.

therefore, we see the way of the desert being further enlarged and adapted, towards the formation of a monastic tradition in which different strands were brought together.

In summary, therefore, we may recall that Gaza was situated at a geographical crossroads, on the highway leading from Egypt to Palestine, Syria and Asia Minor. In the fourth, fifth and sixth centuries it was the centre of a flourishing 'monastic school' which produced the remarkable writings of Abba Isaiah of Sketis, the 'Old Men' Barsanuphius and John, and Dorotheus. It was based firmly and consciously on the way of the desert embodied in the sayings of the 'Fathers' of Egypt. But as time moved on writings and teachings from other places would be circulated, and the monks of Gaza began to incorporate some of the thoughts and practices of other writers into their own monastic life. John Chryssavgis, who edited both the *Discourses* of Isaiah and the *Letters* of Barsanuphius and John, sums it up in this way:

> Abba Isaiah senses that he is part of the tradition of the Desert Fathers, that he has transplanted this tradition from the chosen to an adopted land, and that he is obliged to keep that memory alive in his new homeland. Abba Barsanuphius and his disciples, particularly the gifted Dorotheus, sense that they are part of a new tradition, closely linked to the past and yet at the same time clearly looking to a different experience, and working within a different environment. Abba Isaiah's attitude is backward-looking to the golden age of Egypt; Barsanuphius and Dorotheus are forward-looking to the diverse monastic population that they are addressing and the diverse monastic culture that they are confronting.[17]

The monastery of Thavatha is known to have continued into the seventh century, but probably did not survive for long after the Muslim conquest. Barsanuphius, Seridos and Dorotheus are,

---

17 Chryssavgis, *John Climacus*, p. 9.

however, commemorated in the liturgy of the Eastern Church, and Barsanuphius in the West as well; and their writings are preserved and have been a resource for monastic life in both East and West. And with the help of these writings we can look back at these outstanding spiritual leaders, men of depth, insight and humility, and see how they continued, expanded and developed the way of the desert.

8

Sinai

The third place where the desert tradition was preserved and developed was the region of Sinai, near the southern end of the Sinai peninsula. The mountain known as Mount Sinai, or Jebel Musa, is one of a range of steep, rocky hills in a barren country-side, far from towns or cities, and inhabited, then and now, only by desert Bedouin. A wealth of religious tradition and symbolism has gathered round this mountain. This is believed to be the place where, according to the book of Exodus, Moses encountered God in the Burning Bush, where later the people of Israel experienced the terrifying theophany of God in the midst of the storm, and where Moses received the Law from the hands of God. This was the place to which, according to the book of Kings, the prophet Elijah fled to escape the wrath of the queen, and encountered God in the 'sound of sheer silence'.[1] For the Israelites this was the place in which their life as a people was begun; and for Christians this was a place of unique significance. The origins of the desert movement can be traced to Mount Sinai.

It is not surprising, therefore, that from very early days Christian people visited or went on pilgrimage to Sinai. We are told that a monk named Julian Saba from near Antioch in Syria went there, probably about the middle of the fourth century, believing that 'the deserted character of the place' would give

---

1 In the biblical records Sinai and Horeb appear to be two names for the same mountain. Others identify them as two mountains or peaks adjacent to one another in the same range.

him tranquillity. This was a significant visit because while he was there Julian built the first church at the top of the Holy Mountain.[2] Another monk of Syria, Symeon the Elder, is also reported to have made a pilgrimage to Sinai about the same time.[3] In the following decades the Holy Mountain became an important place of pilgrimage for monks and others from far and wide. The *Sayings of the Desert Fathers* reports that Xoius, a monk of Thebes in Egypt, said that 'one day he went to the mountain of Sinai'.[4] John Moschos tells of various people who paid visits to Sinai: John an anchorite of Palestine, Theodore an anchorite from Jordan, two monks from a monastery near Jerusalem, and a monk of Pontus.[5]

The most famous visitor was Egeria, a lady who during the years 381 to 384 travelled 'from the other end of the earth' – probably either Spain or Gaul – to make a pilgrimage to the Holy Places of Jerusalem and elsewhere, and who wrote a lengthy account of her experiences for her 'beloved sisters' at home. In the course of her travels she visited Mount Sinai, and has left a narrative of her visit and a detailed description of the place.[6] She tells how one Sunday morning, the day after her arrival in Sinai, she made her way, with the guidance of some 'holy men', up to the top of the mountain of Moses, where the Eucharist was celebrated in the little church built by Julian Saba some years earlier. She writes of her enthusiasm at being able to visit all the exact spots where the various events recorded in the book of Exodus were believed to have taken place, including Moses' encounter with God at the Burning Bush, the giving of the tablets of the Law at the summit of the mountain, and all the events that followed. Egeria herself was a passing pilgrim, but she records that there were cells or

2 Theodoret of Cyrrhus, *History of the Monks of Syria*, p. 29.

3 Ibid., p. 65.

4 *Sayings*, Xoius, 2.

5 John Moschos, *The Spiritual Meadow*, 170, 180, 134, 100.

6 *Egeria's Travels*, Chapters 3–4.

hermitages of some 'holy men' who had settled there. 'Late on Saturday,' she reports, 'we arrived at the mountain and came to some cells. The monks who lived in them received us most hospitably, showing us every kindness.' When she reached the top of the mountain, she says, 'Several other presbyters met us too, and all the monks who lived near the mountain, or at least all who were not prevented from coming by their age or their health.' There must have been quite a large number of monks in the area, because on coming down the other side she found a church at the foot of the mountain, 'at the place of the Bush', with a presbyter and a community of monks who gave her hospitality for the night. She also reports that 'there is a little soil at the foot of the mountains, the central one and those around it, and in this the holy monks are always busy planting shrubs, or setting out orchards or vegetable-beds round their cells'.[7] All this suggests that there was quite a well-established monastic community in the area, with constructed cells surrounded by gardens, and with several presbyters and some aged monks who had probably been there for some years.

Other written sources tell of monks living in Sinai. In the *Sayings of the Desert Fathers* we read of Nicon 'who lived on Mount Sinai', of Megethius who 'lived on the river bank at Sinai', and of Joseph of Pelusia who was 'living in Sinai'.[8] In addition there was Silvanus, a Palestinian by birth who after living for a while in Sketis moved to Sinai together with twelve disciples, and later went to Gaza, as we saw earlier. As his move to Sinai was in 380, he and his disciples were probably among the 'holy men' whom Egeria met. One of his disciples was Mark, who opted to stay on in Sinai when the others moved to Gaza.[9] John Moschos also tells of monks living in Sinai, probably at a later period: Abba Zosimos, a Cilician, Sergios who later moved to

7 The quotations in this paragraph are from *Egeria's Travels*, 3:1, 3:4, 4:8, 3:6.

8 *Sayings*, Nicon, 1, Megethius, 2, Cronius, 5.

9 *Sayings*, Silvanus, 4, Mark, 4, 5.

the Rouba desert of Palestine, Orentes, and Abba George, the abbot of a monastery at Sinai who paid a visit to the Church of the Resurrection in Jerusalem.[10] John Moschos himself lived for a time in Sinai, though there is some uncertainty about the date and length of his stay.[11] Two sources, one attributed to a fourth-century monk named Ammonius and the other to Nilus, an influential writer of the early fifth century, tell of marauding attacks by Saracens on the monks of Sinai, but these accounts may come from a later period.[12]

The existence of a sizeable monastic community in Sinai in early days is confirmed by recent archaeological evidence. Uzi Dahari discovered the remains of a large number of monastic settlements in South Sinai in the Byzantine period.[13] The settlements, many of them dating from the fourth century, were mainly communes for small groups of hermits, ranging from two or three up to fifteen or twenty. 'The archaeological remains indicate that colonies of hermit monks composed the main nucleus of monastic activity on the mountain.'[14] The settlements were scattered around the wadis on either side of the twin peaks of Sinai and Horeb, with the larger number on the western side of the hills, the other side from the present monastery of St Catherine, and with chapels at some of the clusters of cells. Dahari identified 62 such settlements, and he reckons that at their peak time, towards the end of the sixth century, there would have been upwards of 600 monks in the area. Their economy was based on the cultivation of fruit and vegetables,

---

10 John Moschos, *The Spiritual Meadow*, 123, 125, 138, 126, 127.

11 The uncertainty centres around the question of the location of the Laura of the Aeliotes, mentioned in *The Spiritual Meadow*, p67 and 134. See Wortley's Introduction to *The Spiritual Meadow*, p. xviii, and Binns, *Ascetics and Ambassadors of Christ*, p. 50 n.49, and references there.

12 See Chryssavgis, *John Climacus*, p. 3; also Paliouras, *The Monastery of St Catherine*, p. 8; Kadloubovsky and Palmer, *Early Fathers from the Philokalia*, pp. 127f.

13 Dahari, *Monastic Settlements in South Sinai in the Byzantine Period: The Archaeological Remains.*

14 Ibid., p. 48.

not on basket-weaving as in other places, and surprisingly he found no sign there of accommodation or arrangements for visiting pilgrims.

Here, then, was a numerous monastic community, apparently mainly living the eremitic or semi-eremitic life in scattered small settlements. Sinai was a place which, because of its biblical associations, attracted monks from far and wide from very early times. It was, indeed, one of the original areas of the desert movement, and could have been included along with the other three areas discussed in Chapters 1 to 3, were it not for the fact that we have no early records describing the life of the community, and we know almost nothing about its leading figures.

The only substantial monastery in Sinai that we know of was the Monastery of St Catherine, as it came to be known. This was an establishment of a coenobitic type located in the valley on the east side of Mount Sinai, at the spot where the Burning Bush was believed to be. As we have seen, at the time of Egeria's visit there was a church on the site, which is said to have been built on the orders of the Empress Helena, wife of the Emperor Constantine. In 556–7 this establishment was enlarged when the Emperor Justinian arranged for the erection of the large fortified structure which forms the basis of the present monastery. It was originally known as the Monastery of the Transfiguration, that being the subject of a huge mosaic in its church; but when the relics of St Catherine of Alexandria, a martyr of perhaps the fourth century, were found to have been miraculously transported to the nearby Mount of St Catherine, the monastery came to be named after her. This is one of the two oldest continuously inhabited Christian monasteries in the world today, the other being Mar Saba in Judea, and it has been an important spiritual centre throughout the centuries down to our own time. With its priceless library of ancient manuscripts in various languages, and an unrivalled collection of ancient icons, it has been the home and base of a number of influential spiritual writers.[15] One of the most significant of these, and one through whom the way of the desert was interpreted and developed, was John Climacus.

John Climacus

Relatively little is known about the early life of John, who was called 'Climacus', or 'John of the Ladder', from the name of his famous work, *The Ladder of Divine Ascent*. He was born probably shortly before the year 579, it is not known where. He appears to have belonged to a noble family and may have been given a good early education. But at the age of sixteen he took himself to the Monastery of the Transfiguration in Sinai. He attached himself to a revered monk named Abba Martyrius as his spiritual father, and lived in a cell for three years under his direction. When John was 20 Abba Martyrius took him to the top of the Holy Mountain to tonsure him as a monk, and then led him to the abbot Anastasius, who immediately recognized him as a future abbot of the monastery. John then went off by himself to a cell at Tholas, at a distance of about five miles to the north of the monastery, where he lived as a hermit for the next 40 years. He seems to have adopted a semi-eremitic life, as he accepted a disciple, Moses, to live with him. In the course of time he became so well known as a person of sanctity that many other monks began to seek his counsel. As a result, some criticized him for speaking too much, whereupon he decided to keep total silence for a year. Sometime during these years he paid a visit to a monastery on the outskirts of Alexandria, and observed the way of life of the monks there. After 40 years his fellow monks brought him to the monastery and, against his will, made him abbot. It is not known how long he lived, but it is thought he may have remained abbot for ten to fifteen years, and died possibly around the year 649.

---

15 For an account of the history and life of the monastery see Paliouras, *The Monastery of St Catherine on Mount Sinai*.

It was during his time as abbot of the monastery that John wrote the *Ladder*. It was written at the request of another John who was abbot of a monastery at Raithou, a place not far away on the Red Sea coast. The *Ladder* is a long work portraying the way of asceticism as a ladder consisting of 30 rungs or steps, which John describes in detail and in a lively style. It is quite different in its presentation and method from other works we have discussed. In each Step John offers not a systematic, reasoned argument or a theoretical discussion but a collection of thoughts, insights, images and illustrations to do with the subject in hand, based on his own experience or on what he had learned directly from others, and presented in such a way as to provide a practical challenge to the reader. Sometimes his style is gnomic, with short sentences like proverbs: 'A man who has heard himself sentenced to death will not worry about the way theatres are run' (S7, p. 143).[16] 'It is hard to keep water in without a dyke; it is harder still to hold in one's tongue' (S11, p. 159). He can wax lyrical in describing a spiritual quality or a demonic passion with a series of graphic phrases. He speaks of prayer in a way reminiscent of a famous poem by George Herbert: 'Prayer is future gladness, action without end, well-spring of virtues, source of grace, hidden progress, food of the soul, enlightenment of the mind, an axe against despair, hope demonstrated, sorrow done away with. It is wealth for monks, treasure of hermits, anger diminished. It is a mirror of progress, a demonstration of success, evidence of one's condition, the future revealed, a sign of glory' (S28, p. 274). Elsewhere he can offer powerful exhortation, or a story about the experience of other monks. He demonstrates deep insight into the working of the passions and the nature of the ascetic life, but always in a way that is practical and relevant to the life of his readers. His aim, according to Kallistos Ware, 'is not to inculcate abstract teaching or impose a formal code of ascetic rules, but to evoke

---

16 The references are to the number of the Step, and the page of the Luibheid and Russell edition of *The Ladder of Divine Ascent*.

in his readers an experience similar to his own'.[17] His work is, in Chryssavgis' words, 'a testimony, not a treatise'.[18]

The ascetical life is seen as a progression. It starts with Renunciation, Detachment and Exile, moves on through the fundamental virtues, Obedience, Penitence, Remembrance of Death, and Sorrow, into a large number of Steps dealing with the passions, then to the higher virtues of Simplicity, Humility and Discernment, finally reaching the aim of Stillness, Prayer, Dispassion and Love.[19] This is a systematic scheme, and Climacus makes it clear that monks should move through it, from one Step to another, towards the top of the ladder. But he is by no means rigid in his thought and presentation, and it is clear that he sees the ascetic life as a whole, and that things which are presented as part of one Step may be relevant to other Steps as well. Love for God is the subject of Step 30, but is urged on his readers in Step 1: 'We should love the Lord as we do our friends' (S1, p. 77). Humility is discussed in Step 25, but is a theme which recurs throughout the work, starting with Step 2: 'You must show humility when you have been condemned' (S2, p. 83).

As John was writing for the monks of the established monastery at Raithou, he does not need to describe the organization of the monastic life, and we learn little from him about life in his own monastery. He also says relatively little about the practical or external features of the ascetic life. 'John usually refrains from giving detailed directions about what food to eat, how much and when, about hours of sleep and the daily programme of manual labour.'[20] He does not discuss the liturgical offices, or methods of prayer. When he writes of withdrawal from the world, eating, sleeping, silence, or solitude, he con-

---

17 Luibheid and Russell, Introduction, p. 8.
18 Chryssavgis, *John Climacus*, p. 163.
19 Based on the discussion in Luibheid and Russell, Introduction.
20 Ibid., p. 9.

centrates on their inner aspects, on the general principles, and on the attitude of mind that is required. Although he is aware of the importance of such practical matters, he does not lay down rules or instructions about them, but emphasizes them by means of precept and sometimes graphic illustration. Frequently he offers brief gnomic summary statements: 'Withdrawal from the world', he writes, 'is a willing hatred of all that is materially prized' (S1, p. 74). 'Control your appetites before they control you' (S14, p. 167). 'Excessive sleep is a bad companion, stealing half a lifetime or more from the lazy man' (S20, p. 197).

Like other writers, John attaches special importance to obedience, the subject of Step 4, to which he devotes more pages than any other. He gives many examples of it in the life of people he has known. In the monastery in Alexandria which he visited, he saw men 'who lived in total obedience for all of fifty years'; and he gives a number of examples from the lives of monks he met there. Obedience is generally assumed to mean obeying the abbot of the monastery, but John nowhere discusses just how the abbot should exercise his authority, or what kind of issues are involved. Obedience is, of course, a practical virtue, but John makes it clear that it is based on an inner attitude of submissiveness, and of obedience not just to the abbot but to Christ. In Step 4 John pre-empts many of the points discussed in more detail later in the book, including the value of silence, the need to 'keep watch on ourselves', the danger of falling to the demons of gluttony and vainglory, and the importance of dispassion or purity of heart. Above all he emphasizes that it is from this inner attitude of obedience that humility is born: 'Humility arises out of obedience'; 'From obedience comes humility' (S4, pp. 109, 114). All this illustrates how Climacus sees the practical life of the monk as a means towards and an expression of the inner qualities which are at the heart of the ascetic life. 'What matters for him', writes Chryssavgis, 'are not external, physical rules of asceticism as such, but the interior disposition, not an uncompromising obedience to ethical rules but humility . . . His purpose is always to indicate the inner spirit and meaning behind and beyond the outward rule.'[21]

When we turn to these inner aspects we find that John Climacus largely echoes and develops what we have found in the desert movement. As with the desert monks, he regards *repentance* as basic to this way of life. The ascetic life starts with repentance, which is 'the renewal of baptism and is a contract with God for a fresh start in life' (S5, p. 121). But it doesn't end there, as one needs to continue to repent throughout one's life. 'Repentance is a way of life',[22] involving 'a cheerful renunciation of every creature comfort' (S7, p. 136). It is 'critical awareness and a sure watch over oneself' (S5, p. 121). With repentance goes compunction and weeping over one's sins. John attaches great importance to tears. To be able to weep tears because of one's sins is a gift of God, but it is a gift given in varying degrees according to one's nature, and one for which one can prepare by 'labouring for' compunction. A special feature of Climacus' discussion is his belief that joy can accompany tears, because 'God secretly brings consolation.' 'I find myself amazed', he writes, 'by the way in which inward joy and gladness mingle with what we call mourning and grief' (S7, p. 141). Nevertheless, compunction must be accompanied by penance, and the acceptance of affliction for one's sins. This penance may be imposed by the abbot or may be undertaken voluntarily, but in some cases it can be very severe, as in John's description of the 'prison' at the monastery in Alexandria in Step 5. It appears that the pardon, forgiveness and release granted by God does not come until one has paid the necessary penalties.

Climacus maintains that if one is truly repentant and sorry for one's sins one will be prepared to endure not only severe penance and affliction but also insults and dishonour, and will

---

21 Chryssavgis, *John Climacus*, p. 25.
22 Ibid., p. 138.

not judge or condemn others for their sins and faults. In saying this he echoes another major feature of the way of the desert. 'Anyone . . . able to see his own faults for what they are would worry about no one else in this life . . . Do not condemn. Not even if your very eyes are seeing something, for they may be deceived . . . To pass judgement on another is to usurp shamelessly a prerogative of God, and to condemn is to ruin one's own soul' (S10, pp. 155f).

To live a life of repentance one needs to be able to recognize one's sins and to diagnose their cause. This requires *discernment*, and this is another of John's major themes, which he discusses at length in Step 26. Discernment means the ability to distinguish between good and evil, to perceive the deceitful tactics of demons that would trap us into sin, to know whether a thought comes from within ourselves, from God, or from the demons, and the willingness to allow God to act within us. Discerning and acknowledging the faults within us requires humility: as Climacus says, 'From humility comes discernment' (S4, p. 114).

Discernment is necessary if we are to guard our hearts against the *passions* and the demons. Like all the desert monks, Climacus attributes the insidious quality of the passions to demonic activity, and draws attention to the need to 'keep watch on ourselves' (S4, p. 110). A large part of his book is made up of a discussion of the various passions. In his identification of them he is obviously indebted to Evagrius, but he extends the latter's list of eight – gluttony, lust, avarice, anger, sadness, acedia, vainglory and pride – to include a number of others: malice, slander, talkativeness, falsehood, insensitivity, fear and blasphemy, while excluding sadness which he regards as being part of despondency or acedia.

He deals with each of these passions, not examining them psychologically and theoretically as Evagrius does, but giving counsel about how they afflict us, and how they can be resisted. For example, in discussing anger he describes it as 'an untimely flaring up of the heart', 'an indication of concealed hatred, of grievance nursed' (S8, p. 146). Anger not resisted leads to 'remembrance of wrongs' and malice or resentment, which is 'a worm in the mind' (S9, p. 152). It 'must be restrained by the chains of meekness, beaten by patience, hauled away by blessed love' (S8, p. 150), and it 'disappears before the fragrance of humility' (S8, p. 146). The way to deal with it is to forget the wrongs, forgive the one who has wronged you, and do some act of kindness for him (S9, p. 153). Interestingly, he also suggests that 'Singing, in moderation, can occasionally ease bad temper' (S8, p. 148). Like other desert writers Climacus pays special attention to vainglory. It is the most insidious of passions, because it comes unawares upon those who have conquered all the others. A vainglorious man is 'apparently honouring God', but 'actually is out to please not God but men' (S22, p. 202). The most devout of people may be secretly seeking human praise while serving God, often not realizing that they are doing so. The only remedy is to keep thinking of one's sins and to remember that we must die (S22, p. 205).

God is not the creator of passions as he is of many natural virtues. These passions are not natural to us, but 'we have taken natural attributes of our own and turned them into passions' (S26, p. 251). We are constantly enticed into doing this by the *demons*. Climacus mentions demons frequently, equating them with the passions or 'thoughts' in a manner characteristic of the desert movement. Monks, he says, must always 'be battling with [their] thoughts' (S4, p. 109), just as they must resist the suggestions and enticements of the demons. Often the reference is to demons in the plural as a collective force for evil, but Climacus also writes of individual demons connected with particular passions, such as the demon of fornication, the demon of avarice or the demon of vainglory. He does not regard demons as beings able to take physical form and mount physical attacks on ascetics: 'he is concerned not with apparitions but with the inward ascetic struggle'. Nevertheless, demons are real, 'basically alien forces, attempting to coerce people into acting against their true selves'.[23] He offers many suggestions about how demons can be outwitted in particular circumstances, including the idea that sometimes they should simply be ignored or laughed at (S14, p. 167; S26, p. 240); but he recognizes that victory over the demons is not finally in one's power, and that sometimes one must 'offer up to God the weakness of [one's] nature' (S15, p. 173). In this struggle all are in need of the grace and help of God.

After the long series of Steps on the subject of the '*logismoi*' and the demons, the *Ladder* concludes with six Steps, numbers 25 to 30, describing the inner state which the monk aims to reach by means of this struggle. These include humility, still-ness, and dispassion or purity of heart, the three elements that make up the 'inner disposition' which is the object or aim of the way of the desert, as it is summarized in Chapter 5. Included along with them are two Steps, on discernment and prayer, which are the final means and requirements for reaching this inner state. In this context *discernment*, discussed earlier, involves not only understanding oneself and other people but also trying to ascertain the will of God (S26, p. 242). *Prayer*, of course, must have a special place in the life of the monks. John Climacus follows the way of the desert in emphasizing the need for unceasing prayer (S26, p. 241; S.28, pp. 277f), but develops his teaching on prayer beyond what we find in the literature of the desert monks. His instruction, 'Do not form sensory images during prayer', and his statement that God 'grants the prayer of him who prays' (S28, p. 279) are reminiscent of Evagrius. And Climacus follows Barsanuphius in attaching particular importance to short prayers using the name of Jesus. He mentions this three times, once using the phrase 'Jesus Prayer' (S15, p. 178; S21, p. 200; S27, pp. 269f), and on one of these occasions he seems to suggest that the name of Jesus can be invoked

---

23 Chryssavgis, *John Climacus*, pp. 174f.

along with one's breathing, in a way that was developed later in the Orthodox tradition.[24]

The qualities of humility, stillness and dispassion are discussed as three separate Steps, but it is clear from the way Climacus writes that they are in fact interrelated and bound up together. Each one helps to produce the other. All the desert writers regard *humility* as the highest virtue, and Climacus is no exception. It is 'the mark of the perfect' (S25, p. 222). It is the best and ultimately the only way of overcoming the demons. Humility leads to dispassion or purity of heart. 'If you wish to fight against the passions, take humility as your ally' (S25, p. 228). Along with humility goes *stillness* or *hesychia*. This can refer to the quiet life led by solitaries or hermits, but also to the inner state of tranquillity which is reached by those who by their humility have subdued the passions. Stillness can be achieved by those living in a coenobium but is in fact attained by very few. 'Stillness is worshipping God unceasingly and waiting on Him' (S27, p. 269). And along with these two there is *apatheia*, dispassion or *purity of heart*, which is 'attained by stillness' (S15, p. 176). Climacus describes this in Step 29 as 'a heaven of the mind within the heart, which regards the artifice of demons as a contemptible joke'. Someone who is dispassionate is 'enraptured, like someone already in heaven' and 'wholly united with God'. 'To have dispassion is to have the fullness of love, by which I mean the complete indwelling of God in those who, through dispassion, are pure of heart for they shall see God' (S26, p. 160).

For Climacus, as for all the desert monks, this inner state, made up of humility, stillness and purity of heart, is the object of the ascetic life; but it does not end there, because this state produces love of God, which is the ultimate end. In discussing this Climacus is at his most passionate and distinctive. The ascetic life is not simply a stony discipline, a cold rational

---

24 On Climacus' use of the name of Jesus in prayer, see especially Luibheid and Russell, Introduction, pp. 43ff.

pursuit. It is impelled throughout by a fervent desire for God, an ardent longing to live with God and be united to God. This is the aim of the ascetic life. 'The ascetic sets out on the long road of spiritual struggle with a view to attaining love.'[25] John speaks of ascetics he has known 'whose flaming urge for God was limitless. They generated fire by fire, love by love, desire by desire' (S27, p. 263). 'There are some', he says, 'who undertake this holy way of life because of a delight in, a thirst for the love and sweetness of God' (S27, p. 265). The last brief Step is devoted to this theme. It speaks of a love which is 'an abyss of illumination, a fountain of fire, bubbling up to inflame the thirsty soul. It is the condition of angels, and the progress of eternity' (S30, p. 289). This love is not only *agape* but *eros*, a passionate desire; and Climacus does not demur from likening this to the love of human lovers, or of a mother for her child. Moreover, this love is never-ending, never completely satisfied, but grows and progresses even beyond this life. To reach this love of God, to be filled with the fire of this love, was the purpose for which all the rigours and hardships of the ascetic life were undertaken with willingness and hope.

It will be clear from the above that in all that he wrote John Climacus was pursuing, and at the same time developing, the way of the desert. Although he spent his monastic life in Sinai, a place which attracted monks from far and wide including Asia Minor and Syria, he shows no sign of having been influenced by the monastic traditions of Basil or of the Syrian monks. But he was indebted to the monks of Egypt, as he demonstrates by quoting their thoughts, by mentioning Antony and Arsenius by name, and by referring to Sketis, and on one occasion to Pachomius' monastery at Tabennesi. He shows that he was aware of the monasticism of the Judean desert by telling at length of John the Sabbaite, who had lived in the monastery of St Sabas in Judea (S4, pp. 115ff). He was also influenced by those who

---

25 Chryssavgis, *John Climacus*, p. 204.

followed the first monks in the desert tradition, making explicit reference to both Evagrius and Cassian.

And, living as he did in the desert of Sinai, he was inevitably conscious of the biblical desert tradition. He mentions Moses several times, and refers also to Elijah and John the Baptist. In the last Step of the *Ladder*, he writes that 'a man commingled with the love of God reveals in his body, as if in a mirror, the splendour of his soul, a glory like that of Moses when he came face to face with God' (S30, p. 288). John Climacus, this last representative of the desert movement, reached back, like all those who came before him, to the biblical desert tradition, which was its source, its origin, and its inspiration.

In conclusion

We may conclude, therefore, by recalling that the desert movement was from first to last a biblical movement. Although there are parallels between early Christian monasticism and the life of some pagan philosophers, the way of the desert is unique in that it was deeply grounded in the Bible. This is true of all areas and all aspects of the movement. The sayings and stories we have are full of biblical references, as David Burton-Christie has shown.[26] All the desert monks spent much of their time reciting and meditating on the Psalms of the Old Testament. Many of the accounts of miracles performed by the leading figures of the desert were told in such a way as to bring miracles of the Bible to mind.[27] Shenoute in Upper Egypt regarded himself, and was regarded by others, as something of an Old Testament prophet. The monks who came to the Judean desert did so partly because it called to mind events of the Old Testament and the lives of John the Baptist and Jesus. Cassian's writings are filled with biblical references, and even the philosophic Evagrius drew up

---

26 Burton-Christie, *The Word in the Desert*.
27 See Ward's Introduction to *The Lives of the Desert Fathers*, p. 44.

a huge list of biblical quotations which monks could use in their struggle with the demons.[28] Sinai was a place of pilgrimage and of multiple monastic settlements because of its strong biblical associations. And as we have seen throughout the preceding chapters, all the monks were conscious that they were following in the footsteps of Elijah and John the Baptist, the heroes of the biblical desert tradition.

We should also recall that the desert movement grew out of this rich soil of the Bible at a particular time and place. We have seen how it was pioneered in the third, fourth and fifth centuries in the three desert areas of Lower Egypt, Upper Egypt and Judea, but was later applied to monastic life elsewhere, principally in southern Gaul, Gaza and Sinai. Here the way of the desert was developed in new ways, but the same principal features which characterized it from the beginning were continued and preserved. The desert movement was, however, a movement of its time, and did not continue for very long in its original form. Although monasteries of different kinds still exist today at Antony's 'Mountain' in Lower Egypt, at Shenoute's centre and other sites in Upper Egypt, at Sabas' Great Laura and three or four other sites in Judea, and at the Holy Mountain of Moses at Sinai, most of the original monasteries disappeared in the years following the Muslim conquest in the seventh century. Nevertheless, the movement has bequeathed to subsequent generations the rich corpus of written records which have been the focus of our study. Through these, and through the remembrance of the saintly men and women who were part of this movement, the way of the desert came to have a significant influence on the monastic life and the spirituality of the church in both the East and the West in later years, and is still an inspiration to people today.

---

28 Evagrius, *Antirrheticus*.

Epilogue: Through Modern Eyes

The monks of the desert lived in a very different age, culture and climate from ours, and we cannot simply adopt their way of life or their spiritual outlook and make it ours. It has not, therefore, been the purpose of this book to identify and describe a 'spirituality of the desert' which can be appropriate and relevant to the twenty-first century, but simply to describe the various aspects of the way of the desert which characterized the desert movement of those early centuries. In this Epilogue, however, it may be appropriate to draw attention to some aspects of the movement which seem to stand out when we view it from a modern perspective.

Difficulties

To begin with there are three aspects which will probably appear to people of today to be strange, and difficult to understand and accept: the extreme asceticism, the belief in demons, and the accounts of miracles.

Asceticism can be defined as the voluntary acceptance of severe abstinence and austerity as a form of spiritual discipline. For many Christians in the modern world, who believe that the good things of life are gifts of God to be enjoyed with thankfulness and that it is right to try to limit pain and discomfort, this is something hard to understand. But in the ancient world ascetic practice of one kind or another was a common feature of religious life, pagan, Jewish and Christian. For the monks

of the desert it took the form of living with very few possessions, renouncing sexual relations, restricting the amount and
the kind of food they ate, and limiting their sleep. These were
common features of the way of the desert, practised in varying
ways in different places, but shared by all the monks of the
desert movement.

Why did they choose to live in this way? They did so for
several reasons. One was that by doing so they were following
the example and the teaching of Christ. Jesus left home and
family, and lived in celibacy and with nowhere to lay his head,
and voluntarily accepted the way of suffering and death. It was
right and appropriate that his followers should do the same.
And he had taught that those who wished to be perfect should
give up their possessions, and live as 'eunuchs for the kingdom
of heaven'. This provided a pattern and model for the ascetical
life. Abba Aaron in the desert of Aswan explained, 'Since God
took it upon himself to suffer on our behalf, it is right that we
too should have every kind of affliction.'[1]

Another reason was that it helped them to fulfil their principal aim of focusing their attention on God and growing in love
for God. In so far as they were attached to worldly possessions,
enjoyed worldly pleasures, pampered and indulged their bodies
or yielded to their physical appetites, it was impossible to give
their whole attention to God. Denying pleasures and creaturely
comforts helped them to overcome the passions which drew
them away from God, and to reach towards the inner state of
humility, stillness and purity of heart which was their object.
Their ascetic practices enabled them to sever earthly attach-
ments and so be free to focus on God.

A third reason for living an ascetic life arose from their conviction that this earthly life should be seen as a preparation for
the heavenly life. Human beings were destined for heaven, to
live like the angels in the presence of God. The heavenly life
was not bodiless and disincarnate but life with a purified body,

1 Paphnutius, *Histories of the Monks*, 94, p. 119.

purged of all excess and of all bodily appetites and passions. The ascetic life was based on the belief that it was possible, in the course of this present life, to prepare one's body for heaven and begin to live the heavenly life. To do so one had not to reject the body as evil or to ignore it as unnecessary and unimportant, but to discipline and train it for its future state. As Peter Brown has shown, the desert monks were not denying the body, but fine-tuning it by cutting out all but the bare essentials for its existence. By their asceticism, and by entering the inner state to which it led, the desert monks were able to share the life of the angels while still living on earth.

It follows from this that ascetic practices were not to be undertaken for their own sake. To do so would lead only to pride, which was a denial of God and the most serious of the passions. This was a constant danger and temptation in the desert. In some places, particularly in Syria, monks adopted extreme ascetical practices, such as wearing heavy chains of iron, shutting themselves up in tiny enclosed spaces, or living without any shelter, but there was little of this among the monks of the desert. The leading figures in all areas of the desert movement warned against excessive asceticism because this could easily lead to pride. Moderate asceticism, however, could lead to humility and purity of heart.

That is to say, asceticism, for all its strangeness to the modern mind, was seen by the desert monks not as something negative, not mainly as a denial and a restriction, but as a way of enabling a fuller and purer inner life, of savouring even now something of the angelic life, and of preparing for the life of heaven.

Demons

Throughout the literature of the desert there are references to demons. These were believed to be evil beings, subservient to their master the devil, whose intention was to deceive human beings and lead them away from God and into evil ways. The demons had their home and dwelling place in the desert: they regarded it as their own territory and resented it when monks came there to do battle with them. Certain places were occupied by large numbers of them, such as the hill of Castellium in the wilderness of Judea, from where Sabas dispelled them. The demons were not physical beings with material bodies, but they could appear in various forms, as fierce animals, as seductive women or as black Ethiopians.

The activities of the demons are described in a variety of ways. Although they were not physical beings they are sometimes described as mounting physical attacks on a monk. Antony is said to have been fiercely battered by demons who tried to frighten him;[2] Evagrius in the desert was 'beaten by demons and sorely tempted by them times without number',[3] and Abba Isaac in the remote wilderness of Upper Egypt was terrified at the sounds of demons roaring in the night and assuming fantastical shapes.[4] Other stories, especially in the more hagiographical writings, tell of people possessed or afflicted with illness by demons, in much the same way as we read of in the Gospels.

The activity of the demons, however, is spoken of more often in psychological than in physical terms, especially in some of the later writers. It was the demons that tried to introduce evil 'thoughts' or passions into the minds of the monks, and indeed they were often identified with the passions. David Brakke, in his important study of demonic activity, writes that in the writings of Evagrius, 'The thoughts are synonymous with the demons and, at times synonymous with the passions.'[5] Sometimes demons were connected with particular passions, so that Evagrius and others could speak of the 'demon of fornication' or the 'demon of gluttony'. The demons did not create the

---

2 *Life of Antony*, 8, 9.
3 Palladius, *Lausiac History*, 38.
4 Paphnutius, *Histories of the Monks*, 95.
5 Brakke, *Demons and the Making of the Monk*, p. 54.

passions, but they attempted, in all sorts of subtle and devious ways, to entice the monks to allow the passions into their hearts, and so lose their purity of heart.

It was because the demonic activity was so insidious that the monks needed to have great discernment, and to 'pay attention to themselves'. They had constantly to be aware of the presence of the demons, and always to remember that even their apparently good intentions might be suggested by demons in order to deceive them and lead them astray, and that visions or dreams which seemed to come from God might be demonic deceptions. The inner life of the monk, therefore, had to be one of constant vigilance. The struggle against the demons went on throughout one's life.

Nevertheless, the monk could take courage from the knowledge that the ultimate power did not lie with the devil and his army of demons but with God, who had overcome them through Christ. Confronted by the name of Christ, or with the sign of the cross, the demons were powerless. Although the demons had to be resisted, they could also be treated with contempt, and could indeed be mocked and laughed at. And the supreme Christian virtue of humility was a weapon which the demons could not withstand.

Belief in demons and their insidious activities was part of the culture of the time, but it falls strangely on the ears of people living in the scientific and rationalistic world of today. It can be seen, however, as a way of representing some important aspects of the nature of evil, which can still be meaningful today. On the one hand, the belief that the demons existed in the world independently of human beings was a way of representing the fact that the power of evil was an objective reality, existing outside and beyond human minds, seeking to deceive, invade, mislead and destroy human beings. On the other hand, the belief that the demons were able to insinuate themselves into human minds and hearts in the form of evil thoughts and passions represented the fact that evil was not only an objective force existing outside us, but a subjective reality deeply embedded in our hearts. The belief in demons also made it easy to understand that evil was a force which had to be resisted and struggled against, but which had been conquered by Christ, and could be overcome in his name.

Miracles

The literature of the desert contains a large number of stories of miracles performed by holy monks, in a way that seems strange to us. As Sister Benedicta Ward has said, 'One of the elements in the whole literature of early monasticism which is perhaps especially unfamiliar to the modern reader is the account it gives of miracles.' These miracles, she indicates, are mainly of three different types.[6] First, there are miracles of clairvoyance. Pachomius in Upper Egypt and Barsanuphius in Gaza in particular were said to have been able to see into other people's minds, and to foretell events, in a way which facilitated their work of spiritual direction. Second, there are miraculous healings, including exorcisms to cure people possessed by demons. Stories of this kind are not common in the *Sayings of the Desert Fathers*, but occur more frequently in the writings of Cyril of Scythopolis and John Moschos. Third, there are 'nature miracles', such as taming wild beasts, receiving bread from heaven, miraculously finding water or causing rain, and more extraordinary deeds such as crossing a river dry-shod and even making the sun stand still. Some of these occurrences are witnessed to directly by the writers concerned from their own experience.[7]

Many of these miracles are reported in ways that recall miracle stories of the Bible – the bread brought to Elijah, the water from the rock supplied by Moses, and the exorcisms and cures

---

6 See the classification in Ward's Introduction to *The Lives of the Desert Fathers*, pp. 39ff; and Binns, *Ascetics and Ambassadors of Christ*, pp. 218ff.

7 Cyril, *Life of Sabas*, 164, 187.

of the Gospels. By framing their accounts in this way the desert writers were demonstrating again the continuity of the desert movement with the biblical tradition.

The significance of the miracles is principally that they demonstrate the power and activity of God. In the person of a dedicated ascetic monk God was close at hand, and able to do wonderful things, just as he had done in biblical times. It was this, not the extraordinary or visible aspect of the miracle, that was important. They were performed not in order to produce a sense of wonder, but as signs of the power of God. They were signs also of the holiness of the miracle worker. With their disciplined ascetic practice and their quest for purity of heart, the monks of the desert were attempting to live the life of heaven. In them some of the powers of heaven had come to earth. The taming of the wild beasts, the casting out of demons and the cure of illnesses were a fulfilment of prophecies of the blessedness of the end time, such as we find in Isaiah 35. They were signs of the breaking in of the kingdom of heaven into human life, and the restoration of Paradise brought about by Christ.

Such stories fail to impress the modern mind in the way they did in earlier times. They do, however, point to an acute awareness of the nearness of the presence of God, and of the reality of God's power over the whole of creation. They show how the minds of devout people of old were not enclosed in the mundane material world, but were open to the wonder of the unexpected and the unusual, to the possibility of incomprehensible occurrences, and things beyond our ken. They testify to an attitude to reality which has been lost to the rational scientific mind, to an awareness that since God is near anything can happen, and so to a dimension of life which is more readily open to the holy.

Fundamental features

It remains only to say a few words about two things that can be seen as the principal and fundamental features which characterize the desert movement as a whole, and which taken together make it unique in Christian history.

Radical and subversive

First, the way of the desert was radical in the original sense of that word: it went to the root of what Christianity was believed to be about. The desert monks took as their basis not only the tradition and example of the men of the desert in the Bible, but also the demanding and challenging aspects of the teaching and example of Jesus. Words of Jesus which most Christians have regarded either as not to be understood literally or as not applicable to everyone, were taken seriously and literally and applied to themselves – sayings such as the invitation to the rich young ruler to 'Sell all that you have and distribute to the poor, and come follow me' (Luke 18.22); or 'Whoever of you does not renounce all that he has cannot be my disciple' (Luke 14.33); or 'If anyone comes to me and does not hate his own father and mother and wife and children . . . cannot be my disciple' (Luke 14.26). The words of Jesus that 'There are some who have made themselves eunuchs for the sake of the kingdom of heaven' (Matt. 19.12) were interpreted as an invitation to celibacy; and the example of Jesus who 'had nowhere to lay his head' (Matt. 8.20) was taken by some as a pattern of monastic homelessness.

They also took very seriously Jesus' teaching that in order to enter the kingdom of heaven it was necessary to humble oneself like a little child, and his saying that those who humbled themselves would be exalted (Matt. 8.3f; Luke 14.11). In the light of this they took humility to be the supreme and essential Christian virtue. It was necessary in every situation and in relation to every other person to humble oneself, and to regard each other person, no matter how apparently despicable and wicked, as better than oneself.

Along with humility there went a radical quest for purity of heart. It was only the pure in heart that would be able to stand in God's presence and look upon the face of God (Ps. 24.4; Matt. 5.8). To reach purity of heart one needed to go to the root of the impurities, the evil and self-centred thoughts, motives and desires which lurked often unrecognized within one's heart. One's heart and mind had to be examined constantly, rigorously and radically, so that every twist and turn of selfish passion could be exposed and uprooted. One had to be always aware of one's own sins and faults, and if one wanted them to be forgiven one had always to be ready not only to forgive the offences of others but to ignore and cover them.

This meant taking a radical view of oneself as a person without rights. The monk had no rights to possessions, to comfort, to the respect, attention or admiration of others, or to a position of importance in society or the monastic community. To regard oneself in this way and to live accordingly was extremely difficult and demanding. There was always a temptation to insist on one's rights, if not outwardly at least secretly within one's own mind, and to resent any usurpation of them. To follow the desert way one had constantly to guard against what Barsanuphius of Gaza repeatedly called 'pretence to rights'.

Living in this way, with this kind of attitude to oneself and to other people, was only possible in so far as one had abandoned and renounced the world, and the ordinary ways and attitudes of society. The desert monks regarded themselves as no longer citizens of this world, but citizens of heaven, living not in the present world but in the next. In this way of life the values and assumptions of society were turned upside-down, and the criteria by which behaviour and thoughts were normally judged were stood on their head.

That is to say, the desert movement was and is subversive. By introducing into the world a bit of the life of heaven, it contravened and challenged the conventional assumptions about the ultimate meaning of life and the fundamental values of society. By anticipating the kingdom of God it stood at odds with much of common life. It was not a movement designed to be popular, to attract many followers and to become an accepted part of human society. It was not proposing a way of life which could be followed by people generally. It stood out as radically different, pointing to a different reality, and in doing so it challenged and still challenges ordinary people, not to follow it precisely but to rethink their lives in the light of it.

Interiority

The second unique characteristic of the way of the desert was its focus on interiority, on the need to pay special attention to one's inner life. In order to do this one needed a measure of solitude and silence, as a means of shutting out external concerns. One had to go into the secret inner chamber of the heart and shut the door. In all areas of the desert movement there were solitaries, men and women anchorites or hermits, people who withdrew completely from other people for a longer or shorter time, and even in the coenobia and the semi-eremitic monastic communities there was always an emphasis on periods of solitude and silence. The monk sitting alone in his or her cell, engaged in manual labour, repeating prayers and chanting psalms, and spending hours of the night in silent vigil, was the true heart and centre of the desert movement.

The main aim of these monks, especially in their times of solitude and silence, was to overcome and exclude the evil 'thoughts' or passions inspired by the demons, so as to reach an inner state of humility, stillness and purity of heart. They did this by 'paying attention to themselves': examining their inner heart and their secret motives with rigour and utter honesty.

This emphasis on interiority differentiated the desert movement from the monastic and ascetic life practised elsewhere.[8]
All forms of monasticism involved withdrawing from the ordinary life of the world, practising asceticism in various ways and
degrees, and engaging in a life of prayer; but not all had the
focus on the inner life that we find in the desert. The important
and influential monastic movement inspired and led by Basil of
Caesarea in Cappadocia placed the emphasis on living 'a life
pleasing to God' through love and service to others, and on
obedience to the scriptural commandments. Basil himself was
strongly opposed to monks living in solitude. The monks of
Syria placed the main emphasis on a life of celibacy and asceticism. In neither of these areas, however, do we find the same
special priority given to the inner life.

It is important to realize that this inner focus of the desert
monks was not an exclusive, narrowly individualistic thing. It
did not cut the monks off from a concern for other people.
Instead it enabled them to relate to others and to God with
truth and utter selflessness, to put into practice proper relationships between people, and so establish the fundamental basis
for genuine community. By paying attention to their inner selves
they were reminded that they themselves were sinful people, in
need of repentance and of the grace and mercy of God. They
knew that they were part of 'torn and broken humanity',[9] and
in laying their little bit of this humanity before God they were
helping to guard the world against the powers of evil. It was
said at the time about the desert monks of Egypt that 'it is clear
to all who dwell there that through them the world is kept in
being, and that through them too human life is preserved and
honoured by God', and that 'the people depend on the prayers
of these monks as if on God himself'.[10] Their withdrawal from

---

8 See the Additional Note, pp. 226ff.

9 This phrase is taken from Ward's Introduction to *The Lives of the Desert Fathers*, p. 13, where this point is further developed.

10 *The Lives of the Desert Fathers*, Prologue, 10.

the world to live the life of heaven in penitence, humility and purity of heart, was not done out of a careless disregard for the world and for others, but out of a concern for the world at a deeper and more fundamental level than that of practical action, the level of heroic struggle against the power of evil in the place where it has its primary operation, the human heart. The object of the interiority of the desert monks was not self-fulfilment but utter loss of self for the sake of God and of other people.

The ultimate reason for engaging in this internal struggle was that it enabled the love of God to grow and flourish within them. The monks of this movement, both those in the original desert places and those in other places who followed them in the way of the desert, were men and women inspired by an intense inner desire for God, before which everything else paled into insignificance, and every hardship was worth enduring. Their aim was to reach towards God, to be drawn closer to God, to find and know and love God, and to overcome everything that stood in the way of their movement towards God. Their goal was to come to that state where, in the words of John Cassian, 'every love, every desire, every effort, every understanding, every thought of ours, everything that we live, that we speak, that we breathe, will be God'.[11] In their pursuit of this goal the monks of the desert movement have provided the basic pattern and model for the contemplative way which has influenced and guided Christian spirituality throughout the centuries.

---

11 Cassian, *Conferences*, 10.7.2.

Additional Note: The Monastic Movements of Cappadocia and of Syria

There are two other areas where monastic movements developed during the period from the fourth to the seventh centuries: Cappadocia in modern Turkey, and Syria, an area comprising both modern Syria and Iraq. It may be asked why they have not been included in this study of the desert movement. A brief look at each of these should provide an answer.

The monastic movement in Cappadocia

This was led by Basil of Caesarea, one the three famous Cappadocian Fathers. Basil was a bishop and a distinguished theologian as well as a founder of monasteries. Born into a Christian family and educated in rhetoric and philosophy, he spent some time living an ascetic life in relative isolation, before becoming a bishop and church leader. The monastic movement he established had its own character, spelled out by him in a body of ascetic writings, which included a series of 'Rules' as well as homilies and discourses. Since Basil was a church leader concerned with the whole Christian community, some of his writings are addressed to Christian people in general, and it is not always clear when he is writing only for monks.

Basil's monasteries had much in common with the desert movement. He too required separation from one's family,

renouncement of the world and of worldly possessions, a measure of ascetic practice, observing times of silence and stillness,
engaging in manual labour, practising constant prayer, obedience to a spiritual director, resisting the passions, and seeking
humility. But the purpose of the monastic life was expressed
differently. The aim was to grow in love for God, to live a life
that was pleasing to God, and to love and serve other people.
To do this one had to concentrate on the scriptures and to
obey the commandments they contained. All the aspects of the
monastic life had to serve these ends.

So it was that although he demanded renunciation this did
not involve withdrawal into remote desert places. 'Because
of the paramount obligation of charity towards one's fellow
man, Basilian coenobia are established in towns instead of in
desert wastes.'[1] The important thing was the life of the monastic community and its relation to the community outside. He
advocated asceticism, including 'a life without house, homeland
or possessions'[2] and regulating and limiting one's eating,[3] but
his was a moderate asceticism which was to be undertaken not
individually but along with others. Its aim was to enable self-
control and so to strengthen the bonds of the community. The
importance of the interior work of the individual was 'so that
it could be expressed usefully in visible behaviour'.[4] Similarly,
spiritual direction must take place in the context of the community. 'Repentance, confessing and healing took place within
the community, the "weaker" confessed to the "stronger", so
bearing one another's burdens.'[5] A monastery should be 'a
hive of activity – weaving, shoemaking, building, carpentry,
metalwork and especially agriculture';[6] but this manual labour
should be undertaken for the good of other people, and the

---

1 Wagner, Introduction to *St Basil: Ascetical Works*, p. xi.
2 Basil, *An Introduction to the Ascetical life*, in Wagner, ibid., p. 10.
3 Long Rules 18, 19, in Wagner, ibid., pp. 274ff.
4 Rousseau, *Basil of Caesarea*, p. 224.
5 Ibid., p. 215.
6 Ibid., p. 203.

produce was to be given away to the poor. Basil makes mention of the passions, but does not analyse them or reflect on how they insinuate themselves into the human heart, and does not regard the struggle against them as a primary aim of the ascetic life. He speaks not of purity of heart, or of *apatheia*, but of *enkrateia*: self-control or continence, the purpose of which was to achieve good behaviour in accordance with the commandments. The lover of God, he says, 'retires to God, driving out the passions which tempt him to incontinence, and abides in the practices which conduce to virtue'.[7] As Augustine Holmes says in his fine study of Basil's Rules, 'In the Evagrian system there is a profound treatment of the ascetic life and the struggle against the passions, but the dynamism is always towards contemplation. For Basil the accent on the practical is stronger and more orientated to community.'[8] And for him even silence or stillness was a corporate thing. It was 'a quiet to be shared: it had a social effect, and the closeness of God's presence was thus made visible to all'.[9]

All this points to a difference of emphasis and purpose from that of the desert movement. This is shown most clearly in Basil's polemic against the solitary life in his well-known Long Rule 7. Here he argues that people should not live in solitude, because in doing so they have deprived themselves of the opportunity to love their neighbour and so fulfil the commandment of Christ. This represents a profoundly different approach to the ascetical life from that of the desert movement. As has been argued in Chapter 5 and the Epilogue of this book, it fails to recognize that a concern for the life of the world can be lived out in a very real, important and profound way through engaging in the solitary struggle against the powers of evil.

Clearly, Basil's approach represents a deeply Christian way of living the ascetic life, and it has had a very great and signifi-

---

7 From a letter of Basil, quoted in Rousseau, *Basil of Caesarea*, p. 227.
8 Augustine Holmes, *A Life Pleasing to God*, p. 64.
9 Rousseau, *Basil of Caesarea*, p. 227.

cant influence on the development of monasticism in both East and West. But it is an approach which, in spite of obvious similarities, differs considerably from the way of the desert, both in its aim and purpose and in its practice. Basil emphasized life in the monastic community, and love and service for others in the wider community, rather than interiority, the struggle against the passions, or purity of heart, which were defining characteristics of the desert movement.

The Monks of Syria

In *A History of the Monks of Syria*, Theodoret of Cyrrhus, a fifth-century bishop and theologian, tells of a large number of monks living in the areas round about Antioch. Most of these lived close to towns or villages, but a few were in the neighbouring desert. 'The typical habitat of Theodoret's holy men was neither town nor desert but the intermediate region of the fringe of inhabited areas.'[10] Most were individuals living alone, but there is some evidence of monasteries, such as that established by a monk named Macrianus in a desert region.[11] The way of life of most of them was one of 'extreme, sometimes histrionic asceticism'.[12] Some wore iron chains weighing up to 120 pounds; some lived in cells too small to stretch out or stand up in; some lived all the year in the open air without shelter; some immured themselves in tiny spaces; some, such as the famous Symeon Stylites, lived at the top of columns; and others afflicted themselves with other severe austerities. Generally they took very little sleep and a minimum of food. Since they lived on the edge of towns, many people came out to see them and to gaze with wonder at their ascetic practices. In Theodoret's account there are no stories of people coming to ask for 'a word' or to seek spiritual counsel, as they came

---

10 Theodoret of Cyrrhus, *A History of the Monks of Syria*, p. 57 n.1.
11 Ibid., pp. 37ff.
12 Ibid., Introduction, p. xxviii.

to the monks of the desert. What he describes is 'a spiritual life that was actually visible, and a direct object of veneration'.[13] There are some references to a love for God and a desire for purity of soul, but generally he has little to say about the inner life of the monks.

Further east, in Mesopotamia, there grew up what has been called a native Syrian ascetic tradition. Here there were men and women who belonged to a group of people known as the 'Sons and Daughters of the *Qyama*', or Covenant, who had taken a vow of chastity and lived a consecrated life. As one early Syriac text says, 'All the *qyama* of men and women were modest and decorous, and they were holy and pure, and they dwelt singly and modestly without spot.'[14] They did not, however, live apart, but 'formed the core of the local church community'.[15] Some of these consecrated ones were known by a word meaning the 'single ones', individuals who were unmarried and celibate, and committed to single-minded devotion to Christ.[16] Their ideals and way of life are described in the fourth-century Syriac *Book of Steps*, which sets out the difference between them and ordinary Christians. At this early stage, however, this ascetic movement was not a form of monasticism but was what Sebastian Brock has called 'proto-monasticism'. There were no monasteries to which men and women withdrew. It appears that sometimes members of the Covenant movement lived in small associations 'forming house communities or informal religious communes'; but these were 'essentially a feature of town and village life, a far remove from the Egyptian monastic model of *anachoresis* or withdrawal from town and village to the desert'.[17] When during the fifth century monasticism did

---

13 Ibid., Introduction, p. xxxiv.
14 Quoted in Murray, *Symbols of Church and Kingdom*, p. 14.
15 Brock, *The Luminous Eye*, p. 135.
16 For a discussion of the meaning of this term see Brock, ibid., pp. 136f.
17 Ibid., p. 136.

develop in this area it did so through Egyptian influence, and was not a native development.[18]

This ascetic movement in Syria, particularly the developments in Mesopotamia, eventually had considerable influence on Christian monastic spirituality, especially in the Orthodox Church, largely through the writings of such leading figures as Aphrahat, Ephrem, and Isaac of Nineveh. But, like the monastic movement in Cappadocia, it arose independently of, and was in important ways very different from, the desert movement.

---

18 Kitchen and Parmentier, Introduction to *The Book of Steps*, p. xvi; Brock, *The Luminous Eye*, pp. 131f.

Bibliography

Primary texts in translation

Athanasius, *Life of Antony*, trans. R. C. Gregg, Mahwah, NJ, Paulist Press, 1980.

Barsanuphius and John, *Letters*, 2 Vols, trans. J. Chryssavgis, Washington DC, CUA Press, 2007.

Besa, *The Life of Shenoute*, trans. D. N. Bell, Kalamazoo, MI, Cistercian Publications, 1983.

Cyril of Scythopolis, *The Lives of the Monks of Palestine*, including the *Lives* of Euthymius, Sabas, John the Hesychast, Cyriacus, Theodosius, Theognius, and Abraamius, trans. R. M. Price, Kalamazoo, MI, Cistercian Publications, 1991.

Dorotheos of Gaza, *Discourses and Sayings*, trans. E. P. Wheeler, Kalamazoo, MI, Cistercian Publications,1991.

Egeria's Travels, trans. J. Wilkinson, Warminster, Aris and Phillips, 1999.

Epistle of Barnabas, trans. J. B. Lightfoot, in *The Apostolic Fathers*, London, Macmillan, 1926, pp. 239–88.

Eusebius, *The Ecclesiastical History*, Vol. 1, trans. Kirsopp Lake, Loeb Christian Classics, London, Heinemann, 1926.

Evagrius, *Antirrheticus* (Selections), trans. M. O'Laughlin, in V. L. Wimbush (ed.), *Ascetic Behavior in Greco-Roman Antiquity*, Minneapolis, Fortress Press, 1990.

Evagrius, *The Praktikos*, and *Chapters on Prayer*, trans. J. E. Bamberger, Kalamazoo, MI, Cistercian Publications, 1981.

Evagrius, *The Greek Ascetic Corpus*, trans. R. E. Sinkewicz, including *The Foundations of the Monastic Life*, *To Eulogius*, *On the Vices*, *On the Eight Thoughts*, *Praktikos*, *To Monks*, *To a Virgin*, *On Thoughts*, and *Chapters on Prayer*, Oxford, Oxford University Press, 2003.

The Gospel of Thomas, in B. Layton, trans., *The Gnostic Scriptures*, London, SCM Press, 1987, pp. 376–99.

Isaiah of Scetis, *Ascetic Discourses,* trans. J. Chryssavgis and P. Penkett, Kalamazoo, MI, Cistercian Publications, 1991.

Jerome, *Life of Hilarion*, in Carolinne White, *Early Christian Lives*, London, Penguin, 1998.

Jerome, *Life of Paul of Thebes*, in Carolinne White, *Early Christian Lives*, London, Penguin, 1998.

John Cassian, *The Conferences*, trans. and Preface Colm Luibheid. Copyright © 1985 Colm Luibheid. Mahwah, NJ, Paulist Press. Reprinted by permission of Paulist Press, Inc.

John Cassian, *The Conferences*, trans. Boniface Ramsey, Mahwah, NJ, Paulist Press, 1997.

John Cassian, *The Institutes*, trans. Boniface Ramsey, Mahwah, NJ, Paulist Press, 2000.

John Climacus, *The Ladder of Divine Ascent*, trans. C. Luibheid and N. Russell, Introduction by Kallistos Ware. Copyright © 1982 the Missionary Society of St Paul the Apostle in the State of New York. Mahwah, NJ, Paulist Press. Reprinted by permission of Paulist Press, Inc.

John Moschos, *The Spiritual Meadow*, Kalamazoo, MI, Cistercian Publications, 1992.

The Letters of Saint Antony the Great, trans. D. J. Chitty, Oxford, SLG Press, 1975.

The Letters of Ammonas, trans. D. J. Chitty, Oxford, SLG Press, 1979.

The Life of Chariton, trans. L. DiSegni, in V. L. Wimbush (ed.), *Ascetic Behavior in Greco-Roman Antiquity*, Minneapolis, Fortress Press, 1990, pp. 393–421.

The Life of Abba Daniel of Scetis, in T. Vivian, *Witness to Holiness*, Kalamazoo, MI, Cistercian Publications, 2008.

The Life of Saint George of Choziba, in T. Vivian, *Journeying into God*, Minneapolis, Augsburg Fortress, 1996, pp. 71–105.

The Life and Activity of the Holy and Blessed Teacher Syncletica, trans. E. A. Castelli, in V. L. Wimbush (ed.), *Ascetic Behavior in Greco-Roman Antiquity*, Minneapolis, Fortress Press, 1990, pp. 265–311.

The Lives of the Desert Fathers, the Historia Monachorum in Aegypto, trans. N. Russell, Introduction by Benedicta Ward, London and Oxford, Mowbray, 1980.

A Narrative about Syncletica who Lived in the Jordanian Desert, in T. Vivian, *Journeying into God*, Minneapolis, Augsburg Fortress, 1996, pp. 46–52.

'St Nilus of Sinai: Short Biographical Note', in E. Kadloubovsky and G. H. E. Palmer, *Early Fathers from the Philokalia*, London, Faber and Faber, pp. 127f.

Pachomian Koinonia: Vol. 1, *The Life of Saint Pachomius,* including the Bohairic and Greek *Lives*; Vol. 2, *Chronicles and Rules*; Vol. 3, *Instructions, Letters and other Writings*, trans. Armand Veilleux, Kalamazoo, MI, Cistercian Publications, 1980–82.

Palladius, *The Lausiac History*, trans. R. T. Meyer, Mahwah, NJ, Paulist Press, 1964.
Paphnutius, *Histories of the Monks of Upper Egypt, and The Life of Onnophrius*, trans. T. Vivian, Kalamazoo, MI, Cistercian Publications, 1993.
Paul of Elusa, *Encomium on the Life of St Theognius*, in T. Vivian *Journeying into God*, Minneapolis, Augsburg Fortress, 1996, pp. 134–65.
Philo, *On the Contemplative Life,* trans. G. P. Corrington, in V. L. Wimbush (ed.), *Ascetic Behavior in Greco-Roman Antiquity*, Minneapolis, Fortress Press, 1990, pp. 134–55.
The Sayings of the Desert Fathers, The Alphabetic Collection, trans. Benedicta Ward, London and Oxford, Mowbray, 1975.
Sozomen, *Ecclesiastical History*, Library of Nicene and Post-Nicene Fathers, Series 2, Vol. 2, Grand Rapids, MI, Eerdmans, 1979.
Ward, B., *Harlots of the Desert*, Kalamazoo, MI, Cistercian Publications, 1987.
The Wisdom of the Desert Fathers, Systematic Sayings from the Anonymous Series, trans. Benedicta Ward, Oxford, SLG Press, 1975.
The World of the Desert Fathers, Stories and Sayings from the Anonymous Series, trans. C. Stewart, Oxford, SLG Press, 1986.

Also:

Augustine Holmes, *A Life Pleasing to God: The Spirituality of the Rules of St Basil*, Kalamazoo, MI, Cistercian Publications, 2000.
St Basil, *Ascetical Works*, trans. M. M. Wagner, Washington DC, CUA Press, 1962.
The Book of Steps, trans. R. A. Kitchen and M. F. G. Parmentier, Kalamazoo, MI, Cistercian Publications, 2004.
Theodoret of Cyrrhus, *A History of the Monks of Syria*, trans. R. M. Price, Kalamazoo, MI, Cistercian Publications, 1985.

Modern works

Binns, J., *Ascetics and Ambassadors of Christ: The Monasteries of Palestine, 314–63*, Oxford, Clarendon Press, 1994.
Bitton-Ashkelony, B. and Kofsky, A., *The Monastic School of Gaza*, Leiden, Brill, 2006.
Bitton-Ashkelony, B. and Kofsky, A. (eds), *Christian Gaza in Late Antiquity*, Leiden, Brill, 2004.

Boud'hors, A., 'Some Aspects of Volume 8 of Shenoute's *Canons*', in G. Gabra and H. Takla (eds), *Christianity and Monasticism in Upper Egypt*, Vol. 1, Akhmim and Sohag, Cairo, American University in Cairo Press, 2008, pp. 13–20.

Brakke, D., *Demons and the Making of the Monk*, Cambridge, MA, Harvard University Press, 2006.

Brock, S., *The Luminous Eye*, Kalamazoo, MI, Cistercian Publications, 1992.

Brown, P., *The Body and Society*, London, Faber and Faber, 1988.

Brown, P., *The Rise of Western Christendom*, Malden, MA and Oxford, Blackwell Publishing, 1996.

Burton-Christie, D., *The Word in the Desert*, New York and Oxford, Oxford University Press, 1993.

Chitty, D. J., *The Desert a City*, Crestwood, NJ, St Vladimir's Seminary Press, 1995.

Chryssavgis, J., *John Climacus: From the Egyptian Desert to the Sinaite Mountain*, Aldershot, Ashgate, 2004.

Chryssavgis, J., *In the Heart of the Desert*, Bloomington, World Wisdom, 2003.

Clark, G., 'Women and Asceticism in Late Antiquity', in V. L. Wimbush and R. Valantasis (eds), *Asceticism*, New York, Oxford University Press, 1995, pp. 33–48.

Dahari, U., *Monastic Settlements in South Sinai in the Byzantine Period: The Archaeological Remains*, Jerusalem, Israel Antiquities Authority, 2000.

Dalrymple, W., *From the Holy Mountain*, London, HarperCollins, 1997.

Elm, S., *Virgins of God: The Making of Asceticism in Late Antiquity*, Oxford, Clarendon Press, 1994.

Emmel, S., 'Shenoute's Place in the History of Monasticism', in G. Gabra and H. Takla (eds), *Christianity and Monasticism in Upper Egypt*, Vol. 1, Akhmim and Sohag, Cairo, American University in Cairo Press, 2008, pp. 31–46.

Fraade, S. D., 'Ascetical Aspects of Ancient Judaism', in A. Green (ed.), *Jewish Spirituality: From the Bible through the Middle Ages*, London, Routledge and Kegan Paul, 1986, pp. 253–88.

Gabra, G. and Takla, H. (eds), *Christianity and Monasticism in Upper Egypt*, Vol. 1, Akhmim and Sohag, Cairo, American University in Cairo Press, 2008.

Goehring, J. E., *Ascetics, Society, and the Desert*, Harrisburg, PA, Trinity Press International, 1999.

Goehring, J. E., 'New Frontiers in Pachomian Studies', in *Ascetics, Society, and the Desert*, Harrisburg, PA, Trinity Press International, 1999, pp. 162–86.

Goehring, J. E., 'Pachomius and the White Monastery', in G. Gabra and H. Takla (eds), *Christianity and Monasticism in Upper Egypt*, Vol. 1, Akhmim and Sohag, Cairo, American University in Cairo Press, 2008, pp. 47–58.

Goehring, J. E., 'Through a Glass Darkly', in *Ascetics, Society, and the Desert*, Harrisburg, PA, Trinity Press International, 1999, pp. 53–72.

Goehring, J. E. and Timbie, J. A. (eds), *The World of Early Egyptian Christianity*, Washington DC, CUA Press, 2007.

Gould, G., *The Desert Fathers on Monastic Community*, Oxford, Clarendon Press, 1993.

Gribomont, J., 'Monasticism and Asceticism: Eastern Christianity', in B. McGinn, B. Meyendorff and J. Leclerq (eds), *Christian Spirituality: Origins to the Twelfth Century*, London, SCM Press, 1989, pp. 89–112.

Harmless, W., *Desert Christians: An Introduction to the Literature of Early Monasticism*, Oxford and New York, Oxford University Press, 2004.

Hirschfeld, Y., 'The Founding of the New Laura', in V. L. Wimbush and R. Valantasis (eds), *Asceticism*, New York, Oxford University Press, 1995, pp. 267–80.

Hirschfeld, Y., *The Judean Desert Monasteries in the Byzantine Period*, New Haven, Yale University Press, 1992.

Hirschfeld, Y., 'The Life of Chariton in the Light of Archaeological Research', in V. L. Wimbush (ed.), *Ascetic Behavior in Greco-Roman Antiquity*, Minneapolis, Fortress Press, 1990.

Hirschfeld, Y., 'The Monasteries of Gaza: An Archaeological Review', in B. Bitton-Ashkelony and A. Kofsky (eds), *Christian Gaza in Late Antiquity*, Leiden, Brill, 2004, pp. 61–88.

Jasper, D., *The Sacred Desert*, Oxford, Blackwell Publishing, 2004.

Keller, D. G. R., *Oasis of Wisdom: The Worlds of the Desert Fathers and Mothers*, Collegeville, MN, Liturgical Press, 2005.

Krawiec, R., 'The Role of the Female Elder in Shenoute's White Monastery', in G. Gabra and H. Takla (eds), *Christianity and Monasticism in Upper Egypt*, Vol. 1, Akhmim and Sohag, Cairo, American University in Cairo Press, 2008, pp. 59–72.

Layton, B. 'The Ancient Rules of Shenoute's Monastic Federation', in G. Gabra and H. Takla (eds), *Christianity and Monasticism in Upper Egypt*, Vol. 1, Akhmim and Sohag, Cairo, American University in Cairo Press, 2008, pp. 73–82.

Louth, A. *The Wilderness of God*, London, Darton, Longman and Todd, 1991.

Luckman, H. A. and Kulzer, L. (eds), *Purity of Heart in Early Ascetic and Monastic Literature,* Collegeville, MN, Liturgical Press, 1999.

Mekhaiel, N., 'Shenoute as Reflected in the *Vita* and the *Difnar*', in G. Gabra and H. Takla (eds), *Christianity and Monasticism in Upper Egypt*, Vol. 1, Akhmim and Sohag, Cairo, American University in Cairo Press, 2008, pp. 99–106.

Meyendorff, J., *St Gregory Palamas and Orthodox Spirituality*, Crestwood, NJ, St Vladimir's Seminary Press, 1974.

Moawad, S., 'The Relationship of St Shenoute of Atripe with his Contemporary Patriarchs of Alexandria', in G. Gabra and H. Takla (eds), *Christianity and Monasticism in Upper Egypt*, Vol. 1, Akhmim and Sohag, Cairo, American University in Cairo Press, 2008, pp. 107–20.

Murray, R., *Symbols of Church and Kingdom: A Study in Early Syriac Tradition*, London, T&T Clark, 1977.

O'Neill, J., 'The Origins of Monasticism', in R. Williams (ed.), *The Making of Orthodoxy*, Cambridge, Cambridge University Press, 1989, pp. 270–87.

Paliouras, A., *The Monastery of St Catherine on Mount Sinai*, St Catherine's Monastery, 1985.

Patrich, J., *Sabas, Leader of Palestinian Monasticism: A Comparative Study of Eastern Monasticism*, Washington DC, Dumbarton Oaks, 1995.

Pearson, B. A., 'Earliest Christianity in Egypt', in J. E. Goehring and J. A. Timbie, *The World of Early Egyptian Christianity*, Washington DC, CUA Press, 2007, pp. 97–112.

Regnault, L., *The Day-to-Day Life of the Desert Fathers in Fourth Century Egypt*, Petersham, MA, St Bede's Publications, 1999.

Rousseau, P., *Basil of Caesarea*, Los Angeles, University of California Press, 1994.

Rousseau, P., *Pachomius: The Making of a Community in Fourth Century Egypt*, Los Angeles, University of California Press, 1985.

Russell, N., *The Doctrine of Deification in the Greek Patristic Tradition*, Oxford, Oxford University Press, 2004.

Ryrie, A. C., *Silent Waiting: The Biblical Roots of Contemplative Spirituality*, Norwich, Canterbury Press, 1999.

Sanders, E. P., *Judaism: Practice and Belief, 63BCE–66CE*, London, SCM Press, 1992.

Stewart, C., *Cassian the Monk*, Oxford and New York, Oxford University Press, 1998.

Swan, L., *The Forgotten Desert Mothers*, Mahwah, NJ, Paulist Press, 2001.

Swanson, M. 'Searching for Shenoute: A Coptic-Arabic Homilary', in G. Gabra and H. Takla (eds), *Christianity and Monasticism in Upper Egypt*, Vol. 1, Akhmim and Sohag, Cairo, American University in Cairo Press, 2008, pp. 143–54.

Timbie, J., 'Once More into the Desert of Apa Shenoute', in G. Gabra and H. Takla (eds), *Christianity and Monasticism in Upper Egypt*, Vol. 1, Akhmim and Sohag, Cairo, American University in Cairo Press, 2008, pp. 169–78.

Tugwell, S., *Ways of Imperfection*, London, Darton, Longman and Todd, 1984.

Waddell, H., *The Desert Fathers*, London, Constable, 1936.

Williams, R., *Silence and Honey Cakes: The Wisdom of the Desert*, Oxford, Lion Publishing, 2003.

Wimbush, V. L. (ed.), *Ascetic Behavior in Greco-Roman Antiquity*, Minneapolis, Fortress Press, 1990.

Wimbush, V. L. and Valantasis, R. (eds), *Asceticism*, New York, Oxford University Press, 1995.

General Index

acedia 84, 156, 166, 207
anachoresis, withdrawal 6, 11,
  40–1, 46, 56, 108, 112, 119–21,
  174, 192, 204–5, 224, 227, 230
anger 107, 156, 158, 166, 188, 193,
  203, 207–8
apatheia 141, 154, 156, 158–61,
  167, 179, 193, 210, 228; see also
  purity of heart
apotaktikoi, renouncers 2, 7, 11,
  100
archaeology 77–8, 97, 173, 181,
  200, 235–6
ascetic practice 2, 22, 58, 79, 83,
  106, 116, 120, 123–4, 158, 165,
  169, 214–16, 220, 227
attending to, watching oneself 23,
  84, 107, 120, 130–1, 133–5, 177,
  193, 205–7, 218, 223–4
avarice 133, 156–7, 166, 207–8

bearing insults, offences 120, 136,
  155, 188, 206, 222
biblical desert tradition 7, 10–12,
  25, 39, 46, 49, 68, 70, 78, 94–5,
  118, 126, 146, 161, 164, 212–13,
  220–1
Book of Steps 230–1, 234

cell, description of 41
cell, staying in one's 34–5, 43, 81,
  120–1, 155, 165, 175, 184, 185
Chalcedon, Council of 68, 87
Coptic language 47–8, 55, 62–3,
  66, 181
Cross of Christ 50, 67, 72, 74, 110,

134, 145, 158, 166, 176–7, 191,
  218

Dead Sea Scrolls 5, 78
deification 189–90, 237
demons passim; see especially 20–1,
  23–4, 131–4, 157–8, 187–8,
  208–9, 216–19
desert, nature of the 48, 75–6
desert as 'mountain' 20, 48, 50,
  52–3
desert as place of the dead 48, 52–3
desire for God 144, 160, 170,
  179–80, 211, 225
detachment 128, 165, 176, 179
discernment 55, 83–4, 120, 131,
  133, 157, 177, 182–3, 187, 204,
  207, 209, 218
disciples and abbas 31, 42–3, 72,
  123, 130–1, 133, 185

early asceticism 1–7
eating 7, 54, 57, 60, 83, 100–1,
  175, 227; see also food and fasting
enkrateia, self-control 84, 227–8
Epistle of Barnabas 3, 232
Essenes 4, 5, 7, 75
Eucharist 42, 44, 51, 57, 65, 72,
  93, 198

families, renouncing 6, 41, 56, 58,
  94, 101, 155, 168, 215, 226
fasting 10, 37, 44–5, 58, 64, 75, 85,
  94–5, 106–8, 113, 123–4, 129,
  133, 138, 142, 155, 165, 168,
  185, 193; see also eating and food

Index of People

Aaron, anchorite 70–4, 118, 121, 124, 125, 132, 215
Abraham, monk 33
Agathon, monk 32–3, 44–5, 134, 194
Alonius, monk 122
Ammonas, monk 28, 39, 44, 131, 141, 144, 233
Amoun, monk 29
Anastasia, patrician lady 105, 132
Anastasius, abbot 202
Anianus, anchorite 70–1
Antony of Choziba 93
Antony the Great ix, 1–2, 12, 19–26, 28–30, 34, 39–41, 46–50, 55, 61–2, 68, 72, 75, 78, 85, 92–3, 95, 101, 118–19, 121, 128, 130–2, 134, 136–9, 141, 145, 160, 169, 172, 187, 194, 211, 213, 217, 232–3
Apollinaris, emperor's daughter 105
Arsenius, monk 31–2, 42–3, 45, 83, 95, 115, 122–3, 211
Athanasius, archbishop 12, 19–22, 24–6, 53, 68–9, 101, 130, 158, 189, 232

Bamberger, J.E. 156, 232
Barsanuphius, monk 177, 181–96, 209, 219, 222, 232
Basil of Caesarea 13, 89, 95, 152, 161, 180, 182, 184, 194, 211, 224, 226–9, 234, 237
Benjamin, monk 126, 160
Besa 62–4, 67–8, 124, 126, 132, 232

Bessarion, monk 35–6, 45, 104, 122
Binns, J. 85, 89, 95, 124, 141, 200, 219, 234
Bitton-Ashkelony, B. 184, 186, 234, 236
Boud'hors, A. 66, 234
Brakke, D. 132, 157, 217, 234
Brock, S. 85, 142, 230–1, 235
Brown, P. 100, 115, 145, 216, 235
Burton-Christie, D. 14, 139, 157, 212, 235

Chadwick, O. 171
Chariton, monk ix, 77–84, 86–7, 92, 95–7, 118, 121, 123–4, 126, 139–40, 145, 233, 236
Chitty, D. 13, 75, 77, 88, 92, 95, 233, 235
Chryssavgis, J. 14, 174, 180, 182–4, 190, 195, 200, 204–6, 209, 211, 232, 235
Clark, G. 99, 115–16, 235
Clement of Alexandria 158
Cyriacus, monk 91–2, 96–7, 111, 118, 121, 124, 232
Cyril of Scythopolis 76–7, 81, 83–5, 88–92, 94, 96, 111, 123–6, 133, 140, 142, 144, 160, 219, 232

Dahari, U. 200, 235
Dalrymple, W. 98, 235
Daniel of Sketis 28, 40, 105, 123, 132, 233
Dorotheus of Gaza 192–5, 232

Egeria 198–9, 201, 232
Elijah 9–11, 25–6, 39–40, 49,

Index of Places